Grammar in ELT and ELT Materials

SECOND LANGUAGE ACQUISITION

Series Editors: Professor David Singleton, *University of Pannonia, Hungary* and Fellow Emeritus, *Trinity College, Dublin, Ireland* and Professor Simone E. Pfenninger, *University of Zurich, Switzerland*

This series brings together titles dealing with a variety of aspects of language acquisition and processing in situations where a language or languages other than the native language is involved. Second language is thus interpreted in its broadest possible sense. The volumes included in the series all offer in their different ways, on the one hand, exposition and discussion of empirical findings and, on the other, some degree of theoretical reflection. In this latter connection, no particular theoretical stance is privileged in the series; nor is any relevant perspective – sociolinguistic, psycholinguistic, neurolinguistic, etc. – deemed out of place. The intended readership of the series includes final-year undergraduates working on second language acquisition projects, postgraduate students involved in second language acquisition research and researchers, teachers and policymakers in general whose interests include a second language acquisition component.

All books in this series are externally peer reviewed.

Full details of all the books in this series and of all our other publications can be found on http://www.multilingual-matters.com, or by writing to Multilingual Matters, BLOCK, The Fairfax, Pithay Court, Bristol, BS1 3BN, UK.

SECOND LANGUAGE ACQUISITION: 164

Grammar in ELT and ELT Materials

Evaluating its History and Current Practice

Graham Burton

MULTILINGUAL MATTERS
Bristol • Jackson

DOI https://doi.org/10.21832/BURTON5270
Library of Congress Cataloging in Publication Data
A catalog record for this book is available from the Library of Congress.
Names: Burton, Graham, author.
Title: Grammar in ELT and ELT Materials: Evaluating its History and Current
   Practice /Graham Burton.
Description: Bristol, UK; Jackson, TN: Multilingual Matters, 2023. |
   Series: Second Language Acquisition: 164 | Includes bibliographical references and
   index. | Summary: 'This book investigates the content of the grammar syllabus
   traditionally employed in English Language Teaching materials. Using a
   mixed-methods approach, the author examines how the existing syllabuses used in
   coursebooks are actually constructed and how valid their contents are as a basis
   for teaching' – Provided by publisher.
Identifiers: LCCN 2023007190 (print) | LCCN 2023007191 (ebook) | ISBN
   9781800415270 (hardback) | ISBN 9781800415287 (pdf) | ISBN
   9781800415294 (epub)
Subjects: LCSH: English language – Grammar – Study and teaching.
Classification: LCC PE1065 .B796 2023 (print) | LCC PE1065 (ebook) | DDC
   425.071 – dc23/eng/20230418
LC record available at https://lccn.loc.gov/2023007190
LC ebook record available at https://lccn.loc.gov/2023007191

British Library Cataloguing in Publication Data
A catalogue entry for this book is available from the British Library.

ISBN-13: 978-1-80041-527-0 (hbk)
ISBN-13: 978-1-83668-256-1 (pbk)

Multilingual Matters
UK: BLOCK, The Fairfax, Pithay Court, BS1 3BN, UK.
USA: Ingram, Jackson, TN, USA.
Authorised Representative: Easy Access System Europe – Mustamäe tee 50, 10621
Tallinn, Estonia gpsr.requests@easproject.com.

Website: www.multilingual-matters.com
Twitter: Multi_Ling_Mat
Bluesky: https://bsky.app/profile/multi-ling-mat.bsky.social
Facebook: https://www.facebook.com/multilingualmatters
Blog: www.channelviewpublications.wordpress.com

Copyright © 2023 Graham Burton.

All rights reserved. No part of this work may be reproduced in any form or by any means without permission in writing from the publisher.

The policy of Multilingual Matters/Channel View Publications is to use papers that are natural, renewable and recyclable products, made from wood grown in sustainable forests. In the manufacturing process of our books, and to further support our policy, preference is given to printers that have FSC and PEFC Chain of Custody certification. The FSC and/or PEFC logos will appear on those books where full certification has been granted to the printer concerned.

Typeset by Riverside Publishing Solutions.

Contents

Acknowledgements		ix
Interviewees		xi
1	Introduction	1
	1.1 Grammar and Language Teaching	1
	1.2 Pedagogical Grammar in ELT	2
	1.3 Rationale for the Book	4
	1.4 What This Book is and What it is Not	5
	1.5 Overall Focus of the Book and Chapter Overview	7
2	ELT Grammar in its Broader Context	10
	2.1 Introduction	10
	2.2 Grammar and Pedagogical Grammar	10
	2.3 Pedagogical Grammar: Content and Design	11
	2.4 Pedagogical Grammar: Sequencing	15
	2.5 Competency Levels	17
	2.6 The Nature of the ELT Publishing Industry	22
	2.7 Summary	25
3	ELT Grammar Canon and Consensus: An Evolutionary Perspective	27
	3.1 Introduction	27
	3.2 Is There an ELT Grammar Canon?	28
	3.3 English Grammars up until the Early 20th Century	30
	3.4 English Grammars into the 20th and 21st Centuries	35
	3.5 Four Key 20th-Century Pedagogical Grammars	40
	3.6 ELT Pedagogical Grammar Today	48
	3.7 Overview	50
4	Interviews with Authors and Editors: The Canon Today	52
	4.1 Introduction	52
	4.2 Methodology: Interviews	52

	4.3	Organising Theme: Norms	59
	4.4	Organising Theme: Publishers	66
	4.5	Organising Theme: Institutions	70
	4.6	Organising Theme: Considering the Market and Users	74
	4.7	Organising Theme: Innovation	80
	4.8	Summary	84
5	Interviews with Authors and Editors: The Canon in the Past and Present		87
	5.1	Introduction	87
	5.2	Organising Theme: Origins	88
	5.3	Organising Theme: Change	97
	5.4	Summary	104
6	Conditionals, Relative Clauses and Future Forms: Contemporary Canon in the Spotlight		106
	6.1	Introduction and Overview of Methodology	106
	6.2	Methodology: Exploring Grammar in Contemporary Coursebooks	107
	6.3	Case Study A: Conditionals	113
	6.4	Case Study B: Relative Clauses	118
	6.5	Case Study C: Future Forms	124
	6.6	Summary	132
7	Conditionals, Relative Clauses and Future Forms: Evolution of the Canon		135
	7.1	Introduction	135
	7.2	Methodology: Exploring Grammar in 'Historical' Publications	136
	7.3	Case Study A: Conditionals	138
	7.4	Case Study B: Relative Clauses	145
	7.5	Case Study C: Future Forms	157
	7.6	Summary	169
8	Conclusion		173
	8.1	How, When and Where did the Consensus on the ELT Grammar 'Canon' Develop?	173
	8.2	What is the Nature of the Canon Today, and the Consensus that Perpetuates and Sustains It?	175

8.3 Does the Canon Reflect Empirical Evidence on how
    Grammatical Competence Develops in English Language
    Learners?   176
8.4 Discussion   177

References   182
Index   193

Acknowledgements

I owe a great deal of debt for the genesis of this book to a number of people. In particular, I would like to thank Anne O'Keeffe, Mike McCarthy, Richard Smith and Deirdre Ryan. I would also like to thank the interviewees in this study for the time they kindly gave me and whose opinions and experiences contribute so much to this title; many have been kind enough to 'continue the discussion' even after the conversations that make up the bulk of the interview data in this study. All had slightly differing perspectives and opinions but I hope that they nonetheless all feel represented in the analysis and overall thrust of this work.

Thank you to the staff at Multilingual Matters and to the series editors David Singleton and Simone E. Pfenninger.

Finally, my thanks also to Cambridge University Press and Oxford University Press for providing copies of coursebooks for some of the analysis in this study.

Note: Every reasonable effort has been made to locate, contact and acknowledge copyright owners. Any errors will be rectified in future editions.

Acknowledgements

Interviewees

The following abbreviations are used in Chapters 4 and 5 to refer to the interviewees.

- **ACA:** Anonymous coursebook author
- **AG:** Adam Gadsby
- **APP:** Anonymous publishing professional
- **BU:** Bart Ullstein
- **DH:** Diane Hall
- **IF:** Ingrid Freebairn
- **JR:** Jack Richards
- **LS:** Liz Soars
- **MS:** Michael Swan
- **PV:** Peter Viney

See pages 53–54 for biographical information on each interviewee.

1 Introduction

1.1 Grammar and Language Teaching

The focus of this book is grammar and, more precisely, the grammar that is used around in English Language Teaching (ELT), particularly for teaching 'General English' in mainstream educational contexts such as state schools and private language schools. Just as the teaching of grammar as part of mother-tongue school education has a rather turbulent history (see Crystal, 2017, for an overview of the situation in the UK), so has the role of grammar in foreign language teaching, with frequent disagreements within academia and within the teaching profession on how and how much grammar should be taught.

The explicit study of grammar was central to the 'grammar-translation method' used in schools from around the turn of the 18th century, which involved the systematic teaching of grammar points, typically (de)contextualised in individual sentences (Howatt & Widdowson, 2004). A century later, the Reform Movement, which involved efforts to reform secondary school language teaching in Europe, with an increased emphasis on spoken ability and a move away from grammar and literature, brought about a paradigm shift. Its proponents argued that teaching should be based on three principles: the prioritisation of spoken language, the use of texts, not sentences, as input and the use of an oral methodology, i.e. speaking the target language in class (Howatt & Widdowson, 2004). None of these necessarily required the abandonment of the teaching of grammar altogether, but it was now no longer a, or *the*, central learning aim. The role of grammar was brought further into question in the 1970s, with the development of ideas of 'communicative competence' (Hymes, 1972), and the 'communicative approach' to language teaching. During this period, some argued for the complete abandonment of grammar teaching yet, just two decades later, such a proposal was already confidently being described as 'a manifest absurdity' in the preface to the edited collection *Grammar and the Language Teacher* (Candlin, 1994: vii).

1.2 Pedagogical Grammar in ELT

Grammar used in the teaching of a foreign language is 'pedagogical grammar'. This term appears to be relatively young, appearing in the *ELT Journal*, for example, for the first time only in 1972 ('Readers' Letters', 1972). The exact definition of pedagogical grammar has been described as 'slippery' (Little, 1994: 99) and will be discussed in Chapter 2; however, broadly speaking, the term 'pedagogical grammar' can be understood in this book to mean descriptions and rules about grammar, constructed to be used in language teaching and typically featured in teaching materials such as coursebooks and practice grammars.

In this book, the main focus is pedagogical grammar for General English. The concept of 'General English' is not unproblematic, as it is used in different ways by different authors, often without definition (Campion, 2016) and when it is defined, it is often described reductively, in terms of what it is not. However, Murray and Muller's (2019: 258) definition is helpful: 'General English is a general competence enabling the individual to negotiate the demands of everyday communication in primarily social contexts[, which] typically includes: an operational understanding of grammar and syntax; an awareness of the socially appropriate deployment of language according to context; an appreciation of the broader discourse structures to which language conforms; and the ability to negotiate meaning and compensate for obstacles to communication'. At a more practical level, it relates to the teaching content found in globally marketed ELT coursebooks and grammars, and in internationally recognised language examinations such as the Cambridge English 'General and higher education' qualifications (which include well-known examinations such as Cambridge First and Cambridge Proficiency).

Scores of ELT grammar practice books are available, with most coursebooks also providing extensive grammar reference sections. There is also no shortage of resources offering grammatical explanations for free online. The totality of grammar rules and descriptions for ELT is characterised by O'Keeffe and Mark as a 'smörgåsbord of items', a mix of syntactical analysis and description alongside 'thematic and functional clusterings' (2017: 466) and it has been argued (e.g. Carter & McCarthy, 1995, 2017; McCarthy & Carter, 2002) that much of this content reflects written, rather than spoken, conventions. Nevertheless, the evidence from published teaching materials suggests that teachers, materials writers and syllabus designers are in broad agreement about what should be included in this smörgåsbord, suggesting the existence of a 'canon' of grammar for ELT, a term also used by both R. Ellis (2006) and O'Keeffe and Mark (2017).

The word 'canon' – which I will use throughout the book – comes to English from Ancient Greek, via Latin, and originally referred to an ecclesiastical rule or doctrine, before being applied to rules and laws in a more general (i.e. secular) way. The relevance of the word 'canon' to discussions of pedagogical grammar is perhaps most apparent in the Oxford English Dictionary's definition of the 'canon' in literacy criticism: 'those works of esp. Western literature considered to be established as being of the highest quality and most enduring value' (OED Online, 2021a), a sense that appeared only in the 20th century. Just as over the decades a collective agreement has developed as to which works are the most important in literature, this book will argue that within the ELT profession an understanding and consensus has emerged over the decades as to which grammar points need to be taught. This canon of grammar points is, rather like the canon of Western literature, 'considered to be established' as being of the greatest importance and value.

One important characteristic of pedagogical grammar is that its contents are typically sequenced into what is believed to be a logical order for teaching and learning. This is in contrast to descriptive grammars, whose entries may be organised alphabetically, by area of grammar or so on, since users of such works are only ever likely to need to access specific sections irregularly, rather than reading them from cover to cover. Sequencing is not typically described in the literature as a property of pedagogical grammar itself; possibly it is perceived as simply a by-product of grammatical content being published in print, for use in classrooms, rather than as an inherent property of pedagogical grammar itself. However, the sequencing of grammar across coursebook levels (often referred to as 'scope and sequence') and, in some cases, across grammar practice books, is a firmly established practice in ELT and I therefore view it as a key element of ELT pedagogical grammar. The 'canon of ELT grammar' under examination in this book can therefore be understood to be the catalogue of grammar items used in mainstream ELT contexts, such as in General English language courses in state schools and private language schools around the world, often with the support of coursebooks produced by local or international publishers. The canon also includes the shared understanding of the optimum way this catalogue should be ordered – in other words, at which language competency level each point in the catalogue should be taught and, in some cases, how these points should be sequenced within a level.

In this book, I frequently use the words 'canon' and 'consensus' when talking about grammatical descriptions used in ELT. I consider them closely connected, but not synonymous. The **consensus** on ELT grammar is the shared understanding that is posited to exist within the ELT profession and industry; the 'totality' or 'catalogue' described in the previous paragraph. This consensus informs the **canon**, which is the physical embodiment of the consensus and can be found in the contents pages of popular, mainstream ELT coursebook series and practice grammars. To investigate the consensus and the canon, we need to use different research methods; the latter is best investigated by analysing primary sources such as coursebooks and grammars, while the former is best investigated by talking to professionals involved in the production of these. Both methods are used in the research presented in this book.

This book seeks to trace the origins of the consensus on ELT pedagogical grammar by using historical and contemporary written sources, as well as interviews with key ELT authors and publishing professionals who have helped to define the field. It explores how pedagogical grammar explanations evolved over the 20th century and up to the present, investigates the factors that sustain the consensus in the present day and explores whether the consensus actually reflects evidence on how learners use grammar. Essentially, the book sets out to answer the questions, 'Why is ELT grammar the way it is?' and 'Should it be this way?'.

1.3 Rationale for the Book

If there is indeed an understanding and consensus on grammar content, a key question is whether or not it is based on sound foundations. While some detailed accounts of the history of ELT have been produced (for example, Howatt & Smith, 2014; Howatt & Widdowson, 2004; Richards & Rodgers, 2001), they do not shed light on exactly where the grammar canon originates. There is not, and never has been, an ELT 'ruling body' that sets out what grammar should be taught and in which order; nor has there ever been an equivalent for English of linguistic 'regulating' bodies like *Académie française* for French, the *Real Academia* for Spanish or the *Academia della Crusca* for Italian. Consequently, no official document exists that presents to practitioners or learners a list of grammatical structures that should be taught, or the order in which they should be taught. Instead, a number of different institutions and organisations exert influence on ELT pedagogy: these include publishing houses, organisations such as the British Council and examination boards and education ministries.

Given its ubiquitousness, there would seem to be very good reasons for investigating the teaching of grammar in ELT. To a great extent this does indeed occur; the field of Second Language Acquisition research regularly investigates the questions of how grammar is acquired by language learners and how the learning of grammar (and often lexis) can best be supported in the classroom. The overwhelming focus in research, however, has tended to be on 'how' to teach rather than 'what' to teach (Sheen, 2003). The question of which grammar points should be taught for a given language is not typically addressed, and when such issues are explored, the responses tend to be speculative or inconclusive. R. Ellis, for example, in answering the question, 'What grammar should we teach?' in his (2006) review of issues in the teaching of grammar, discusses different grammatical models that can be employed and principles that can be used to select grammar points. Overall, however, he defines the question of the choosing which grammar points to teach as 'controversial' (2006: 87) and 'very problematic' (2006: 89); his most concrete advice is that grammatical content could be based on typical learner errors, but this does not seem to be an approach that has ever actually been used to create a complete pedagogical grammar syllabus – including typical ELT grammar syllabuses. Similarly, Hinkel, in her (2017) chapter 'Prioritizing Grammar to Teach or Not to Teach', makes and reviews recommendations on selecting pedagogical grammatical content, but does not attempt to account for the system widely in use in ELT. This is not to criticise such studies, but simply to point out that the focus in the literature on ELT pedagogical grammar tends to either provide only an overview of current and historical practice, or discuss how a grammatical syllabus *could* be constructed, rather than how any specific syllabus *has been* constructed.

1.4 What This Book is and What it is Not

This study is, at its core, about 'practice', that is to say, 'the actual application or use of an idea, belief, or method, as opposed to the theory or principles of it' (OED Online, 2021b). It focuses on what we have said is an under-researched area of investigation: the canon of grammar that is actually employed in classrooms around the world. The contemporary mainstream ELT profession has inherited and maintains a widely accepted tradition – a grammar canon, operationalised across competency levels. A practitioner needs to know, however, what this tradition is based on and whether it offers a valid basis for teaching.

Given the paucity of sources addressing these questions, this study draws on different, but overlapping, domains of enquiry, to provide a framework for investigation. Firstly, this is a study of pedagogical grammar, seeking to investigate questions of the utility of grammatical descriptions and the teachability of grammar in the classroom. It is also in part a historical investigation. It seeks to provide an account of how the canon of grammar used in ELT evolved over time, in the belief that this can tell a practitioner something about suitability of the canon when put into practice in the classroom today. Finally, given the focus I place on primary sources – in particular, coursebooks and pedagogical grammars – it is also a study on materials and syllabus design, and includes the opinions and experiences of those actually involved in this enterprise, that is to say in the practice of ELT publishing. While the study is not located wholly in any one of these three domains, all three are crucial in providing the practitioner-oriented account that lies at its core.

I should make it clear from the outset that it is *not* my principal aim in this book to critique the canon or to suggest an alternative to it. Rather, I attempt to explore and understand it. There are two main reasons for this. Firstly, as outlined above, as a phenomenon the ELT grammar canon has never been examined in any depth. That is to say, despite its ubiquity and importance – the fact that it is employed in ELT classrooms around the world every day – its origins have never been explored in detail and nor have the factors and forces that perpetuate it. Given its importance in practice around the world, I believe that a book investigating and exploring needs little further justification. Secondly, there is the question of the (perceived) 'disconnect' between research and practice in ELT (see, for example, Block, 2000; Nassaji, 2012). As Howatt and Widdowson (2004: 369) argue, 'the actuality of practise is for the most part unrecorded' and is largely unaffected by 'shifts of thinking' among theorists. Continuing, the same authors note that there has been a tendency to 'see actual practice as a constraint on the effective implementation of the proposals of expert opinion', with teachers 'coaxed, or even coerced, into changing their ways' (2004: 369). If we as researchers feel dissatisfied with current practice and wish to make the case for changes to it – and, crucially, have any expectation that our arguments are listened to – I believe that our starting point should be to fully understand current practice and ideally use it as a starting point for calls for change, rather than simply dismiss it. I certainly do not believe that the canon is perfect and should not be critiqued, or that alternative proposals should not be made. However, that is not my aim in this book. In any case, I would suggest that any new proposal acknowledge and attempt to work with the status quo rather than attempt to replace it if there is a real desire to influence mainstream ELT pedagogy.

I take three key positions in this book, and I believe it is important to acknowledge them from the outset as they guide the book's structure and content and the research presented within it. These positions are as follows:

(1) **The importance of primary sources.** In this book, I take the position that evidence on the consensus on grammar in the ELT profession – a key element of the practice of ELT around the world – is most readily and reliably found in the primary literature, which is typically published teaching materials such as grammars and coursebooks but might also include online resources such as videos or interactive materials. As discussed above, it is in these sources that we can find the canon, the 'physical manifestation' of the consensus. Coursebooks are particularly important as they have such a wide reach in the profession, with sales reaching hundreds of thousands a year (Gray, 2002; Littlejohn, 1992). They can therefore be assumed to be highly influential on the practice of ELT in schools and classrooms around the world, particularly as in many cases a coursebook is used simultaneously as a de facto syllabus and exam specifications document (Harwood, 2014; Mares, 2003).

(2) **The value of historical research.** Although this book does not attempt to provide a purely 'historical' account of the canon, I believe that considering its history and evolution is essential in order to have a full understanding of it. As Smith argues in his (2016) article setting out the case for the 'historiography of applied linguistics', historical evidence has a role to play in Applied Linguistics in developing 'historical sense' within language teacher education, in putting modern conceptions in perspective, potentially revealing their limitations and, perhaps most importantly, in providing a basis for reform efforts. Again, primary sources are crucial here: as Smith notes, existing historical accounts tend to over-rely on secondary sources or simply on 'hearsay or handed-down mythology' (2016: 75).

(3) **The importance of understanding the views of the practitioner and the realities of current practice.** In order to fully understand the nature of the consensus on grammar in ELT, I believe that it is crucial to seek out the views, perspectives and experiences of those directly involved in its development and perpetuation. For this reason, I give space to the voices of professionals within the ELT publishing industry and provide an 'insider' account of decisions on grammar content in ELT publications which both seeks and values the perspectives of those responsible for them. Similarly, I seek to understand and respect the realities of current practice as much as possible, rather than seeing them as – to use Howatt and Widdowson's words again – 'irksome obstacles to the implementation of imported wisdom' (2004: 369). Essentially, I attempt in this book to provide the reader with an *emic* perspective (Pike, 1967) on the canon, allowing the views of those responsible for it to emerge, in addition to the *etic* perspective provided through the analysis of primary sources with the external lens of the researcher.

1.5 Overall Focus of the Book and Chapter Overview

The questions this book attempts to address are as follows:

(1) How, when and where did the consensus on the canon of ELT grammar develop?
(2) What is the nature of the canon today, and the consensus that perpetuates and sustains it?
(3) Does the canon reflect empirical evidence on how grammatical competence develops in English language learners?

Although all three questions are closely related, this book uses mixed methods to address them. As I have argued, primary sources are of particular importance, and a content analysis of both historical and contemporary teaching materials is therefore used to address, in part, both questions 1 and 2. The insights from the analysis of primary sources are supplemented by a discussion and an analysis of interview data with ten professionals working within the ELT publishing industry with direct experience of writing or editing (and in one case marketing) coursebooks and grammars. Finally, parts of the content of the canon are assessed through a comparison with empirical evidence, in the form of the 'English Grammar Profile' (see Chapter 6 for details), on how learners' grammatical competence develops as their English improves. One aspect of the analysis therefore focuses on similarities and differences between how content is sequenced in the ELT grammar canon, and the order at which learners typically start producing it. Information about the methodology used in this study can be found at the beginning of Chapter 4 (for the interview data), Chapter 6 (for the analysis of contemporary teaching materials) and Chapter 7 (for the analysis of 'historical' teaching materials).

The remainder of the book is structured in the following way. **Chapter 2** explores the overall context of the study, primarily that of studies on pedagogical grammar and on materials design/analysis, also considering these domains from a historical perspective. The chapter begins by discussing previous attempts to define the nature of pedagogical grammar and how it differs from other accounts of grammar. As this study considers sequencing to be a crucial aspect of pedagogical grammar, a more general discussion of principles of syllabus design and of proficiency frameworks is also provided, including recent perspectives based on findings from learner corpus research. The chapter continues by considering previous studies on the nature of the ELT materials and the ELT publishing industry, crucial for understanding the forces that have shaped and perpetuate the ELT grammar canon.

Chapter 3 sets out the historical context for the main research presented in this study. It begins by discussing existing empirical evidence for the existence of a canon of grammar in ELT. Following this, it provides a broad overview of the evolution of grammars of English, from Bullokar's 16th-century *Pamphlet for Grammar* through school grammars and the turn-of-the-20th-century 'scientific grammars', before turning to 20th-century pedagogical grammars. It identifies key milestone texts that served to solidify the consensus on ELT pedagogical grammar; these same grammars will be referred to in the case studies in Chapter 7.

Chapters 4–7 present the main research and analysis in the study by synthesising information from the interviews and the primary written sources (coursebooks and grammars). **Chapters 4** and **5** present the interview data. **Chapter 4** contains the first part of the analysis of the interview data and the methodology used, presenting a thematic analysis of views and experiences related to what lies behind the existence of the canon today and how it is perpetuated, while **Chapter 5** focuses on the origins of the canon and on changes in practice reported by the interviewees to have occurred since the mid-20th century. **Chapters 6 and 7** then present the three case studies (of pedagogical grammar accounts of conditional forms, relative clauses and future forms). **Chapter 6** presents the methodology used in the case study analysis; it then explores the treatment and sequencing of the three areas of grammar in five contemporary coursebook series and compares this with the descriptors of learner competency in the English Grammar Profile (EGP); **Chapter 7** investigates how descriptions and sequencing of the three areas of grammar under examination have changed and evolved, from Jonson's 17th-century grammar up until late 20th-century coursebooks.

Finally, **Chapter 8** draws together the research and introduces conclusions, returning to the three main research questions posed in Chapter 1. The chapter concludes by examining the role that learner corpora – particularly 'quasi-longitudinal' (Granger, 2002) learner corpora – may have as a source of renewal and inspiration for innovation. It also reviews how the historical research presented throughout the book tells a somewhat different story about the how the role of grammar teaching in ELT materials has changed over the decades compared with standard accounts, arguing that what many might consider as 'traditional' grammar syllabuses in ELT are a relatively recent phenomenon, only really taking a familiar shape in the last quarter of the 20th century.

2 ELT Grammar in its Broader Context

2.1 Introduction

Before we turn our focus directly to the canon itself, it is worth taking some time to consider some concepts and issues that surround it. In this chapter, I set out some foundations for the content of the rest of the book by considering what constitutes a 'pedagogical' grammar and how this differs from other types of grammatical account, before looking at the idea of competency levels in language teaching and how teaching content can be sequenced. Finally, we will consider the nature and importance of the ELT publishing industry: although this book is not intended as an analysis only of the grammar content of language teaching materials (we will see in the coming chapters that the grammar canon appears to have a 'life of its own' away from the printed page), an understanding of how the ELT publishing industry works and the conditions within which it operates is important in understanding the forces that sustain and influence the ELT grammar canon.

2.2 Grammar and Pedagogical Grammar

The meaning of the word 'grammar' has shifted significantly over the years. The original Greek term covered a wide range of disciplines, and over the centuries the meaning has changed significantly, becoming progressively narrower and closer to the modern conception of the term, such as that provided in the *Longman Dictionary of Language Teaching and Applied Linguistics*: 'a description of the structure of a language and the way in which linguistic units such as words and phrases are combined to produce sentences in the language' (Richards & Schmidt, 2007: 230). However, this comparatively narrow definition is still relatively recent; many grammars of the 19th century still included discussions of prosody, for example (Michael, 1970).

Even today, the word 'grammar' can mean different things. One variation is the countable form of the noun, meaning 'a book describing the grammar of a language'; the *Oxford English Dictionary* attests this usage for the first time in 1530. A further basic distinction is often made between descriptive and prescriptive grammars, with the former attempting to describe actual usage, and the latter attempting to influence it. To descriptive and prescriptive grammar can be added pedagogical grammar, the grammar of language learning and teaching, which combines aspects of both descriptive and prescriptive grammars. (Both the terms 'pedagogic grammar' and 'pedagogical grammar' have been used in the literature; there do not seem to have been any attempts to differentiate them but as the more frequent of the two is 'pedagogical grammar', this is used in this book.)

A number of differing definitions and characterisations of pedagogical grammar have been offered; these include the following:

- a form of grammatical description to be used by teachers rather than learners (Corder, 1975, cited in Chalker, 1994);
- the 'types of grammatical analysis and instruction designed for the needs of second language students' (Odlin, 1994: 1);
- the 'framework of definitions, diagrams, exercises, and verbalized rules which may help a learner to acquire knowledge of a language' (Allen & Widdowson, 1974);
- a textbook that teaches the grammar of a foreign language (Greenbaum, 1987);
- grammatical descriptions that are 'practical, selective, sequenced, task-orientated, etc.' (Leech, 1994: 17);
- 'a grammar developed for learners of a foreign language', drawing on (i) descriptive models of grammar, 'which can be incorporated into pedagogical reference grammars and teaching materials and formulated in ways which make the description accessible to the learner' and (ii) theories of second language acquisition, 'which will provide the basis for classroom methodology' (Newby, 2000: 459).

So while there is agreement in the literature that pedagogical grammar aims to assist language learning, there is disagreement on whether discussions of it should also consider processes of grammar teaching, and on whether it is for teachers or learners (or both). The use of the term 'pedagogical grammar' in this book is largely aligned with the first part of Newby's definition; pedagogical grammar is understood as descriptions of grammar written for English language learners, incorporated in teaching materials.

2.3 Pedagogical Grammar: Content and Design

How can one decide on the content of a pedagogical grammar account? One crucial characteristic of pedagogical grammar is that, as noted by Leech (1994) it is deliberately, and perhaps unavoidably, selective. Language learners simply cannot learn (and teachers cannot teach) all the grammar of a language in the time they have available, a point discussed by Swan:

> [A] pedagogic grammatical description of a language is necessarily fragmentary. Time constraints do not allow language learners to learn, or their teachers to teach, anything approaching the whole of a language. [...] While a descriptive grammar will aim at complete coverage, a pedagogic grammar will consequently miss out or simplify material of lesser practical importance. (Swan, 2011: 565)

One difficulty here is the question of how, and by whom, it is to be ascertained exactly which materials are of 'lesser practical importance'. One approach – certainly not new (see Chapter 3) – is to consider the learners' L1. A proponent of such an approach, Swan argues that pedagogical grammars should aim to impart knowledge 'which learners do not already possess, glossing over or leaving out what they already know by courtesy of their mother tongue' (Swan, 2011: 565). Towell (2016) makes similar arguments, suggesting in addition that the grammatical content selected for inclusion be based on L1–L2 differences that are most likely, according to the experience of the grammar author, to 'create genuine learning difficulties' (2016: 1).

In terms of teaching materials, this would clearly require the publication of many different versions of grammars aimed at different L1 groups – unlikely with 'international' products such as global coursebooks and grammars. Such an approach also does not address Kellerman's (1978) 'psychotypological hypothesis', which posits that learners are less likely to transfer features of the L1 if they perceive it to be 'distant' (in terms of typology) from the L2 being learned; this occurs even in the case of features that in fact exist in both languages. The danger of assuming that learners do not need to be taught areas of grammar common to both the L1 and L2 by virtue of the fact that they can or will automatically transfer it from the L1 to the L2 is that, in some cases, such transfer does not occur.

Overall, the question of selection of grammatical items in a pedagogical grammar is perhaps surprisingly untheorised. What, then, of the general characteristics of the rules and descriptions found within pedagogical grammars? Again, a number of suggestions and recommendations have been made, but as Newby (2000) notes, there has been comparatively little development of theory on how pedagogical descriptions – particularly rules – should be formulated. Perhaps the richest set of guidelines are Swan's (1994) six 'design criteria for pedagogic language rules', which are as follows:

- truth: Swan argues that it is desirable that rules be true. Although this requirement at times will conflict with other criteria, he argues that 'it

is best if language rules correspond reasonably well to the linguistic facts' (1994: 46);
- demarcation: this mainly refers to predictive value. Swan states that rules should 'show clearly what are the limits on the use of a given form' (1994: 47), and should hence provide learners with a basis to predict when to use one form rather than another;
- clarity: rules should be clear and avoid 'unsatisfactory terminology' (1994: 48);
- simplicity: rules should be simple, even if at times this may lead to 'some trade-off with truth or clarity' (1994). Swan argues simplicity is one way in which pedagogical grammars differ 'sharply from general-purpose descriptive rules';
- conceptual parsimony: pedagogical grammarians should consider the concepts and terminology with which the target learners are familiar and explanations should be written with this in mind;
- relevance: every explanation given should answer a 'question, real or potential, that is asked by a learner, or that is generated by his or her interlanguage' (1994: 51). Consequently, a pedagogical account of grammar is likely to be 'fragmentary' and 'partial' rather than 'complete'. Selectivity therefore goes beyond contrastive analysis, and considers what learners want to know and what they are perceived to want to know.

Swan's conception of 'demarcation' represents an important characteristic of pedagogical grammars when compared with descriptive grammars: learners need pedagogical grammars to tell them when and how to choose between two formally correct possibilities, something which descriptive grammars do not necessarily do. A similar dichotomy is outlined by Carter and McCarthy's (2006), who contrast 'grammar as structure' and 'grammar as choice', and in Williams' (1994) conception of 'constitutive' and 'communicative' grammar rules. An example of the former is fixed word order (for example in phrases such as 'my name' or in the *be* + *-ing* structure), the third person singular *-s* in the present simple or the unacceptability of the sentence 'I am eat'; these are formal areas of grammar which learners must simply learn. In contrast, the correct choice between the sentences 'I didn't eat at midday' and 'I don't eat at midday' is not a matter of formal correctness, but of 'communicative' grammar rules. Both types of rule are likely to be useful to foreign language learners, yet providing sufficient coverage of the latter type represents one of the challenges of producing an effective pedagogical grammar. Also related to the question of demarcation is Johnson's (1994) argument that pedagogical rules should be both 'generalisable' and 'proceduralisable'. Generalisability is important because learners need to be able to go beyond the small subset of language to which they have been exposed; a good pedagogical grammar explanation will therefore tell a learner how to form, for example, the present perfect of any verb, rather than only of a limited number of verbs. Rules should be proceduralisable in the sense that they should be formulated in such a way that the language they instruct on can eventually be produced by the learner automatically, without conscious attention to the rule. The desired 'transformation' here is from 'declarative knowledge' to 'procedural knowledge', and pedagogical grammar should, for Johnson, be able to aid this process of 'automatisation', potentially by 'increasing the burden to be placed on the learner's attention, leaving less attention available for focus on the form being practised' (Johnson, 1994: 127). This is in line with the arguments put forward by DeKeyser (2014) for the relevance of Skill Acquisition Theory to language acquisition. According to DeKeyser, the learning of a foreign language shows a 'similarity in development' to many other types of learning, with explicit knowledge – such as that which can be developed through studying pedagogical grammar rules – playing 'a *causal* role in the development of procedural knowledge' (2014: 103, emphasis added).

Swan's criteria also suggest that the content of pedagogical grammar may not always be completely accurate, and that there may often be underlying reasons for this (of which the authors themselves are probably aware). Furthermore, the question of selectivity is again raised; there may be features of language that can be described but that at the same time might not actually be of use to learners, and pedagogical grammarians, for Swan, should be ready to disregard these. The difficulty here is perhaps in how to establish with confidence what is of use to learners, particularly when teachers, grammarians, administrators, and indeed the learners themselves, have become used to the status quo.

To these difficulties can be added James' (1994: 207) suggestion that the areas of grammar that are comparatively easily to teach and explain 'perhaps do not need to be explained because they are so obvious', whereas the more complex areas, those that learners would benefit most from being taught, are more difficult to explain. Evidence for this comes from a study by Zhou (1991), which reports that Chinese learners appeared to learn from explicit instruction of the English passive (a comparatively easy area of grammar for Chinese learners of English as Chinese uses a parallel structure to front topics) but not from the teaching of the use of auxiliary *do* and of the morphology of tense and aspect. Such a phenomenon, if generally true, perhaps interacts with both Swan's criteria of simplicity (the most complex areas of grammar may be difficult to explain adequately because of the need for simplicity), and conceptual parsimony (if one is to bear in mind learners' familiarity, or otherwise, with particular concepts, it will presumably be more difficult to write explanations of grammar that relate to concepts with which learners are not familiar).

Finally, a discussion of the content of pedagogical grammar must acknowledge the fact that developing such a grammatical account inevitably involves choosing to provide information on the grammar of one particular language variety, or at least a very limited selection (for example 'British English' and 'American English'). The question of which variety of English is most suitable for ELT – and, indeed, the complex issues surrounding language standards in general – lie beyond the scope of this book and will not be addressed directly. Readers interested in how these issues pertain to ELT in particular might consult the literature on the teaching of 'International English' (for example, Marlina, 2018; Phan, 2020; Rose et al., 2020; Sharifian, 2009).

2.4 Pedagogical Grammar: Sequencing

As we said in Chapter 1, a further key characteristic of pedagogical grammar is that the various elements of which it is made up tend to need to be ordered in some way, typically to follow some kind of (expected) developmental sequence, perhaps most obviously in the case of the grammatical content in a coursebook and across books in a coursebook series.

This kind of sequencing is, of course, not exclusive to the teaching of English. An early title to make use of what is sometimes termed a 'graded syllabus' of this type was Ollendorff's 19th-century *New Method* series – a hugely successful book series consisting of self-study titles for a number of European languages. Ollendorff's titles were innovative in that they introduced areas of grammar one by one, with different aspects of each area often split across several chapters, unlike grammar translation courses, which tended to introduce entire paradigms at the same time (Howatt & Widdowson, 2004). The principles with which grammar was graded across the whole books was, for Howatt and Widdowson, 'convention and "logic"' (2004: 163) – for example, present is taught before past, and both before the imperative.

Harold Palmer, in his (1921) *The Principles of Language-Study*, offers perhaps the first detailed theoretical discussion of how decisions on sequencing can be made. After an initial characterisation of sequencing (or 'gradation', using Palmer's choice of term) in general as 'passing from the known to the unknown by easy stages' (1921: 113), Palmer sets out some more specific criteria that can be used for the sequencing of grammar:

> Certain moods and tenses are more useful than others; let us therefore concentrate on the useful ones first. In a language possessing a number of cases, [...] we will select them in accordance with their degree of importance. As for lists of rules and exceptions, if we learn them at all we will learn them in strict order of necessity. In most languages we shall probably find certain fundamental laws of grammar and syntax upon

which the whole structure of the language depends; let us first learn these essentials and leave the details to a later stage. (1921: 115)

For Palmer, then, sequencing takes into account usefulness, importance and necessity, prioritising the 'essentials' over the 'details'. While this appears to be common-sense advice, he does not go into any more detail about what exactly would characterise a 'useful' grammatical structure and how, and by whom, it should be identified; similar doubts can be levelled against the other characteristics he lists. We thus return to the point made earlier: it is ultimately a subjective decision, made by the grammar writer, on what grammar should be selected for teaching.

More recently, questions of sequencing have been revisited, typically as part of wider discussions of 'syllabus design' or 'curriculum design'. For example, Nunan, in his (1988) *Syllabus Design*, notes in his discussion of grammatical syllabuses that syllabus items are typically sequenced 'according to grammatical notions of simplicity and complexity', with the most 'rigid' syllabuses introducing items one by one, each item needing to be mastered before the next step can be taken' (1988: 28). Nunan does not define how exactly grammatical simplicity or complexity can be ascertained, but he does make the important point that grammatical difficulty does not necessarily equate to learning difficulty, noting that the third person singular *-s* in the present simple, for example, is 'fairly straightforward [...] [but] notoriously difficult for learners to master' (1988: 33), something Ellis explains in relation to its relative lack of 'salience' in the language stream available to the learner (Ellis, N.C., 2006).

Two further authors (and academics) to have discussed grammatical sequencing in some detail are Keith Johnson and Jack Richards, who, writing in two separate publications (Johnson, 2001; Richards, 2001), nonetheless converge on five main principles for sequencing, as follows:

- simplicity and centrality;
- learnability;
- frequency;
- linguistic distance;
- communicative needs.

Like Nunan, neither Richards nor Johnson attempt to define the terms 'simplicity and centrality', just as Palmer did not elaborate on what exactly 'the essentials' and 'the details' of a language are. The inclusion now of frequency as a criterion possibly reflects the ease with which frequency counts can be made using corpora (in Section 2.6, we will see some studies to have used frequency data from corpora to critique existing ELT grammatical descriptions and syllabuses). With 'linguistic distance', we are returning to the question of the differences between the

L1 and target language; these differences can be used not only as a basis for selecting items, as we saw above, but also for sequencing them within a syllabus. 'Communicative need' echoes to an extent Palmer's concept of necessity, with Richards noting that 'some structures will be needed early on and cannot be postponed, despite their difficulty' (2001: 13).

Finally, the principle of 'learnability' relates to the claimed existence of an 'internal syllabus' – the idea that learners acquire structures in a natural order, regardless of the order in which they are taught, and that this natural order should be reflected in teaching materials (see, for example, Long, 2015). There are two main sources for this claim: firstly, Dulay and Burt's (1974) morpheme study, which appeared to show that all learners of English acquire grammatical morphemes in largely the same order; secondly, Pienemann's processability theory (Pienemann, 1989), which suggests that certain syntactic structures are acquired in a predictable order in a number of languages. However, more recent work (Luk & Shirai, 2009; Murakami & Alexopoulou, 2016) has called into question the validity of the original morpheme studies, suggesting that the claimed 'universal' order of acquisition is to a great extent L1 dependent, while DeKeyser (2014) has noted that most studies on acquisition order use data from learners acquiring the language implicitly (often children), with very large amounts of exposure – learning conditions that do not apply universally in language teaching. Overall, it is perhaps worth noting Richards' assertion that 'little reliable information on acquisition sequences has been produced that could be of practical benefit in planning a grammar syllabus' (Richards, 2001: 12).

One difficulty with ordering is that no single principle can of course be entirely satisfactory. A syllabus designer may use a number of different principles, which may themselves at times be in conflict with one another; for example, it may be considered desirable to teach a relatively 'complex' structure early on if it is communicatively very useful. It is therefore likely that the design of any structural syllabus will have involved the materials designer weighing up the various principles and deciding, case by case, which principle to prioritise. The existence during the writing process of competing demands and the need for compromise has been reported by a number of different materials authors (see, for example, Bell & Gower, 1998; Johnson, 2001; Mares, 2003; McGrath, 2013; Timmis, 2014).

2.5 Competency Levels

The kind of sequencing described in the previous section gives the impression of a syllabus or curriculum being organised along a single developmental line. However, most language courses and teaching materials are of course not structured in this way; instead, teaching and learning is typically divided into levels and thus the language items that are selected for inclusion are divided into groups, with each group allocated to a particular level. Hence, a beginner level course or coursebook will contain the first 'chunk' of teaching items in the sequence, an elementary level course or coursebook will contain the next chunk, and so on. There are some fundamental questions about organising teaching and learning in this way; for example, we might ask on what basis any particular level system lies; whether there is an optimum number of levels for language teaching; and whether particular areas of language should be taught at particular levels. However, an examination of existing frameworks reveals an almost bewildering range of level systems in use, with sometimes limited empirical basis.

The basic premise of levels – that learners gradually progress through levels of competency on their way to whichever level of ability they eventually ascertain – appears superficially straightforward. For example, Brindley (1999) argues that it is 'reasonable enough to assume that learning a language consists of an evolution through progressive levels of mastery, each approximately more closely to the target' (1999: 116). What is more, according to Brindley, it should be possible to describe language competence at these different levels: 'a cross-sectional of description of typical behaviours at each level would by definition constitute a picture of the developmental process over time' (1999: 116). Yet, as we will see below – and as Brindley himself notes – the empirical basis for rating scales, if it indeed exists, is rarely provided by the providers of exams.

One major examination board for ELT is Cambridge English and the examinations they administer may have been influential in developing the perception of levels in ELT. Cambridge exams were originally offered at only two levels: the 'Certificate of Proficiency in English', equivalent to the modern 'Cambridge English: Proficiency' examination, was introduced in 1913, and the 'Lower Certificate', equivalent to the 'Cambridge English: First' examination, was introduced in 1939 (Weir, 2013). The offering was expanded relatively recently, with three extra levels added in the 1980s and 1990s. This expansion reflected, according to Weir *et al.* (2013), a perceived need 'on the part of intergovernmental agencies in Europe to define language teaching and learning goals more precisely and to make a start on delineating the stages of progression across the language proficiency spectrum' (Weir *et al.*, 2013: 421; a similar explanation is also provided by North & Schneider, 1998).

No single explanation is given, however, as to why Cambridge English examinations came to be offered at five levels, rather than six, or eight or twenty. Weir *et al.* (2013) argue that insights from research in applied linguistics and pedagogical developments made it possible for examination boards to achieve 'a more explicit specification of the constructs underlying their English language tests at differing levels of proficiency' (2013: 421–422). Yet, while they discuss in detail the various elements that make up the constructs for the five levels in the different papers of Cambridge examinations (for example, the text types and exercise types featured in reading paper, task demands in the speaking paper and the changing cognitive demands made in the listening paper at different levels), they do not explain what, if anything, the five levels at which Cambridge English examinations are offered actually represent in a broader sense.

Moving outside of Europe, the United States has an equally long history of language assessment, with various entities currently setting standards and offering certifications. The Interagency Language Roundtable (ILR) scale is highly influential, even in Europe (North & Schneider, 1998), and describes competence in 'foreign languages' (i.e. not English) at six levels, from 0 to 5. The labels 0+, 1+, 2+ etc. can also be used 'when proficiency substantially exceeds one skill level and does not fully meet the criteria for the next level' (Interagency Language Roundtable, 2011). The American Council on the Teaching of Foreign Languages (ACTFL) offers its own set of 'proficiency guidelines', based on the ILR scale, which set out bands of proficiency at five levels (Swender et al., 2012). The lower three of these levels are themselves divided into three sub-levels, creating a total system of 11 levels. Specifically for English, the TOEFL examination offered by the English Testing Service (ETS) has been in existence since the early 1960s. Candidates taking the test simply receive a score out of 120 (the examination is not offered at different levels as such), but ETS provides an interpretation document which divides the scores for the four papers which make up the overall examination into either three or four bands (for example, for the Reading paper there are three bands – Low, Intermediate and High, whereas for the Speaking paper there are four – Weak, Limited, Fair and Good) (Educational Testing Service, 2014). Again, however, it is not clear how the number of levels and bands was decided on to start with.

The *Common European Framework for Languages* (Council of Europe, 2001, 2017) was an independent (at least ostensibly) development from the work of examination boards. The CEFR is widely used within Europe and beyond (Chalhoub-Deville, 2014; Hulstijn, 2014; see also Negishi, 2022, for a detailed account of its influence in Japan, for example) and is now also influential on published ELT materials, as there is an increasing tendency for ELT coursebooks to align themselves with CEFR levels (Timmis, 2015). Language competence in the CEFR is described through the use of 'can do' statements, setting out what learners can do at six different levels (labelled A1, A2, B1, B2, C1 and C2). As in the ILR scale, 'plus levels' are sometimes identified in the CEFR, with, for example, the A2 level divided into A2.1 and A2.2 (or sometimes A2 and A2+). Conversely, the six levels themselves are grouped into three 'broad levels': 'Basic User' (A1, A2), Independent

User (B1, B2) and Proficient User (C1, C2). Some justification is given in the CEFR for the choice to divide competence into six levels; it is described in the CEFR as reflecting a 'a wide, though by no means universal, consensus on the number and nature of levels appropriate to the organisation of language learning and the public recognition of achievement' (Council of Europe, 2001: 22–23). However, we might ask from where this consensus originated to start with, and on what basis it was developed.

Various criticisms have previously been made into the use of levels in assessment and course design. For example, the ACTFL guidelines have been criticised in that they are not based on research into how languages are actually acquired (Kramsch, 1986; Savignon, 1985). As for the CEFR, Hulstijn (2007, 2014) has underlined the fact that the scaling of the CEFR descriptors (the 'can do' statements) was based on judgements by teachers and experts, not on learner data. He also points out that there is no empirical evidence that learners actually progress up through the CEFR levels as they are defined. Chalhoub-Deville (2014: 250) also suggests that level frameworks often lack an empirical basis, stating that 'tradition, politics and practical demands' played a significant role in deciding on the six CEFR levels, just as they did on the ACTFL Guidelines. Such criticisms are echoed by McCarthy (2021: 128), who notes the potential circularity in the interplay between publishers and examination boards, both creators of products based around a level system (in the case of publishers, coursebooks offered for learners at a series of competency levels; for examination boards, examinations intended to test learners' competency at these levels). Both stakeholders can 'lean on' the other to 'validate its position', even though neither of the two systems in play may be 'fully objectively or empirically founded'.

The use of scales and bands has also been called into question from the point of view of psycholinguistics. Long (2015: 76), for example, dismisses 'global proficiency levels' as 'opaque and psycholinguistically meaningless'. Bialystok (1991) relates language proficiency to processing skills, arguing that it is a mistake to conceive of proficiency quantitively:

> Language proficiency is not a single achievement marking some quantitative level of progress with language learning. Rather, it is the ability to apply specific processing skills to problems bearing identifiable cognitive demands. (1991: 75)

One consequence of this, for Bialystok, is that a learner may 'exhibit a range of proficiency with the language that is determined by the impact of the task demands on the processing abilities of the learner' (Bialystok, 1991: 75). In other words, not all aspects of an individual's language proficiency are likely to fit neatly into a single descriptive proficiency band.

Related concerns were also expressed by John Trim, a key figure in the development of the CEFR, who noted his original reluctance to using the word 'level' in the original 'threshold' description[1] from which the CEFR eventually grew, and also his reluctance to provide competency descriptions at multiple levels, as was eventually carried out in the CEFR. However, again, practical and political considerations won out:

> We used the term 'level' originally despite deep misgivings concerning the concept. We could see no reason to break the process of language learning into a series of steps and did not like the image of learning poured into an empty vessel, with skills and knowledge like sand in an hourglass. [...] Over time, it became apparent that our reasoning took little account of the realities of the social organization of language learning. State education systems were organised into primary, lower secondary and upper secondary, further and higher educational sectors, and their interfaces called for assessments of proficiency that would provide objectives for one sector and starting points for the next. Similarly, the major institutions of adult education had to cater for large numbers of students at different stages of development, to sort them into financially and organizationally viable groups with realistic common objectives. (Trim, 2012: 28)

As far as ELT is concerned, the majority of coursebooks deploy a *de facto* six-level system, typically aligned to CEFR levels A1–C1 (C2 is not typically covered, with B1 split into two coursebook levels). This, however, is a relatively recent development; the first major coursebook series to have been published at six levels appears to have been *Headway*, in the 1990s. Previous to this, it was most common to publish coursebooks at four levels.[2] Initially, though, only two levels of *Headway* were published – Intermediate and Upper Intermediate, in 1986 and 1987 respectively – before an advanced level was added, followed by the three lowest levels. According to the series' authors, the expansion to six levels occurred only because of the (commercial) success of the original two levels, and was not initially planned (International House World Organisation, 2011). It therefore appears to be the case that the currently ubiquitous division of coursebook series into six levels is simply a case of publishers following the precedent set by *Headway*, rather than a reference to some kind of pedagogical or theoretical foundation. The practice certainly predates the six-level CEFR.

The concept of competency levels clearly goes beyond just the teaching of grammar, yet as any level system will impact on how the teaching of grammatical items is organised, it is nonetheless crucial. The literature on pedagogical grammar is largely silent on the question of levels, perhaps unsurprisingly given that the broader question of sequencing is generally ignored. Despite the theoretical concerns and limitations, it is clear that proficiency levels serve important practical purposes in language teaching. Given the influence of examinations on teachers and teaching, in addition to documents such as the CEFR and the ACTFL scales, it seems likely that the construct of the proficiency level is readily perceived by teachers, course designers and learners, even though they represent an 'oversimplification of the language learning process' (Brindley, 1999: 134). It is interesting that issues such as 'tradition' and 'practical demands' emerge when looking at levels; we will see that the same issues emerge again and again when we look at other aspects of the ELT grammar canon.

2.6 The Nature of the ELT Publishing Industry

As we have said, this book takes the approach that analysing primary sources such as coursebooks and grammars is crucial. But such publications do not exist in a vacuum, and it is therefore worthwhile considering what the literature on the ELT publishing industry has to say. Although ELT publishers produce a variety of materials, it is coursebooks that are said to be the most influential and receive the most attention in the literature, and this section will focus mainly on their characteristics and on discussion investigating their production. Sales of popular coursebook series reach hundreds of thousands a year (Gray, 2002; Littlejohn, 1992), and in many cases a coursebook is used simultaneously as a de facto syllabus and exam specifications document (Harwood, 2014; Mares, 2003). What, then, is the nature of the publishing industry that produces these products?

ELT publishing is often described as being inherently conservative, favouring tried and trusted approaches over innovative ones. Littlejohn argues that the aim of publishers 'is largely to replicate the design characteristics of existing market leaders' (Littlejohn, 1992: 235), meaning that the amount of variation between titles is likely to be limited, while Burton (2012: 97) makes the point that publishers essentially have no interest in promoting change, and simply do their best to provide markets with the kinds of materials they want: 'publishers investigate current practices through market research, and produce materials to best facilitate these existing practices'. On the question of grammatical content in particular, Ellis notes that most grammatical syllabuses are very similar and have changed little over the years, the reason for this being that 'it is safer to follow what has been done before' (Ellis, R., 2006: 89). This sentiment is echoed by Stranks (2003), who describes grammatical content in many ELT publications as 'comfortingly familiar', reflecting an attitude in those who make decisions on the choice of syllabus and books to use as 'better the devil you know than the devil you don't' (2003: 338).

The explanation for these conservative tendencies is said to be the commercial imperatives that most publishers operate under. The investment costs of producing coursebooks are extremely high, and publishers are therefore under pressure from shareholders not to jeopardise them by producing materials that may not sell well (Amrani, 2011; Bell & Gower, 2011; Littlejohn, 1992; Maley, 2003; Tomlinson, 2011). There appears to be a contrast here with some other types of publishing. A literary publisher, for example, takes a far lower risk in publishing a novel by an unknown author because it will incur only limited – if any – costs while the author writes a manuscript. Literature is also less time sensitive; a publisher can produce a limited run of a novel and if it proves successful print more copies. An educational publisher cannot afford to take such a tentative approach as it needs good sales figures to justify the original investment and would not want to miss out on mass adoptions of a coursebook series at the beginning of a school or academic year. Littlejohn (1992: 221) describes the need to avoid risk as being '[a]t the heart of the premises adopted in the commercial publication of a main course [i.e. a coursebook]'.

An interesting account explaining an author's perspective on these commercial imperatives is Mares (2003), who describes his own journey from a novice writer with 'enthusiasm and unfettered idealism of youth' to a more experienced author who understood that publishers wanted material that was 'new and different, but not too new and definitely not too different' (2003: 136–137). In terms of grammar, this more experienced writer also accepted that market requirements – mediated by marketing departments – meant that he would need to write materials using a graded grammar syllabus, even if this did not, in his opinion, match research findings on language acquisition, and at times seemed arbitrary:

[We] were told that the grammar syllabus needed to be graded accordingly, apparently to precedent, which as far as we could tell meant that the simple past could not be addressed until around Unit 7. This seemed odd to us, but apparently it was a market constraint. (Mares, 2003: 137)

Accounts directly from publishers are more limited, but do shed some light on the issues. Amrani's (2011) 'insider' description of the processes employed by publishers to pilot and evaluate materials also contains some more general observations on the publishing processes; one issue identified by Amrani is the difficulty of creating materials to be used by many different groups of learners in different markets (the same observation is made by the author accounts of Bell and Gower, 2011 and McCullagh, 2010), with a publisher only being able to make 'educated guesses' on learners' likes and dislikes. Like Littlejohn and Burton, Amrani (2011) also notes the need for a publisher to consider the 'commercial attractiveness' of a product, but claims there is no contradiction between having such a focus and producing quality, pedagogically sound materials: 'Publishers are also aware that they have a responsibility to deliver high-quality materials which will teach language students effectively, so that their reputations as professional experts in materials development are maintained' (Amrani, 2011: 269). Littlejohn (1992: 221) is less optimistic, arguing that '"Satisficing" or the finding of solutions which are "good enough" will be evident in both the pedagogic aspects of the materials and in the production aspects'.

As we have seen, a frequent theme to emerge from author accounts is the sense of needing to work to requirements imposed by publishers. Amrani's account offers an interesting counterpoint to this, suggesting that, rather than being the source of the restrictions, publishers are themselves restricted by external factors: 'course content, approach and task design is often already established by exam syllabus guidelines or standards [...] [P]ublishers have less of a free hand than previously as there are clearly defined international market expectations which they now need to work within to secure course adoptions' (Amrani, 2011: 268). This is a perspective which is perhaps not sufficiently appreciated in the literature, which tends to place the blame squarely at the feet of publishers. On the actual topic of her chapter – the piloting and evaluation of materials – Amrani notes that development cycles have become much shorter, leaving less time for the testing of books: '[M]ost publishers are now working to development cycles of only two or three years. This leaves little if no time for full piloting [...]' (2011: 268). Presumably such time restrictions would tend to increase the attraction of tried-and-tested content and syllabus structures that have been known 'to work' previously.

Overall, the picture to emerge from the literature is of an ELT publishing industry that has very specific needs and operates under a number of restrictions. The high investment costs associated with the production of coursebooks mean that risks have to be eliminated, or at least limited as much as possible, in a way that is presumably not true for all types of publishing; the consequence of this is a tendency towards conservatism, a preference towards the publication of materials that are similar to those that have already seen commercial success. Simultaneously, publishers need to consider the needs of many different markets, many of which sometimes have apparently arbitrary requirements. Published materials are therefore the result of compromise between different actors and different needs. They must also tread carefully when considering innovation, preferring the 'minimally evolutionary' to the revolutionary (Littlejohn, 1992: 206). As far as grammar is concerned, the pressure to produce materials that are similar to those already on the market leads to the use of graded grammatical syllabuses populated with tried and trusted structures, using a tried and trusted sequence.

As for the actual grammatical content of coursebooks, a number of studies have criticised various aspects of the grammatical descriptions and representations they contain. As we said in Section 2.4 above, frequency is often suggested as a key criterion for sequencing items in a syllabus, and many such studies have used frequency-based critiques. For example, For example, Biber and Reppen (2002) analyse coverage in six ELT grammar books of noun premodifiers and the progressive aspect, and the lexis used to exemplify grammatical features. They show that these features are either over- or under-represented in ELT materials when compared with frequency in corpus data, arguing that materials authors 'make pedagogical decisions based on their beliefs about language use' (2002: 200) and that '[b]y using information based on actual frequency and context of use (e.g. register differences), materials developers and teachers should be able to increase the meaningful input that is provided to learners' (2002: 207). A similar example is Shortall's (2007) study, which compared spoken data in the Bank of English with coverage in coursebooks of present perfect aspect forms, again finding a difference between the two when frequency is considered: coursebooks appear to over-represent the active forms of the present perfect simple and continuous but under-represent present perfect passive and modal perfect forms. Some time adverbials (e.g. *since* and *for*) were also found to be over-represented, while the adverb *now* was under-represented. A further example is Römer's (2005) study, which compares treatment of progressive forms in coursebooks with data from the BNC and Bank of English. Coverage in coursebooks was shown to simplify and misrepresent many aspects of actual usage of progressive forms, under-representing, for example, the function of 'repeatedness', found to be very frequent in the corpus data.

Other studies to compare grammar coverage in coursebooks with empirical evidence in corpora include: Barbieri and Eckhardt's (2007) investigation into coverage of reported speech in coursebooks; Conrad's (2004) discussion of the (lack of) coverage in coursebooks of *though* as a 'linking adverbial'; critiques of the traditional coursebook treatment of conditional forms found in Burton (2022), Gabrielatos (2006), Jones and Waller (2011) and Maule (1988); and Holmes's (1988) analysis of the (mis)representation of doubt and certainty in coursebooks. Equally significant are areas of language that are not established in the ELT grammar canon but which nonetheless seem to have pedagogic value, for example, the features of 'spoken grammar' identified by Carter and McCarthy (1995), or phraseological patterns (Hunston et al., 1997).

2.7 Summary

The aim of this chapter has been to contextualise the study presented in the rest of this book. As we have seen, the investigation into the ELT grammar canon presented here builds on research in a number of fields, specifically previous work on pedagogical grammar, on syllabus and curriculum design (in particular, discussions of how materials might be sequenced in a structural syllabus), on competency levels in language teaching and on investigations into and critiques of the ELT publishing industry and analyses of ELT materials.

There already exists an extensive body of research on pedagogical grammar. Views have been put forward on how pedagogical grammars should be structured, how the elements of which they are made up can be selected, how the rules and descriptions related to these elements should be written and presented and how these elements can be sequenced. However, as we saw, many aspects of the advice put forward essentially rely on subjective judgements to be made on issues such as complexity, communicative need and so on. As we said, the sequencing of grammar content also tends to inevitably involve the assignment of each teaching item to a particular 'competency level', a construct which appears to be an accepted practice in language teaching and materials design, but is not in itself unproblematic.

The existing literature on pedagogical grammar can aid an understanding of the nature of ELT pedagogical grammar in only a relatively limited way, as it has not set out to explain why the ELT grammar canon at present is the way it is, but rather discusses how it – or indeed, the pedagogical grammar for any language – *should* be. Similarly, previous studies on ELT publishing – while offering useful critiques and helping to explain the context within which materials publishers and authors work – have not explored the origins of the ELT grammar canon or attempted an in-depth analysis of its contemporary state. For an explanation of the nature of the ELT grammar canon, we need to look elsewhere. In the next chapter, we will begin to fill this gap by attempting to establish a broad history of the evolution of ELT pedagogical grammar, supported by primary sources.

Notes

(1) The 'threshold level' was a concept developed in the 1970s, 'a metaphor which is designed to capture the notion of "crossing over" from the dependency of a learner to the self-sufficiency of a trained language user' (Howatt & Widdowson, 2004: 338). The term 'threshold' is used in the CEFR to describe the B1 level.
(2) For example, all of the following successful coursebook series – covering the period from the 1920s to the 1990s – were published at four levels: *New Method* (Michael West, 1926–1938), *Oxford English* (Laurence Faucett, 1933), *Essential English* (C.E. Eckersley, 1938–1942), *New Concept English* (L.G. Alexander, 1967), the second editions of *Strategies* (Abbs & Freebairn, 1977–1982), *The New Cambridge English Course* (Swan & Walter, 1990–1992) as well as *Streamline* (Hartley & Viney, 1978–1982).

3 ELT Grammar Canon and Consensus: An Evolutionary Perspective

3.1 Introduction

The aim of the previous chapter was to establish a basis on which an analysis of the ELT grammar canon can be carried out. The 'ecosystem' within which the ELT grammar canon resides is complex and traverses a number of different fields of research. As we saw, this study builds on previous studies on pedagogical grammar, on syllabus and curriculum design and on materials analysis, and will attempt to contribute to these with an approach that puts the analysis of primary sources at the forefront, in addition to considering the perspectives and experiences of those involved in the creation of primary sources.

We can now turn to the canon itself. As we saw in Chapter 1, there is very little research that directly addresses the content of ELT pedagogical grammar either as it is now, or how it developed historically. The aim of this chapter is therefore to provide a broad historical account of the evolution of the canon, starting from early (non-ELT) accounts of English grammar, examining 'traditional' school grammars and the grammars of what became known as the 'Great Tradition', before arriving at 20th pedagogical grammars. I will identify a number of 'milestone' books which I consider to be crucial in the development of the canon. We will see that the canon did not spring out of nowhere but should be seen as a continuation – perhaps one particular branch – of the ongoing evolution of accounts of English grammar. The historical account will bring us up to the pedagogical grammar found in contemporary coursebooks and practice grammars.

It must be acknowledged that in this book I have thus far only asserted the existence of a canon of ELT grammar. We will therefore begin this chapter by considering an existing study, the *British Council – EAQUALS Core Inventory for General English*, which constitutes strong evidence for the existence of a grammar canon (and indeed, a strong consensus on many other aspects of teaching content in ELT), before turning to consider the processes which lead up to this current consensus.

3.2 Is There an ELT Grammar Canon?

The existence of a consensus on ELT grammar in mainstream ELT practice has been widely asserted in the research literature. The word 'canon' to refer to the grammar content used in ELT and in ELT materials is used by both R. Ellis (2006) and O'Keeffe and Mark (2017), while Thornbury (2013: 216), in talking of the 'endless reproduction of what is essentially the same grammar syllabus in coursebook after coursebook', uses the term 'grammar McNuggets' to refer to the mass (re)production of grammar syllabus items. Equally often, it is the totality of coursebook content – including grammar – which is critiqued, with the content of coursebooks described as 'standardised' (Copley, 2018; Littlejohn, 2012) and said to represent a part of the 'commodification' of language education (Copley, 2018; Thornbury, 2013). Long (2011: 7), in his criticism of coursebooks (and synthetic syllabuses more generally), states that publishers justify selling coursebooks 'around the world to learners of all sorts […] on the grounds that they teach "the structures of a language," which are "the same for everyone"' (quotation marks in original).

Despite this, I am aware of no study produced by a critic of coursebooks or of the consensus on syllabus content to have systematically investigated the canon and set out its contents, in order to safely establish the premise – that coursebook content *is* indeed largely homogenous across titles and publishers – on which such critiques are based. Although I believe that the analyses provided in the following chapters will show that strong forces exist within both the ELT profession in general and within ELT publishing industry which tend towards maintaining homogeneity in grammatical content, a wide-ranging analysis of the canon is also beyond the scope of the current study. Fortunately, there nonetheless exists an empirical study which provides very strong evidence for the existence of agreement within the mainstream ELT profession on which language should be taught to English language learners and at which level; this is the 'Core Inventory for General English' (North et al., 2010).

The Core Inventory sets out 'the core of English language *taught* at Common European Framework of Reference (CEFR) levels A1 to C1 in English' (North et al., 2010: 11, emphasis added), providing 'a simple overview of the *apparent consensus* on what constitutes the most important content for teaching and learning at each level' (2010: 20, emphasis added). To establish this consensus, the investigators examined the language implied in the CEFR level descriptors, content found in syllabuses created by EAQUALS (Evaluation and Accreditation of Quality

Language Services) members,[1] coursebook contents, and teacher surveys. Points 'common to a strong majority (80%) in each of the data sources' were defined as 'core', while 'other points common to different sources that were considered significant' were defined as 'less core' (North *et al.*, 2010: 9). Following this initial stage, the Cambridge ESOL, City & Guilds and Trinity examination boards were invited to provide their input, before the exponents making up the inventory were created by the project team 'at an iterative series of workshops' (North *et al.*, 2010).

The purpose of creating the Core Inventory was not to critique the consensus, but quite the opposite: it is said to provide 'a documentation of a consensus in good practice', showing 'the area of overlap in what people do' in ELT (North, 2010: 6). Although it covers more than just grammar (also listed for each CEFR level are functions, discourse markers, vocabulary and topics), the document sets out clearly the consensus on major grammar points, for example tenses, verb forms, conditionals, modal verbs and articles. As per the data sources outlined in the previous paragraph, the focus is on what coursebooks cover and what teachers teach, not what learners actually produce or understand. The authors of the publication report being 'genuinely surprised at the extent of agreement between the different types of sources: course books, teachers, examination boards, syllabus writers' (North *et al.*, 2010: 18). Presumably, those researchers who have claimed the existence of such a strong consensus would not have been so surprised.

An example from the Core Inventory can be found in Table 3.1 below, which sets out the consensus on the levels at which different future forms should be taught. The lighter shading at C1 represents 'a lower, but still very significant, level of consensus' (North *et al.*, 2010: 182010).

The exact contents of the Core Inventory need not detain us; the document is freely available for download from the EAQUALS or British Council websites for any reader that would like to examine the wider consensus it establishes. What is most important is that it exists to start with. The fact that the research team were able to 'track points

Table 3.1 Consensus view on future forms reported in the Core Inventory, from North *et al.* (2010) © British Council

	A1	A2	B1	B2	C1
Future					
Future Time (going to)					
Future Time (present continous)					
Future Time (will & going to)			Prediction	Prediction	Prediction
Future Continous				Prediction	Prediction
Future Perfect					Prediction
Future Perfect Continous					Prediction

of commonality across the profession' (North et al., 2010: 18) – despite referring to a diverse range of data sources – is a remarkable insight into its strength. If there did not exist such a broad agreement (a phrase also used by the authors in the document) on content across the profession, then the suggestion that there could exist a 'core inventory' of best practice would be difficult to sustain.

3.3 English Grammars up until the Early 20th Century

The data presented in the Core Inventory makes us reasonably confident that there does indeed exist, within contemporary ELT profession, a canon of ELT grammar, and we can now begin to consider how we arrived at this point. This chapter – or indeed, book – cannot hope to attempt to provide a full account of English grammars over the centuries. Ian Michael's (1970) account of grammars only up until 1800 runs to over 600 pages, and 856 grammars were published in the 19th century alone (Michael, 1991). What we can do, however, is focus on a small number of titles that might be considered broadly representative of the different periods of grammar writing, or that are interesting for other reasons. We will also return to many of the titles described here in the case studies presented in Chapters 6 and 7.

3.3.1 The earliest accounts and Latin influence

The first formal description of English grammar is said to be William Bullokar's 1586 *Pamphlet for Grammar* (Linn, 2006). It is said that Bullokar's intention in producing his grammar was to show that the English language was rule based and could be analysed in the same way as Latin (Linn, 2006), but even he expresses doubts as to how sophisticated the rule system in English actually was: 'As English hath few and short rules for the declining of words, so it hath few rules for joining words in sentence or in construction' (Bullokar, 1586, cited in Michael, 1970: 467). Doubts about whether English actually had syntax continued in works until the last decades of the 18th century (Linn, 2006).

Latin was the language of science at the time and its influence can be seen in the metalanguage chosen to describe English grammar (for example, 'verb' from Latin 'verbum', 'clause' from Latin 'clausa' and 'perfect' from Latin 'perfectus'). Latin was also used as a framework through which descriptions of English grammar were presented, meaning that descriptions of the structure of the English language was sometimes stretched to fit around structural categories used for Latin. In his treatment of English nouns, for example, Bullokar claims the existence of a case system within which nouns are 'declined with fi[v]e cases in both numbers' (Bullokar, 1586, cited in Linn, 2006: 74) whereas in reality, nouns in English at the time were marked only for number and possession, as in modern English.

While the influence of Latin in the teaching of English grammar in this period was in part the result of reverence towards the classical language, and the desire to follow an educational tradition going back centuries, there were two other contributing factors. Firstly, in this period there was believed to exist a kind of universal grammar (not to be confused with Chomsky's universal grammar) which governed most or all languages (Michael, 1987) and it made sense to 'tap into' this and base descriptions of previously undescribed languages like English on the systems already used to describe Latin and Greek. Secondly, there were practical considerations: the authors, in the 17th century, of the first pedagogical grammars of English as a foreign language made references to Latin equivalents of English grammar as a way of explaining it to foreigners, who were expected to already have a firm grounding of Latin grammar (Howatt & Widdowson, 2004); we will see an example of this later in the chapter.

The number of grammars of English published increased exponentially over the centuries, with the market exploding in the 18th and 19th centuries. In the 19th century alone, 856 grammars were published, hence the title of Ian Michael's chapter on 19th-century titles, 'More Than Enough English Grammars' (Michael, 1991). The increasing number of publications suggests that, by the 19th century, descriptions of English grammar had reached a high level of maturity and confidence, if not always agreement among themselves (Michael, 1970, passim). Whereas 400 years previously no grammar of English had existed, hundreds of titles were now available, and Bullokar's doubts over whether English actually had syntax were long forgotten.

3.3.2 An early pedagogical title: Jonson's *English Grammar*

Jonson's grammar came less than 100 years after Bullokar's, in 1640. Although not especially well known, it is fascinating as it is an early example of a pedagogical grammar. The title is relatively short, at 149 pages. Of these, the first 75 pages deal with the letters of the English alphabet, as was common in grammars of this period (Howatt & Widdowson, 2004). This section covers pronunciation (ostensibly of the letters themselves, although in reality the section provides a phonemic inventory), making comments on etymology and comparisons with contemporary languages. The remainder of the book is closer to what a modern day reader would likely expect of a 'grammar'. Many of the language points chosen for description would be familiar to a teacher working in ELT today. Its contents include, for example, nouns, articles, pronouns (possessive, relative and reflexive), comparatives and superlatives, the passive, linking words and information on word order. On the other hand, the section on 'syntax' is patchy and says little about overall sentence structure in English, while certain analyses (for example, the division of parts of speech into those that are marked for number, and those that are not) would certainly not be familiar to most contemporary practitioners. Some very familiar language points, such as conditional forms, are missing, while modal verbs are only mentioned in passing.

It is also noticeable that explanations of usage are rather lacking, for example advice on when to use one tense rather than another, or when to prefer the passive voice over the active. As mentioned above, however, grammars of this period could let Latin do much of the work for them. The following example is instructive, where Jonson appears to consider the use of translations into Latin to be sufficient for explaining tense and aspect in English:

> The futures are declared by the infinitive and the Verb, *shall*, or *will*: as *Amabo: I shall, or will love.*
> *Amavero* addeth thereunto *have*, taking the nature of two divers Times; that is, of the Future and the time Past:
> *I shall have loved*: or
> *I will have loved.*
> The Perfect times are expressed by the Verb *have*: as,
> *Amavi. Amaveram.*
> *I have loved. I had loved.*
> *Amaverim* and *Amavissem* add *might* unto the former Verb: as,
> *I might have loved.* (Jonson, 1640: 35)

3.3.3 Murray's *English Grammar*

In examining Lindley Murray's grammar, we enter more familiar territory in the history of English grammar. Hugely successful both in the USA and Britain, the title is representative of what became known as 'school grammar' or 'traditional grammar', and was highly influential on titles that followed it (Michael, 1991). The book's aims as a schoolbook for English-speaking children are reflected in its content. For example, no attempt is made to distinguish the meanings of different modal forms when they are covered; a brief note later (Murray, 1795: 90) states that 'learners will readily perceive' the difference, suggesting an intended readership of native speakers. Also present are warnings against 'errors' that seem likely to be features of dialect or vernacular forms; for example, one section covers the misuse of double comparatives (e.g. *worser conduct, more superior*), while elsewhere readers are warned not to confuse irregular past forms and past participles (e.g. 'He would have spoke'). As McCarthy (2021) notes, many of the features that Murray warns against are alive and well today in many parts of the world.

The moralistic tone found throughout the work is also noteworthy, with example sentences frequenting dealing with issues of good governance and self-control; for example, just a single page (p. 75) offers us the following examples to illustrate how verbs can be used with reference to an indefinite time period in the past, present and future: 'Virtue promotes happiness'; 'The old Romans governed by benefits more than by fear'; 'I shall hereafter employ my time more usefully'.

Despite the fact that his title was aimed at English-speaking school children, Murray describes in great detail aspects of English that a native speaker would reasonably be expected *not* to need instruction in. The section on syntax runs to over 70 pages. Elsewhere, a note in the section on the 'infinitive mood' advises that '[i]t may not, however, be generally proper for young persons beginning the study of grammar, to commit to memory all the tenses of the verbs' (1795: 84). So, while the book is written with native speakers in mind, the book's aim often seems to be to 'reteach' them the language: grammar had become a school subject, separated from children's existing language competencies and taught dogmatically. Michael (1991: 11) notes the peculiarity of a school subject in which native speakers are taught 'linguistic skills which, unknown to them and their teachers, they already possessed', adding that this phenomenon, 'if it were unfamiliar, would be regarded with astonishment'.

Grammars from this period had rather limited aims; Murray's intention does not appear to be to provide a full account or description of English grammar, but rather to clear up doubts in marginal cases. Indeed, Murray himself states that there is little point in grammarians attempting to influence established usage, and that they should instead instruct only on 'cases which custom has left dubious' (Murray, 1795: 145). Indeed, a reader that perseveres with Murray's text will find that he is sometimes surprisingly progressive, or at least, non-prescriptive. For example, he notes that *none* can be treated as either singular or plural, in contrast to modern prescriptive accounts, which tend to view a plural verb form as incorrect. Similarly, phrase-final prepositions are said to prevail 'in common conversation, and [...] the familiar style in writing' (1795: 173), instead of being proscribed altogether. However, prescriptivism in grammars certainly increased over the next 100 years, with the gradually emergence of what Linn characterises as the 'popular association of grammar study with inviolable rules and, by association, with rules of propriety and morals' (Linn, 2006: 77).

3.3.4 'The Great Tradition': Late 19th- and early 20th-century 'scientific' grammars

By the end of the 19th century change was on the way, in the form of the Reform Movement (see Chapter 1) and, related to this, a new wave of

English grammars, which what has subsequently been termed 'The Great Tradition' (Chalker et al., 2014). Grammars of this type and period are often referred to as 'scientific', a word chosen by Henry Sweet, one of the most famous grammar authors of the time, in the preface of his (1892) *A New English Grammar*. The new titles took an evidence-based and descriptive approach, representative of what Linn (2006) describes as the professionalisation of language teaching in the 19th century. Whereas in the past, examples were used in grammars principally as way of illustrating grammar 'mistakes' (including those asserted to have been made by respected writers), grammarians now used textual evidence as the starting point of analyses. Otto Jespersen, for instance, in his (1909) *A Modern English Grammar on Historical Principles*, used examples taken from his personal 'corpus' of hundreds of sources, stating that these were 'in many ways more satisfactory than even the best made-up examples' (Jespersen, 1909: vi)

In addition to Sweet and Jespersen, other well-known and important grammarians from this period include E. Maetzner, H. Poutsma, E. Kruisinga, A.P. Erades and R.W. Zandvoort. As the reader can readily apprehend, non-native speaker grammarians were the 'key players' in this period and dominated grammar writing in English until the 1970s (Aarts, 1988); as McCarthy (2021: 53) notes, they remained 'at the forefront' even after the advent of corpus linguistics informed grammar writing at the end of the 20th century. The prevalence of grammars written by non-native speaker grammarians might be surprising to those acquainted with (the authors of) modern ELT pedagogical grammars. However, it is significant beyond simply being a 'fun fact': the role of non-native speakers may have been key in the development of grammatical accounts – particularly pedagogical ones – of English, due to the insight that non-native speaker grammarians possess from having learnt English as a foreign language. Comments to this effect can be found, for example, in an anonymous ELT journal review, from 1949, of Zandvoort's (1945) *A Handbook of English Grammar*, in which the reviewer argues that 'Continental' scholars produce the most useful grammars for English language learners, because they are able to notice features of language that 'English' (i.e. native-speaker) authors do not:

> Most of the others [i.e. grammar books not written by non-native speaker grammarians from mainland Europe] were written for those with English as their mother tongue, and do not meet the special needs of those to whom English is a foreign language. Throughout the book the author is able to explain and illustrate points of usage which no English [sic] author, writing for English people, would think of referring to. [...] It is on such points as these, to which the Englishman gives no conscious thought because usage comes to him without the need for reflection, that the Continental investigator of our language can be and is so helpful. ('Book reviews', 1949: 53–54)

The Great Tradition constitutes a crucial phase in the history of grammatical accounts of English. The grammars from this period played an important role in developing a modern understanding of the grammar of English, and appear to have provided a basis from which 20th-century ELT practitioners could produce more targeted pedagogical accounts. This sentiment is confirmed by the contemporary pedagogical grammarian Michael Swan, who argues that '[m]uch of what we know about English grammar was established by early twentieth-century scholars from Jespersen (1909) onwards' (Swan, 2011: 565).

3.4 English Grammars into the 20th and 21st Centuries

This section will focus mainly on *pedagogical* descriptions of English grammar from the turn of the 20th century. While we will at time make references to developments outside of ELT, the beginning of the 20th century represents the time period which Howatt and Widdowson (2004) characterise as the start of the 'modern era' of ELT; from this point, ELT pedagogical grammar can therefore begin to be seen as a standalone strand in the history of English grammar(s). We will begin by examining the work of Harold Palmer and A.S. Hornby in Japan and beyond, before outlining the work of Charles C. Fries and colleagues in the United States, the shift to Chomskian grammars, and then the re-emergence of descriptive accounts. Finally, we will return to primary sources, and will examine four key titles in the history of pedagogical grammar for ELT.

3.4.1 Harold Palmer and A.S. Hornby

In the early stages of the 'modern' era of ELT, there was inevitably a lack of a strong, theoretical base in terms of pedagogy. In addition, there was also a lack of consensus on or knowledge of exactly *what* aspects of the English language should be taught to English language learners. In terms of grammar, there had been, as we have seen, a long (and infamous) tradition of English grammar taught to English-speaking schoolchildren followed by the revolution represented by the new, scientific grammars of the 'Great Tradition' (although see also Quirk (1957) for a discussion of how these scientific grammars were in any case often lacking useful, prescriptive accounts for language learners).

One of the first people to address the issue of *what* needed to be taught to English language learners was Harold Palmer, in his (1921) title, *The Principles of Language Study* (also referred to in Chapter 2). Palmer's book discusses a wide range of issues related to language learning and teaching, but of most interest to us here is his discussion of grammar and the content of grammars. In the first chapter, in which he discusses the question of the unconscious learning of a language, Palmer asks the following questions:

> Do you say *I go always there* or *I always go there*? You certainly use the latter form. Why? Have you ever been told that a certain class of adverbs (among them the word *always*) is placed before and not after the verb? Have you been told that there are twenty-three exceptions to the rule, and have you ever learnt these exceptions ? [...] In what cases do you replace the word *far* by the expression *a long way*? What are the precise laws governing the respective uses of *went* and *did go*? Which are the English 'postposition's, if any? In what cases do we use nouns unpreceded by any article or other determinative word? What is the exact difference between *had you* and *did you have*? (Palmer, 1921: 38–39)

Continuing, Palmer states that these examples 'are not contained in any manual of English grammar nor even taught as a school subject' (1921: 39). While Palmer's intention in this section is actually to make the point that speakers often have no explicit knowledge of many areas of their own grammar, and must therefore have learned such 'rules' unconsciously (see Goldberg, 2019 for a contemporary perspective on this), he also seems to be – perhaps unintentionally – making the case for the need for pedagogical descriptions of English grammar. The examples chosen surely emerged from his own direct experience of the kinds of problems his own learners had experienced, and his point that 'manuals of English grammar' do not address them shows that published accounts of grammar for learners at that time were extremely limited.

Palmer published in 1924 his own pedagogical grammar, *A Grammar of Spoken English*, which we will look at in more detail below. However, the 'flavour' of pedagogical grammar that Palmer became more commonly associated with is that of 'patterns'. Palmer's approach was to identify the 'grammatical peculiarities pertaining to individual words' (Palmer, 1938: 3) – essentially, the syntactic context(s) in which they typically appear – and use these as a basis for teaching and practice. In his (1938) *A Grammar of English Words*, Palmer focused on the typical patterns associated with 1000 words. There was a strong synergy between content and methodology with patterns. In an earlier publication, Palmer had explained the use of 'substitution tables', such as that shown in Table 3.2, which put such patterns into practice:

Table 3.2 Example of a substitution table (Palmer, 1916: v)

I	saw	two	books	here	yesterday.
You	put	three	letters	there	last week.
We	left	a few	keys	on the table	on Sunday.
They	found	some	good ones	in this box	this morning.

In class, learners would at first repeat verbatim whole sentences spoken by the teacher, and then again but with various elements changed in order to create 'novel' sentences (see King, 1959 for a detailed account of different possible techniques).

Palmer's research on patterns had started while he was director of the Institute for Research in English Teaching (IRET) in Tokyo, Japan, and was continued by colleague A.S. Hornby upon Palmer's return to the UK (see Smith (2004) for a full account of IRET's activities). While perhaps largely forgotten today, two titles which were the fruit of research at IRET – Palmer's (1938) *A Grammar of English Words* and Hornby's (1954a) *A Guide to Patterns and Use in English* – are said to have been 'corner-stones' of ELT in the decades subsequent to their publication (Smith, 2004: 169), with the latter becoming a standard reference work for ELT materials writers of the period (Richards, 2017). The approach also bears many similarities to the corpus-based Pattern Grammar approach of Susan Hunston and colleagues (Hunston & Francis, 2000; see also Hanks, 2008, for an account linking Hornby's work to that of Hunston and Francis). Interestingly, Hornby did not consider such patterns to be a type of 'grammar' (a word which he seemed to believe had negative connotations, harking back to the traditional school grammars discussed above), and preferred to use the term 'structure'.

A.S. Hornby was also a key figure in the launch, in 1946, of the *ELT Journal*. A revealing insight into the knowledge level of pedagogical grammar among teachers in the first half of the 20th century can be found in the journal's 'Question Box' feature, which ran from the first issue and in which readers – typically teachers based outside of the UK (Smith, 2007) – could send in queries about any aspect of ELT (responses were initially anonymous, whereas later on A.S. Hornby was identified as 'responder'). Particularly in the first decades (the feature ran until the early 1980s) many questions were about grammar, and the following five are typical in style and content:

> Will you please explain the difference between *each* and *every*. ('The Question Box', 1947: 111)
>
> Is it possible to give any general rules for the use of the helping verb *do* in the formation of the negative and interrogative? ('Question Box', 1948: 25)
>
> We usually say: 'Have you read this book?' Is it wrong to say: 'Did you read this book?' If it is not wrong, what difference is there? (Hornby, 1951: 30)
>
> Must *any* always be used in interrogative and negative sentences? Can *some* ever be used? (Hornby, 1953a: 138)
>
> Are there any rules about the use of infinitives and gerunds after verbs indicating like and dislike? (Hornby, 1953b: 27)

It is fascinating how simple, from a contemporary perspective, many of the questions in the *Question Box* feature appear to be. Answers to the five questions listed above could be found easily in coursebooks or grammar practice books, or simply online and a reasonably experienced teacher could probably answer all of them without difficulty. The fact that such 'simple' questions were asked and, more importantly, that it was considered worthwhile publishing answers to them, suggests very strongly that in this period a body of knowledge on ELT grammar had yet to be formed and that figures such as Hornby were to be key in developing it.

Overall, we can see Palmer and Hornby as two key figures in the move towards the modern understanding and consensus of pedagogical grammar. Their work (and we should acknowledge that they also collaborated with a number of colleagues, such as the textbook authors and theorists Lawrence Faucett and Michael West) can be seen as a bridge between the turn-of-the-century scientific grammars and contemporary ELT pedagogical grammar.

3.4.2 The United States: Structuralism and the audiolingual approach

The outbreak of the Second World War put an end to the research activities at IRET in Japan, and the focus for research on how to teach languages scientifically shifted to the United States, more specifically to the English Language Institute (ELI) at the University of Michigan and the figure of Charles C. Fries (Howatt & Smith, 2014). Although the work carried out in this period is often associated with what are often described as 'discredited' (Kumaravadivelu, 2006) approaches to teaching such as audiolingualism, it nonetheless had its part to play in the development of ELT pedagogical grammar.

The basis of the research carried out at ELI rested on the structural approach to linguistics, which viewed spoken language as primary and sought to identify the different elements underlying a particular language (phonemes, morphemes and elements of syntax) and establish their relationship to each other. One key element of the structural approach, and something which dated back to Ferdinand de Saussure's work at the beginning of the 20th century (Joseph, 2016), was the distinction between syntagmatic and paradigmatic axes of language. Joseph offers the example of the phrase 'Crime pays', where 'pays' and 'crime' have a syntagmatic relationship: in English, 'crime', as subject, comes before 'pays' the verb, and the third person singular -*s* form of 'pays' is a result of the fact that 'crime' is singular. At the same time, 'crime' is in a paradigmatic relationship with the words 'criminal', 'misdemeanour' and 'legality', among many others. This underlying foundation neatly matched both with the research at IRET on patterns and the existing pedagogy based on the use of substitution tables. Fries and colleagues advocated for the same approach, which effectively practises both entire paradigms (through the repetition of entire sentences), and also teaches syntagmatic choice (through the replacement of single elements in sentences in order to produce new sentences). This eventually became known as the 'audiolingual' approach.[2]

In addition to practice based on sentence patterns, another key element of audiolingualism was the 'contrastive analysis' (CA) hypothesis (Lado, 1957), developed by Fries' ELI colleague Roberto Lado. The hypothesis stated that many production errors in language learners could be explained as a result of differences between the L1 and the L2 (although, as Swan, 2007, notes, subsequent claims that the CA hypothesis posited that *all*, or even *most*, errors are explainable in this way are a misrepresentation of the CA position). The logical consequence of this for the grammatical content of learning materials was that they should be designed with specific L1 groups in mind, targeting the differences between the L1 and target language. For Fries, this meant potentially very different materials – and grammatical content – would be needed for different L1 groups of learners: '[A] different set of teaching materials must be prepared for each linguistic background. [...] [The features of English] present very different problems for those whose native language is German and those whose native language is Japanese' (Fries, 1959: 44). There therefore needed to be strict synergy between the activities of the researcher and the materials designer, with the former carrying out research directly relevant to the latter; this was in fact the case at ELI – the institute carried out research and also ran language courses using teaching materials developed in house. Although rarely now an overarching principle in syllabus design, the influence of the CA hypothesis can still be seen in teaching materials produced specifically for particular local markets, by both local and international publishers and some modern pedagogical grammars.[3]

Fries himself wrote a major (non-pedagogical) grammar, the (1952) *The Structure of English*. The grammar was based in part on an analysis of a 250,000-word corpus of recorded telephone conversations, making it the first grammar to be based on live, spoken data (Linn, 2006). However, the theory-driven approach to grammar associated with the rise of Chomskyan linguistics in the mid-20th century meant that such a data-driven approach, and traditional descriptive grammars in general, were beginning to be considered old-fashioned. Newer accounts of grammar in the Chomskyan tradition were far more narrow in scope, focusing on specific aspects of English grammar to an extent that the word 'grammar' no longer meant what it had done just decades earlier (Linn, 2006).

3.4.3 The return of descriptive grammars

The last quarter of the 20th century saw the return of descriptive grammars, perhaps the best known of which is Quirk *et al.*'s (1972)

A Grammar of Contemporary English, updated in 1985, becoming the *Comprehensive Grammar of the English Language* (Quirk *et al.*, 1985). Another significant title in the period is the highly successful *A Communicative Grammar of English* (Leech & Svartvik, 1975), aimed, at least in part, at English language learners, and with a strong focus on communication. Linn (2006: 87) argues that, along with Halliday's systemic functional approach, Leech and Svartvik's grammar helped to put communication 'firmly at the heart of English grammars for non-native and native speakers alike at all levels' .

At the end of the 20st century and into the 21st, grammars such as Biber *et al.*'s (1999) *Longman Grammar of Spoken and Written English* and Carter and McCarthy's (2006) *Cambridge Grammar of English: A Comprehensive Guide* represented a significant methodological shift in their extensive use of corpus data (although, it should perhaps be said, also a return to the kind of approach pioneered by the likes of Fries). Biber *et al.*'s (1999) title is significant in that it brought to the forefront the question of how register interacts with the distribution and frequency of grammatical features; the grammatical descriptions it contains are based around four different registers – fiction writing, news writing, academic writing and conversation – and frequency data is provided throughout to illustrate how the 'behaviour' of different grammatical elements changes in these different contexts. Similarly, as the subtitle – 'Spoken and Written English Grammar and Usage' – of Carter and McCarthy's (2006) grammar suggests, this work was particularly innovative in its focus on both written and spoken grammar conventions. Although less prominently than in Biber *et al.*, differences in distribution of grammatical features across different registers, both written and spoken, are also explained.

3.5 Four Key 20th-Century Pedagogical Grammars

We will now turn to look in detail at some key titles in the evolution of pedagogical accounts of English grammar in the 20th century. In a way somewhat reminiscent of the explosion of school grammars in the 19th century, the number of pedagogical grammars increased exponentially in the 20th century and we will 'sample' this development by examining four titles: three pedagogical grammars and an inventory of grammatical structures aimed at materials authors and syllabus designers. As with the grammars of Murray and Jonson described earlier, we will also return to these titles in the case studies presented later in this book (in Chapters 5 and 7); the reader may also note that the latter three of the titles described here are mentioned several times by the interviewees whose experiences and opinions are presented in Chapters 4 and 6, testifying to their historical significance. The titles we will examine are as follows:

- *A Grammar of Spoken English On a Strictly Phonetic Basis* (Palmer, 1924).
- *Living English Structure* (Allen, 1947).
- *A Practical English Grammar* (Thomson & Martinet, 1960).
- *English Grammatical Structure* (Alexander et al., 1975).

These titles are chosen for different reasons. Palmer's grammar is one of the first modern grammars to be written specifically with ELT in mind (Linn, 2006), and Palmer himself was a key figure in the development of the ELT profession (Howatt & Widdowson, 2004). The grammars of Allen and Thomson and Martinet are chosen primarily because of their influence and commercial success – a fifth edition of the former was published in 1997, over 50 years since its first edition, while the latest edition of Thomson and Martinet was published as recently as 2017. It can reasonably be assumed that since their publication, both titles have influenced millions of teachers and learners around the world. Finally, *English Grammatical Structure* is said to have been highly influential on the grammatical content of coursebooks since its publication (Richards, 2017); as we will see in the coming chapters, this claim is confirmed by more than one of the coursebook authors interviewed for this study. The publication dates of all four titles cover six decades of the 20th century, from the period in which the idea of a pedagogical account of English grammar was essentially an innovation, to the era of contemporary pedagogical grammars, to which we will turn immediately after.

3.5.1 A *Grammar of Spoken English on a Strictly Phonetic Basis* (Palmer, 1924)

We have already referred to Palmer's thoughts on language teaching several times in this and the previous chapter and it is interesting to see how he put these into practice. In the introduction to his grammar, he states that the principal target audience of the book are advanced learners of English as a Foreign Language, or teachers of it, making it one of the earliest modern pedagogical grammars of English:

> Now this *Grammar of Spoken English* is intended to be used chiefly (but not exclusively) by foreign adult students of English, and by all teachers of spoken English. The fact that it is written *in English* shows that it is not intended to be put into the hands of beginners; it is designed to help (a) those who are already able to understand written English, and (b) the English teachers who serve as the medium of instruction in living English speech. (1924: xxx–xxxi)

It is interesting how Palmer chooses to hedge this description of intended audience with the phrase 'but not exclusively', leaving the door open for native speakers as users. Most modern pedagogical grammars would be highly unlikely to describe themselves in such a way, and indeed, Palmer's grammar is considered by some to form part of the Great Tradition (Linn, 2006), arguably placing it closer to a title like Quirk *et al.*'s (1985) *Comprehensive Grammar of the English Language* than to the other two titles discussed in this section. In any case, it goes to show that the line between native speaker grammars and pedagogical grammars had, in this period, perhaps not become as fixed as it is today.

The precise genesis of Palmer's title is somewhat mysterious. He does not include a list of references or explain in any way which sources he referred to, although he does make occasional in-text references to other grammars, most frequently to Henry Sweet's work. In the introduction, Palmer seems to suggest that he is attempting to provide a bridge between the longer, more scholarly grammars such as Sweet's, and the needs of learners of English as a foreign language, by choosing and explaining those areas of grammar he felt most important:

> [T]he foreign student will find *a selection* [emphasis added] of what the author considers to be the most useful grammatical categories of spoken English. [...] A serious endeavour has been made to give proportionate treatment to each subject according to its importance. (1924: xxxiii).

Palmer also makes clear in the introduction that his grammar is descriptive not prescriptive, spending several pages in the introduction citing Sweet in support, to justify his focus on 'the standard of usage'.

Arguably, Palmer's grammatical explanations are not always particularly clear. For example, his explanation of article usage is surprisingly equivocal, stating that 'in many cases such distinctions [between the use of definite and indefinite articles] *can hardly be formulated at all*, and the English usage *can only be acquired by dint of continual observation and imitation*' (Palmer, 1924: 50, emphasis added). It seems unlikely that a contemporary grammar would so quickly 'throw in the towel' in trying to provide an explanation, suggesting that the development of a set of rules for this area of ELT grammar was still in its infancy, and perhaps not satisfactorily covered in the grammars of the 'Great Tradition'. The utility of the title for a learner also seems to be limited by the lack of index (there is, instead, a 17-page table of contents to navigate) and practice activities.

Nevertheless, Palmer's work has been described as 'ground-breaking' (Smith, 2004: 38), and constituted the major body of work for which Palmer was subsequently awarded a doctorate by Tokyo Imperial University. Striking features of the book are the lengthy focus on a full range of phonological issues (including phonemes, stress, features of connected speech and intonation), and the fact that example words and sentences are in phonetic script only.[4] Palmer's grammar also makes extensive use of tables; particularly notable are the 12 pages of verb conjugations and six pages of syntactical patterns, reminiscent of the substitution tables found in his earlier publications described above.

3.5.2 *Living English Structure* (Allen, 1947)

W. Stannard Allen's *Living English Structure* appears to have been a key piece in the jigsaw that is the development of ELT pedagogical grammar, and to have achieved great commercial success (a fifth edition was published as recently as 2009). From a contemporary perspective, it in some ways seems unremarkable – its combination of grammar explanations and practice exercises can now be found in scores of publications. However, this is one thing that set it apart from pedagogical grammars of the era – as we have just seen, Palmer's *Grammar of Spoken English* contained no practice exercises. Equally significant is the way the explanations are written, with a more user-friendly approach adopted; compare, for example, Allen's 'streamlined' explanation of the past perfect with the equivalent explanation in Palmer's grammar:

> The *Past Perfect* tense is related to a moment in the past in the same way that the *Present Perfect* is related to the present moment, i.e. it describes an action completed before some special past moment we have in mind. (Allen, 1947: 145)

> A sharp distinction is made in English between *pastness* and *anteriority*. An action is considered to be, and is treated, as *past* when it is associated with a point (or a series of points) of time situated entirely in the past. When, however, the action is not so associated with such points of time, but is considered merely to have taken place before (*i.e.* anterior to) another given point of time, it is expressed by one of the *Perfect Tenses*. (Palmer, 1924: 272)

There are a number of section titles in Allen's book which would be unfamiliar to modern eyes, for example, 'emphatic connectives', 'phrase openings' and 'accepted phrases'. Its single section covering the 'present tense' would also be unusual now, with modern grammars typically separating out the present simple and present continuous. Also of note is the lack of a discreet, labelled focus on articles; they are instead covered in the section on countable and uncountable nouns, the first in the book. On the whole, though, the contents list is similar to that of contemporary pedagogical grammars. An index at the back aids navigation.

The choice of the word 'structure' instead of 'grammar' in the title is interesting. How much, if at all, Allen was influenced by structural linguistics or Hornby's conception of 'structure' is unclear – the first edition was published three years before Fries' *The Structure of English,* and a 1959 review in the *ELT Journal* of a special schools version of *Living English Structure* criticises it for having a 'misleading' title: 'there is no special emphasis on "structure" in the sense in that word is commonly used nowadays' ('Book reviews', 1959: 85). Nevertheless, Allen's introduction makes it clear that he believes that he is moving away from the idea of 'grammar' as it was widely understood at the time:

> An English schoolboy does 'grammar' as an analytical exercise, but the foreign student needs to learn the mechanics of the language. Most existing grammar books are designed for the English schoolboy, and even a large number of those that are intended for foreigners have not managed to free themselves entirely from the purely analytical point of view. (Allen, 1947: vii)

This is followed by an assertion that the book is descriptive rather than prescriptive – again, a clear attempt to distance the title from older grammars:

> Teachers will find in this book a great deal that is unconventional, perhaps even revolutionary, for it does not pretend to tell the student what he OUGHT to SAY in English, but tries to show him what is ACTUALLY SAID. (Allen, 1947: vii)

As with Palmer's title, the precise genesis of Allen's grammar is a mystery. Allen provides a list of 'some useful books for further reference' in the introduction (Allen, 1947: x), including various grammars from the Great Tradition, which implies that he had read at least some of them and that they had informed his work. The introduction cryptically states that many of the exercises 'are based on the results of personal "structure-counts" [...] carried out while listening to the speech of educated English people over considerable periods' (1947: vii–viii), but no further information is given on this research. It is known, however, that Allen was a teacher at the British Council (Hornby, 1966; Smith, 2005), so it seems possible that some of the content may originally have been material that he and/or colleagues had developed for British Council courses. This would go some way to explaining how he was able to create a work that appears to be so much more accessible and practically orientated compared with what had come before.

Another aspect of note is that the title contains a grading system for the practice exercises. Each one is labelled as being for Elementary ('Up to 1 ½ or 2 years of English'), Intermediate ('Up to about the standard demanded for the University of Cambridge Lower Certificate in English') or Advanced ('Up to about the standard demanded for the University of Cambridge Proficiency in English Examination'). To a certain extent the content is also graded, with certain explanations and footnotes placed with the more advanced exercises. This is one of the first clear examples of the important characteristic of sequencing and grading in pedagogical grammar. It also represents a further departure from older titles like Palmer's, and presumably increased the book's usefulness, meeting students' and teachers' need for practice material differentiated for competency level.

3.5.3 *A Practical English Grammar* (Thomson & Martinet, 1960)

Thomson and Martinet's grammar is very much in the same style as Allen's, and was apparently also very commercially successful (the latest edition was printed in 2017) and widely used. It is more detailed and comprehensive than Allen's; although over 70 pages shorter, the dimensions of the pages are larger, and, more importantly, the book contains only grammatical descriptions, explanations and examples. Exercises were provided in two separate practice books, allowing more detailed explanations in the main book. Like Allen's title, there is a detailed index at the back.

The overall contents list would be entirely familiar to a modern reader, with none of Allen's more 'esoteric' section headings included. Compared with Allen's title, a number of additional grammar points are included. These include, among others, a dedicated section on articles, a section on conjunctions and a much longer and more detailed section on comparatives. Although Thomson and Martinet do not make any specific claims about level, in the Preface they seem to position the book as being appropriate for more advanced learners, stating that '[t]his grammar aims to be particularly helpful at the point where the more complicated structures of spoken and written English are first being acquired' (Thomson & Martinet, 1960, Preface).

There is perhaps less to say about this title than Allen's because the style is now familiar: the explanations are streamlined and learner focused, as the authors explain in the preface: 'the style and organization of the Grammar facilitate the student's comprehension and make the information he or she requires readily accessible' (Thomson & Martinet, 1960, Preface). However, the preface also contains the remarkable claim that '[o]bsolete structures and irrelevant concepts from Latin grammar have been given the briefest treatment or are bypassed completely' (Thomson & Martinet, 1960, Preface). It is not clear which parts of the book this comment relates to, and while the writers' intention seems to be to paint their title as being modern and as having left behind the contents of traditional grammars, the logical implication that *some* obsolete structures and irrelevant concepts from Latin *are* in fact included, albeit briefly, is incredible, and would be unthinkable in a modern pedagogical grammar. Once again, it seems to indicate that in the mid-20th century, the delineation between traditional school grammars and modern pedagogical grammars had perhaps not yet been definitively established.[5]

Looking across the three titles examined in this section thus far, it is possible to trace certain trends. Firstly, it is notable that all three titles are at pains to distance themselves from older, prescriptive grammars; as we saw, Palmer and Allen are explicit in making the case for basing their descriptions on usage, while Thomson and Martinet feel the need to make it clear that concepts from Latin are 'bypassed'. Secondly, there is a clear move towards a learner-focused approach, with more concise explanations, along with indexes (in both Allen's grammar, and that of Thomson and Martinet). Finally, the provision of practice exercises in Allen, and Thomson and Martinet (albeit in a separate book in the latter case) again positions the titles as more learner-centred, and perhaps also indicates a move away from substitution as the preferred teaching methodology. In his introduction, Palmer had stated that 'the chief function of a grammar book [is] to furnish the student with a selection of those categories which will enable him to perform the greatest number of useful substitutions' (1924: xxxii). This is not a belief expressed at any point in Allen's or Thomson and Martinet's grammars, and is broadly in line with the familiar narrative of pattern-practice based pedagogies such as the audiolingual method being abandoned from the period around Chomsky's famous review (1959) of B.F. Skinner's (1959) *Verbal Behaviour*.

3.5.4 *English Grammatical Structure* (Alexander et al., 1975)

Alexander *et al.*'s (1975) title is rather different from the previous three. In fact, we might well not call it a grammar at all. Described in its introduction as 'an inventory of sentence patterns and grammatical structures which has been compiled for the purposes related to the teaching of English as a foreign language' (Alexander *et al.*, 1975: v), it was aimed at, among others, the writers of coursebooks, graded readers and tests, and teachers. Its authors were all also authors of other pedagogical grammars and coursebooks, and included W.S. Allen.

The book is essentially a detailed catalogue (running to 245 pages) of pedagogical grammar points, divided into six 'Stages' (in other words, levels); the authors' statement that the inventory is 'limited and selective' (Alexander *et al.*, 1975: v) rather than comprehensive recalls the discussion in Chapter 2 on selectivity as a key characteristic of pedagogical grammar. As stated in the book's introduction, the content was decided on not by statistical analysis, but 'on the basis of [the authors'] combined experience of teaching English and of compiling English-teaching materials'. (Alexander *et al.*, 1975: v), indicating that the book is very much grounded in practice. Example sentences are provided for each grammar point and, for many of the items, notes and advice on usage, exceptions and so on are given. The style and wording makes it clear that these are addressed at materials authors and curriculum designers rather learners; the excerpt in Figure 3.1 is representative of the style, content and structure.

It in some respects seems remarkable that it was possible for *English Grammatical Structure* to be written in 1975. As we saw,

---

II.13 *Will* and *shall* with future reference; choice between *will* and *be going to*

Models
The 12.15 train will leave from Platform Four.
We shall arrive at the North Station at 6.45.

Notes

1 A Will there be a holiday on Monday?
  B Yes, there will. There will be.
    There *will* be a holiday on Monday.
2   The 12.15 train for Liverpool will leave from Platform Four.
    It'll leave from this platform.

1 See II.12.9: *'ll* replaced by *will* when initial or final, or when *will be* is final, or for emphasis or in formal style.
2 *will* + INFINITIVE, referring to the future, in formal style.
  will frequently contracted to *'ll* in informal style.

3 There will not be a holiday next Monday.
  There'll not be a holiday.
  There won't be a holiday.
  There won't be. There won't.
4 A When will the train arrive?
  B It'll arrive soon.
  A What will the passengers do?
  B They'll go to a hotel.
  A Who'll meet them?
  B /I/you/he/she/we/ will.
    /I/you/he/she/we/'ll meet them.
5   /I/We/ shall arrive by air.
    /I/We/ shall not be late.
    /I/We/ shan't be late.

3 *will not*, formal or emphatic.
  Contraction, *'ll* + not.
  Contraction, NEGATIVE informal.
  Can occur initially and finally.
4 *will* frequently reduces to the sound /l/ after *Wh*-question-words, especially *Who*, after PERSONAL PRONOUNS and *there*.

  will permissible after all PRONOUNS.
  'll permissible after all PRONOUNS.
5 *shall* reduces to /ʃəl/ in fluent speech except when final, optional replacement for *will* after *I* and *we* in plain FUTURE.
  shall not = shan't informal typical of British English.

6 A Will George be home for dinner?
  B George won't, but /I/we/ shall (be).
    John and I will be.
7 A Are you going to get up?
  B Yes, I think I /will//shall/.

6 *Will*, *won't* for 2ND or 3RD PERSON;
  will or *shall* after *I* and *we*;
  but only *will* after [*somebody*] and *I*.
7 As in II.12.4.
  /*will*//*shall*/ normal here: intentions not highlighted.

Notes on choice between *be going to* and *'ll*, *will*, *shall*:
  i Throughout II.13 /*will*/*shall*/ is grammatically replaceable by *be going to*, except in 7B. However—
  ii prefer *be going to* in informal style when emphasis is on present intentions, or indication of what the future will bring;
  iii use *'ll*, *will* or *shall* when there is no such emphasis, though exclude *'ll* when initial, final or before final *be*;
  iv use *will* in any case in formal written style, but—
  v treat *shall* as optional replacement for *will* after *I* or *we*.

Figure 3.1 Excerpt from Alexander *et al.* (1975: 49)

just two decades earlier the *ELT Journal* was having to provide its readers with answers to questions on how *any* and *some* are used in interrogative and negative sentences. Yet here, less than 25 years later, four authors were able to come together and agree on the content of a comprehensive, 245-page book setting out a grammatical catalogue of grammar teaching points, across six levels. This appears to confirm Howatt and Widdowson's (2004: 300) assertion that a key principle in ELT in the period 1950–1970 was that that courses should be built around 'a graded syllabus of structural patterns to ensure systematic step-by-step progress'. *English Grammatical Structure* appears to be the natural outcome of this principle and may also have gone some way to formalising it, given that the book was widely used by coursebook authors after its publication (Richards, 2017; see also the interview data in Chapter 5 of this book). Indeed, the lead author of *English Grammatical Structure*, the highly successful and prolific L.G. Alexander (who in 1977 set a world record for book sales by a single author) might well be considered as one of the most important figures in the developmental of pedagogical grammar for ELT, particularly in the field of sequencing of content.

3.6 ELT Pedagogical Grammar Today

ELT publishers today produce a huge number of pedagogical grammars.[6] Perhaps the best known of the contemporary grammars, particularly in parts of the world where 'British English' is used as a model, is *Grammar in Use*, published by Cambridge University Press. An equivalent for American English is the *English Grammar Series* by Betty Azar and Stacy Hagen, published by Pearson Education. Interestingly, the publishers of both make little effort to describe or outline the grammatical contents of the publication: Azar-Hagan is said to offer 'comprehensive coverage of English grammar' (Pearson, 2021), while *Grammar in Use* is simply described as a 'grammar series' and a 'grammar reference and practice book' (Cambridge University Press, 2021). It seems that the contents of an ELT pedagogical grammar are so well known and well established that no further explanation is required; once the terms 'English grammar' or 'grammar reference' are used in a mainstream ELT title, the content is a given, even though, as we have said, pedagogical grammar accounts are by necessity selective and presumably very different selections could potentially be made by different grammarians. As we saw with the Core Inventory, this consensus also runs through the grammatical content of coursebooks.

This is not to say that pedagogical accounts of English have remained completely unchanged since the four titles described in the previous section were published. In particular, we might note the influence of the functional-notional approach in the 1970s, which involves identifying the different notions (e.g. time, location, duration) and functions (e.g. suggesting, describing, explaining) that can be present in conversations, and then pinpointing the (kinds of) linguistic structures typically used to realise them; this language could then become the teaching points in a language course.[7] Similarly, the notion of discourse and cohesion, which had been set out in publications such as Halliday and Hasan's (1976) *Cohesion in English*, also appears to have been quickly taken on board by ELT materials authors. For example, coursebook series published from the second half of the 1970s, such as *Strategies* (first edition published in 1975), *Streamline* (first editions published 1978–1981) and *The Cambridge English Course* (first editions published 1984–1987) all cover an extensive range of linking words and phrases. The difference is striking when compared with slightly older series such as *New Concept English* (first published in 1967) or *Kernel Lessons* (first editions published 1971–1972), which teach almost none.

The development of large, and easily searchable corpora in the 1980s has also had an effect on the information available to materials writers and teachers; we mentioned, for example, two particularly innovative corpus-based descriptive grammars in Section 3.4.3 above. Yet while publishers moved quickly to incorporate this new kind of information into learner dictionaries,[8] and vocabulary practice titles,[9] John Sinclair's (1985: 252) prediction that 'we must expect substantial influence [of corpora] on the specification of syllabuses, design of materials, and choice of method' does not appear to have come to pass, at least for General English. With the exception of the *Touchstone* series (McCarthy *et al.*, 2005a, 2005b, 2005c, 2005d), and the much older (and commercially unsuccessful) *Collins Cobuild English Course* (Willis & Willis, 1988a, 1988b; Willis *et al.*, 1988), the authors and publishers of coursebooks appear to be reluctant to make use of corpus data; the same observation can be made about the pedagogical grammars described earlier in this section. As we saw in Section 2.6, the result of this can be inaccuracies in content. Different reasons for this reluctance have been suggested in the literature, including questions of whether corpus data taken outside its original context is still authentic (Prodromou, 2003), or whether non-corpus data might be favoured over corpus data for pedagogical reasons (Carter, 1998; Cook, 1998; Shortall, 2007). Burton (2012), in contrast, reports that many coursebook writers simply do not have the time or training to use corpora, do not have access to corpora, and, in some cases, report having little interest in or motivation for using them. And while corpus linguistics may have something to tell us about the accuracy of current grammatical representations, publishers are likely to be hesitant about changing or updating grammatical descriptions, for reasons explored in the previous chapter and that we will return to in the coming chapters.

3.7 Overview

This chapter began by reviewing evidence, in the form of the EAQUALS Core Inventory for General English, pointing to the existence of a broad consensus on the learning content – including grammar – generally included in materials and teaching programmes used in mainstream ELT. It then attempted to provide a broad outline of the tradition of grammatical descriptions of English, from the first grammar in the 16th century, up until modern descriptive and pedagogical accounts. We saw that at the beginning of the 'modern' era of ELT, a group of influential teacher-authors such as Harold Palmer and A.S. Hornby had scientific accounts of English grammar from the 'Great Tradition' to draw on. However, these accounts had not been written with language learners in mind, and it was necessary to select from them and mould their contents in order to provide learners with accounts of grammar that these teacher-authors felt best met their needs. The range of grammatical content typically included in ELT materials has developed and increased over the decades, with ever more detailed pedagogical accounts being published, and the addition to the canon in the last few decades of grammatical features related to discourse (see also contributions from Michael Swan in Chapter 5). At the same time, there has been an increasing level of consensus, perhaps due to the influence and endurance of key ELT publications such as those outlined in Section 3.5 above.

While useful in providing a historical framework for the evolution, the broad analysis provided in this chapter can, however, only give us a general idea of how the ELT grammar canon has evolved to arrive at its current state. A key problem in developing a more detailed account is that commercial publications such as teaching materials do not typically cite their sources – only very early pedagogical grammars, for example Palmer's (1924) *Grammar of Spoken English*, made any reference to sources examined, and at best only sporadically. The result is that the decisions about the content of the grammatical canon have invariably taken place 'out of sight'. Writers – including those who have written pedagogical grammars – have offered over the years principles with which particular items can, or should be, chosen, focusing on concepts such as usefulness, centrality and so on. However, the decision-making processes behind individual works, including those that appear to have been cornerstones in the history of ELT pedagogical grammar, were not recorded. We have very little idea why the content of the grammar canon is as it is, or why, given that there appears to be a great deal of subjectivity involved in decisions on content selection, there is so little variation across both coursebooks and pedagogical grammars.

There therefore appears to be a need for both a more in-depth analysis of primary sources, to provide a more complete picture, and, simultaneously, an investigation in the perspectives and experiences of those involved in creating and sustaining the consensus on ELT grammar. The following four chapters will attempt to fill this gap, through the analysis of interview data with 'key players' in the ELT profession, and the analysis of grammar coverage in both contemporary and older grammars and teaching materials.

Notes

(1) 'EAQUALS members' are 'language centres which have achieved [according to the EAQUALS association] the highest international standards', associate members, or individual 'language education professionals' (EAQUALS, 2021).

(2) Contemporary accounts often suggest that audiolingualism was developed as a result of the application of findings from behavioural psychology (see, for example, Richards and Rodgers's account (2001: 54–55) of the theory of learning in audiolingualism). Howatt and Widdowson (2004: 306), however, argue that the idea that researchers at Michigan 'applied behaviourist psychology to language teaching [...] is a rather doubtful claim', partly because Fries made no reference to it in his (1945) monograph *Teaching and Learning English as a Foreign Language*, but also because a 'listen and repeat' approach does not sit particularly well with the complexity of behaviourist theory. Howatt and Smith (2014) argue that references to behaviourist psychology were 'added in' later by advocates of the approach and language laboratories associated with them, presumably to boost its credentials.

(3) See, for example, Swan's *Practical English Usage* (Swan, 2016), which contains multiple references to aspects of language of interest to 'people who speak some languages' (e.g. the entries on 'actual(ly)', 'eventually', articles and the present perfect).

(4) The question of whether or not phonemic transcriptions should be used in teaching materials was one area of disagreement during this period: 'teachers influenced by phoneticians like Sweet believed that transcribed texts were essential, but others remained unconvinced, and their use fell from favour (Howatt & Smith, 2014: 83). Palmer states that the use of 'phonetic spelling' is 'the only possible procedure to follow when dealing with the spoken form of a living language whose orthographic and phonetic systems are mutually at variance' (Smith, 2004: 33–34).

(5) A year before Thomson and Martinet's title was published, A.S. Hornby had been at pains to emphasise that Latin terms like 'accusative' and 'dative' were unnecessary for ELT (Hornby, 1959).

(6) At the time of writing, there are 18 grammar titles in Cambridge University Press's ELT catalogue, 11 in Oxford University Press's catalogue and five in Pearson's catalogue. The actual number of pedagogical grammar books produced by these publishers is far higher, as many of these titles are made up of several offerings at different levels.

(7) Coursebook series that made extensive use of notions and functions include well-known titles such as *Strategies* (Abbs *et al.*, 1975) and *Functions of English* (Jones, 1981). Materials writers and syllabus designers had titles such as Van Ek's (1976) *The Threshold Level* and Wilkins' (1976) *Notional Syllabuses* (1976) at their disposal; these provided large catalogues of such language, in theory allowing the creation of entire syllabuses organised around notions and functions.

(8) The *Collins Cobuild English Language Dictionary* was the first, in 1987, to be based on corpora data (Leech, 1997).

(9) See, for example, the *English Vocabulary in Use* series (Cambridge University Press).

4 Interviews with Authors and Editors: The Canon Today

4.1 Introduction

This chapter presents the first part of the analysis of the interviews carried out with a number of key figures in the ELT publishing industry. As we saw in Chapter 2, various accounts of the writing process already exist, in addition to a smaller number of publisher accounts, but these tend to address rather broad issues in the publishing process. By comparison, the interviews in this study address a very specific area of investigation – how and why decisions are made on the choice of level system, on grammatical content, and on the level assignment of this grammatical content. In order to investigate the issues underlying (i) how the current consensus on ELT grammar is maintained and (ii) the historical development of this consensus, including the level system, interviews were carried out with a number of key figures in ELT publishing. This chapter deals with the first part of this analysis, focusing on the contemporary situation.

4.2 Methodology: Interviews

4.2.1 Interviewees

As the question of sequencing and level assignments of grammar points is considered in this study to be an important characteristic of ELT pedagogical grammar, I decided to approach, as interviewees, only people who had direct experience of multi-level coursebook production, although some of these also had experience in writing pedagogical grammars. The full cohort of interviewees was made up of two broad groups: (i) people who had experience of producing contemporary coursebooks, and (ii) people who had experience of producing coursebooks before the 1990s. This decade was used somewhat arbitrarily as a cut-off point, with coursebooks from the mid-nineties onwards – the period when the six-level system came into use – deemed as no longer being 'historical'. However, in many cases, the experience of the interviewees spanned the two time periods.

For the historical perspective, coursebook authors were favoured, but for the contemporary period, 'publishing professionals' were sought out – I use this umbrella term to refer to someone who works, or has worked, within ELT publishing, in a role that would allow them significant insight into the creation of coursebooks. The decision to focus on this group of professionals rather than authors for the investigation into contemporary practice was made on the basis of my own personal experience – having worked both as an ELT materials author and an editor – of the publisher-led approach currently favoured in the industry. As was also confirmed in many of the studies reported in Chapter 2, contemporary ELT publishing practices place the publisher rather than author in the central position in terms of content selection, meaning that authors now have comparatively limited input into decisions on overall syllabus content. In any case, a number of the 'publishing professionals' selected work as both editors and authors, so the contemporary author perspective is nonetheless represented.

The final list of interviewees is as follows. Note that the initials/codes in brackets after each name are those used, for the sake of brevity and clarity, in the analysis presented in this chapter and the next. This list can also be found on page ix, for easy reference.

(1) Michael Swan (**MS**): ex-teacher and teacher trainer. Author of numerous pedagogical grammar titles including *Practical English Usage* and *Basic English Usage*, co-author of *How English Works* and *The Oxford English Grammar Course* (all Oxford University Press), and the coursebook series *The Cambridge English Course* and *The New Cambridge English Course* (Cambridge University Press).

(2) Liz Soars (**LS**): ex- teacher and teacher trainer, former Director of Teacher Training at International House London, ex-co-chief examiner for the Cambridge/RSA DELTA examination. Co-author of the *Headway* coursebook series (Oxford University Press; fifth edition published in 2018).

(3) Bart Ullstein (**BU**): sales and marketing professional at Longman ELT division in the 1970s, initially in Greece, Turkey, Cyprus and Israel, subsequently establishing a global marketing function at Longman. Responsible for the development of a marketing strategy for and launch of the *Longman Dictionary of Contemporary English*.

(4) Ingrid Freebairn (**IF**): ex-teacher and teacher trainer, ex-RSA examiner and inspector for the British Council Accreditation scheme. Author of numerous coursebook series including *Strategies, Discoveries, Blueprint, Snapshot* and *Sky* (all Longman).

(5) Peter Viney (**PV**): ex- teacher and teacher trainer. Author of numerous coursebook series including *In English, Streamline*

English, *Grapevine* and *Handshake*, and the co-series editor of the *Storylines* series of graded readers (all Oxford University Press).

(6) Jack Richards (**JR**): Honorary Professor of TESOL at the University of Sydney; previously held positions at the Chinese University of Hong Kong, University of Hawaii, City University of Hong Kong and the University of Auckland. Author of over 150 articles and books in the field of second language teaching; co-author of the *Interchange* and *Passages* coursebook series (Cambridge University Press).

(7) Diane Hall (**DH**): ex-teacher and in-house ELT publisher, now freelance ELT editor. Co-author of the pedagogical grammars *Longman Advanced Learners' Grammar* and *MyGrammarLab* (both Longman), and of coursebook series including *Total English* (Longman) and *Pacesetter* (Oxford University Press).

(8) Adam Gadsby (**AG**): ex-Director of Strategic Partnerships, Cambridge University Press; ex-editorial director at Pearson Education.

(9) Anonymous publishing professional (**APP**): highly experienced ELT publishing professional with international experience.

(10) Anonymous coursebook author (**ACA**): ELT coursebook author and former in-house ELT publishing professional.

In this list, interviewees 1–6 represent the group of people who have experience of the historical period, whereas interviewees 7–10 are those with experience of the contemporary period. However, the distinction between each group is not black and white, as some of the first set of interviewees are still active today as authors, and some of the second set are authors in addition to being publishing professionals.

4.2.2 Interview procedure

Semi-structured interviews (Dörnyei, 2007) were used: a set of questions was prepared, and these were asked to all participants, but the interview itself was 'open-ended', meaning that interviewees were encouraged to elaborate on their answers to allow an full exploration of the issues that arose. Six questions were devised that would allow the area of investigation to be adequately explored, but at the same time would be open enough to allow a certain amount of digression. Two slightly different sets were created for the authors and publishing professionals, to reflect their differing roles in and experience of the writing and publishing process. The two sets of questions were as follows:

Questions for authors

(1) How was it decided that [name of coursebook series] would have [number of levels]?
(2) How did you decide which grammar points to include in [name of coursebook series]? Where did they come from?

(3) How did you decide at which level to include this grammar?
(4) Did you include or exclude any grammar content that you would have preferred not to? What happened?
(5) In terms of the choices you made about grammar – both selection and the level it is included in – have you even been influenced by developments outside of ELT?
(6) Is there anything I should have asked but didn't? Or anything else you'd like to add?

Questions for editors

(1) In your experience, how does a publisher or author decide how many levels to publish of a new coursebook series?
(2) In your experience, how does a publisher or author decide which grammar points to include in a new coursebook series? Where do they come from?
(3) In your experience, how does a publisher or author decide at which level to include each grammar point?
(4) Do you feel that there is any space for innovation in terms of the number of levels a coursebook series is published at? What about in terms of the grammar points included? Why (not)?
(5) In your experience, has there been any influence from outside of ELT on the choices made about grammar in coursebook production – either in terms of selection of grammar to be taught or the level it is included at?
(6) Is there anything I should have asked but didn't? Or anything else you'd like to add?

Questions 1–3 were designed to explore, respectively, the issues of the choice of number of levels, overall grammatical content and level allocation of each grammar point. Question 4 was quite differently worded in the author and publishing professional versions of the questions, but was intended to address the same issue: the strength of influence from the publisher to conform to expectations, and whether it is possible to resist this. Question 5 was intended to explore influences from outside ELT on grammatical content, while Question 6 – the most open question – was incorporated simply allow the interviewee to have a final say, if they wished. Interviews were recorded and transcribed for analysis (see below). There was no set time limit, but each interview lasted from around 45 minutes to one hour.

4.2.3 Thematic analysis

After transcription, a thematic analysis of the interview data was carried out. Such an analysis involves identifying recurring themes within textual data in order to identifying overarching commonalities and patterns. For the study reported here, the textual data was the transcriptions of the interviews; themes were identified and then coded for analysis using *NVivo* software, a widely used software package for the analysis of interview data in qualitative and mixed methods research. There are many ways to carry out a thematic analysis (Ryan & Bernard, 2003). I draw on the work of Braun and Clarke (2006), who suggest an iterative process as set out below:

(1) becoming familiar with and transcribing the data;
(2) generating initial codes;
(3) searching for themes;
(4) reviewing themes;
(5) defining and naming themes;
(6) producing the report.

I also embrace the concept of a 'thematic network' (Attride-Stirling, 2001), a representation of the hierarchy of themes identified during coding, with 'basic themes' subordinate to 'organising themes', and these in turn subordinate to 'global themes'. Thematic analysis is necessarily subjective and interpretative (Attride-Stirling, 2001). Its 'exploratory and explanatory power' rests on 'methodological rigour at all stages of the research process' (Attride-Stirling, 2001: 403). In the case of the analysis presented in this study, a number of steps were taken to ensure methodological rigour. Firstly, a choice needed to be made between a deductive and inductive approach to thematic analysis (Braun & Clarke, 2006). The current study takes a broadly deductive approach to coding and analysis: my own experience in publishing, and the literature reviewed, led me to expect certain themes to emerge, and this was a useful base from which to begin the analysis. However, an inductive approach was also used at times, in order to identify any unexpected themes and code them. In fact, many of the themes discussed in these chapters were unexpected to me and would have not been identified had a purely deductive approach been employed. Secondly, there was the question of how to identify a theme. Here, a slightly flexible approach was taken. Braun and Clarke (2006: 91) recommend first identifying 'candidate themes', before later deciding whether there is enough data to support them as individual themes, and this was adopted as an approach. However, the thematic analysis carried out in this study is somewhat different from most thematic analyses, in that experienced experts within the field were sought out, and were asked specific questions on topics that have thus far received relatively little attention in the literature. Within the data, in addition to 'themes' there are often highly significant answers and explanations, and these were felt to be extremely important in the context of the research. Because of this, the analysis at times takes into account data mentioned once by a single informant, which in other thematic analyses might be excluded because of insufficient coverage across informants.

After my own initial analysis, I worked with another researcher with specialist expertise in thematic analysis, but no experience in ELT; their feedback was useful in ensuring that choices made on themes were robust, particularly as the analyst consulted was not likely to be influenced by the status and reputation of the informants interviewed. The themes and thematic network under development were then shared with a further two analysts, both of whom were experienced in ELT, before the final list of themes and thematic network were finalised. Overall, I believe that while the thematic analysis I present here is by necessity subjective and interpretative, the methodology used to arrive at it was at the same time rigorous.

The analysis of the interview data revealed two broad, global themes: 'influences and input' and 'ELT past and present'. The first relates to factors perceived by the interviewees to have an influence on, or provide some kind of input into, the structure and content of ELT grammar syllabuses; here we are essentially talking about the 'modern' period in which the canon has become fixed within the profession and is resistant to change. The second theme relates to differences between the past and present in ELT – in particular the ELT publishing industry – and to changes that interviewees have experienced. Again, these changes or differences are those that appear to be, or to have been, influential in some way on the structure and content of grammar syllabuses. The thematic network built around these two global themes can be found in Figure 4.1.

This chapter focuses on the first global theme: 'influences and input'; the second global theme ('ELT past and present') will be discussed in Chapter 5. However, as we have said, the use of the 1990s as a cut-off point between contemporary and historical issues is admittedly somewhat arbitrary, and additionally all but one of the interviewees selected for their ability to provide insight into pre-1990s coursebooks have remained active in coursebook writing in the present (or at least were active until very recently). As a consequence, this chapter at some points makes reference to comments made that relate to past practice, just as Chapter 5 occasionally makes reference to comments made relating to current practice.

The remainder of this chapter discusses the insights related to contemporary practice that arose from the interviews. Here, as much as possible, I will let the interviewees do the talking. Although they are a somewhat disparate group, with often competing interests, it will be seen that they nonetheless aggregate to form a consensus on many issues. The aim of the research presented here is to identify and present points of this consensus, rather than to critique it.

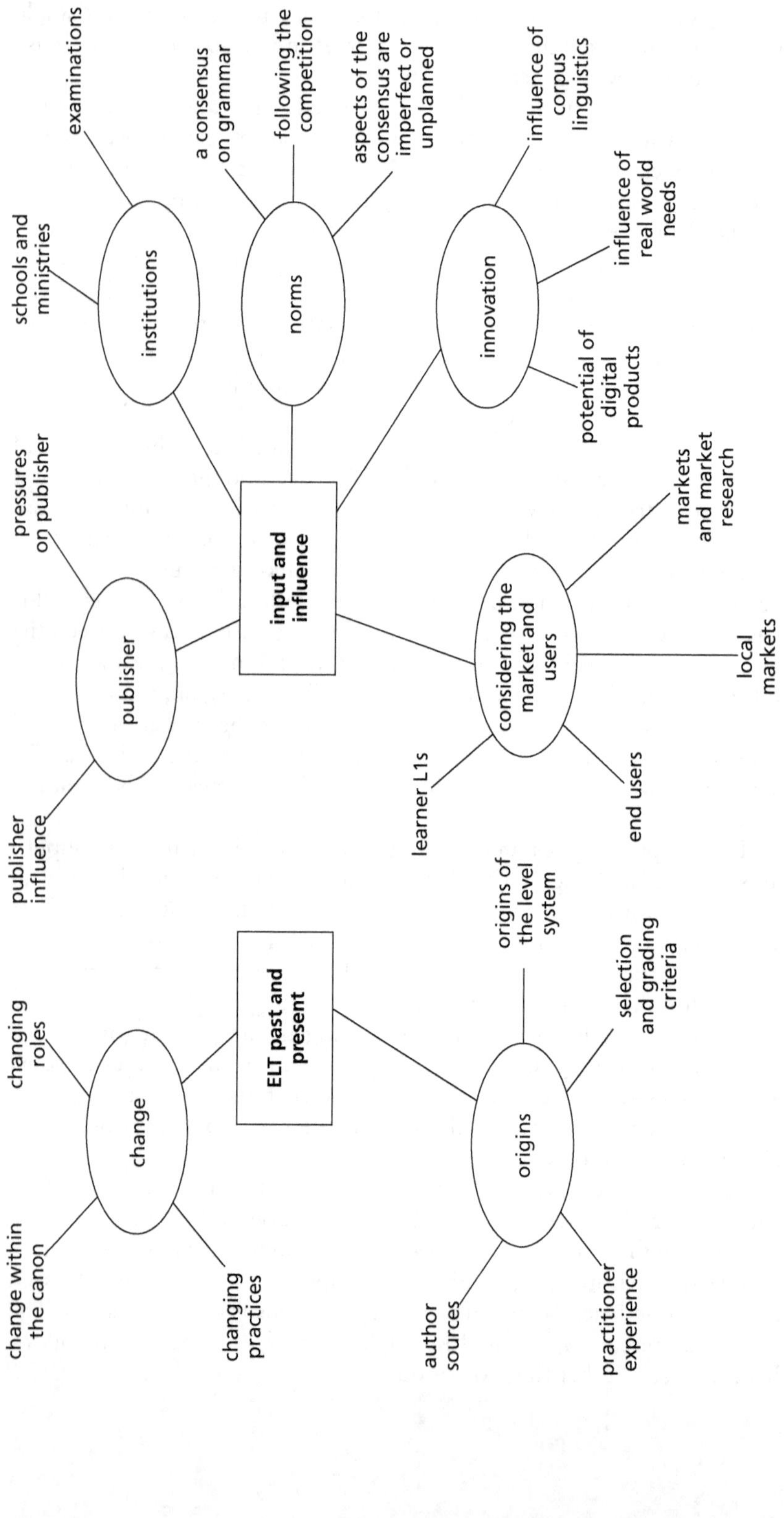

58 Grammar in ELT and ELT Materials

Figure 4.1 Thematic network

As we have said, this chapter focuses on the first global theme in our analysis: 'influences and input'. This relates to a number of different factors that emerged from the interviews, which appeared to have, or to potentially have, an influence on or input into grammar content. These were divided into five organising themes, as follows:

- norms;
- publishers;
- institutions;
- considering the market and users;
- innovation.

As can be seen, each of these organising themes has a number of basic themes associated with them. The remainder of this chapter presents the data from the interviews related to these themes, and concludes by providing a summary of what, as a whole, they tell us about the contemporary 'ecosystem' within which the consensus on ELT grammar resides.

4.3 Organising Theme: Norms

The first organising theme to be identified relates to the existence of norms within the ELT profession. The ideas to emerge under this theme relate to a key point we will return to several times in this book: that while the publishing industry certainly has a key role in sustaining the consensus that supports the ELT grammar canon, the latter should not be conceived of exclusively as an invention of publishers and has – at least to an extent – a life of its own, independent of published ELT materials.

4.3.1 Basic theme: A consensus on grammar

A very common basic theme associated with the organising theme was 'a consensus on grammar'. All interviewees currently involved in the production of coursebooks made reference to the absolute imperative of closely following the existing consensus on grammar. APP puts the situation clearly: 'Publishers are not willing to deviate much from the norm'.

AG, in two different parts of the interview, mentions the existence of a consensus, which he suggests exists – and must be followed – both in terms of overall grammatical content and the level system.

> AG: I think with general adult courses it's become the norm to publish six levels, generally.

> AG: I still think that the teachers will look first at the grammar syllabus and see if fits their 'folk expectation', and 'Does it have the things that I expect to cover at this level and if it doesn't, I'll use something else'.

Key in AG's account is the idea of 'expectation' – publishers perceive that there are norms, and that they are expected to follow them. The words 'expect' and 'expectation' are both used by a number of other interviewees – both authors and publishing professionals:

> APP: I think there's a kind of standard menu these days of grammatical expectations at any one level.

> IF: We would have looked at Louis, Robert and other ones [coursebook syllabuses], and decided, 'OK, that's what is expected at this level' – that you start with present and past, etc., etc., and then you go on.

> MS: [In response to being asked why he would refer to the consensus version of grammar, even if he disagreed with it.] Well, because that's what readers expect. If readers think there are three kinds of conditional, because that's what they've been learning all their lives, teachers particularly, and then along comes this madman, who says there are two main categories of conditional, obviously you don't take him seriously – everyone knows there are three conditionals.

> JR: So partly it [decisions on matching grammar points to levels] was guided by the editors and also just looking at expectations, seeing things like, for example, the present perfect must appear at level 1, and the past tense, and so on.

Interestingly, precisely where or in whom these expectations lie is generally not specified; only MS specifically mentions teachers, although this group of professionals is perhaps implied by all of the interviewees. Although not clearly defined, the sense of expectation is very strong; when JR was asked whether the need to follow expectations and the consensus was troublesome to him as an academic, his reply suggests there was simply no other viable option:

> JR: It didn't bother me particularly because there weren't too many other reference points really. So, you know, common practice was probably a good way to go, because if you depart too much from it, you're likely to lose your target audience.

Similarly, LS, when discussing the merits or otherwise of including the structure *have got* in a grammar syllabus, uses a somewhat vague reference to pressure coming from 'within ELT':

> LS: [And with *have got*, where's the pressure coming from?] The pressure comes from within ELT. Somewhere many, many years ago within ELT, somebody made the discovery that in the English language we say 'I've got a cat', that we use *have got* in informal English. Which of course, we do. But for some reason [...] it's interesting as well, the things that aren't given prominence to in grammar syllabuses, isn't it?

At times, the existence of norms appears to be so accepted as to lie almost undetected. For example, DH, in describing the use of a four-level system in the 1980s, describes the consensus on the level system in terms of acceptance rather than expectation:

> **DH:** It just seemed to be accepted. I don't remember there ever having been a discussion – going back to the first ones [coursebooks] I worked on, I don't remember there being a discussion of why it was four levels.

Similarly, while ACA does not mention expectation explicitly, the reference to the need to 'do what everybody else does' appears to amount to the same thing:

> **ACA:** People want familiar, but done in a fresh way. So you do what everybody else does. [...] In terms of the six level system, the markets want six levels. That's the message. [...] When they've suggested adding a level, it's not been a goer. Six levels is what the institutions want.

4.3.2 Basic theme: Following the competition

As we said, the quotations reported above tend to refer to norms and expectations in somewhat abstract terms. The second basic theme, by contrast, refers to a specific vehicle for the promulgation of norms: other coursebooks. The practice of referring to competition titles was reported by a number of interviewees, suggesting that they play a key role in setting and maintaining norms associated with the level system, grammar selection, and level assignment of grammar points. ACA's observation on this is unequivocal – new coursebooks must reflect the content of older coursebooks in order not to seem 'deficient', while both DH and AG describe the process of surveying competition titles during the writing of a coursebook series – a crucial early step in the production of a new series:

> **ACA:** A lot of it is historic. You put in the grammar points that other coursebooks do. Because if you don't, your title will seem deficient.
>
> **AG:** I know when they started a new course like *SpeakOut* at Pearson or *Empower* at CUP, one of the things you do at the beginning is look at all the other courses and sort of decide on a structure.
>
> **DH:** [Interviewer: How do you decide on the grammar points to include and where do they come from?] I think from other books! And it just seems to be [...] I don't think they're even taken, I've never known a course where it's just taken lock, stock and barrel from another course – obviously you wouldn't do that – but generally it's sort of a survey of courses for the same market, at the same level, etc. and looking at what they cover. [...] [Interviewer: And how do you decide which levels to include the grammar points at?] Much as the above.

APP makes similar points on deciding on both the level system and grammar content.

> APP: I think the number of levels is determined by the competition, to some extent market research, market feedback. [talking about the selection of grammar points] I think generally the publisher decides these days, and very much with an eye on the competition, on the established competition, on the successful competition.

Later in the interview, APP appears to confirm the idea of coursebooks as being the physical manifestations of the consensus, returning again to the idea of expectations:

> APP: Because the competition, to be fair, gives people [...] you know, if it's successful competition, that means they probably haven't got their grammar totally wrong, that it meets the expectations of the teachers, and in terms of level, exactly the same.

As we saw in Chapter 2, the practice referred to by participants is nothing new; over two decades ago Littlejohn's study found that the aim of publishers 'is largely to replicate the design characteristics of existing market leaders' (1992: 235). IF and PV's comments both confirm that a similar approach was taken with older coursebooks:

> IF: We would have used [in designing the grammar syllabus for *Strategies*], I guess, Robert's syllabus, or we would have looked at Louis, Robert and other ones,[1] and decided, 'OK, that's what is expected at this level' – that you start with present and past, etc., etc., and then you go on.
>
> PV: Let's take [the coursebook series] *Kernel Lessons* to start with. Because that was our bible, for everybody. Robert O'Neill [author of *Kernel Lessons*] was the great. [...] Robert and Bernie [Hartley – PV's co-author] worked together for years. And Bernie was very, very heavily influenced by Robert.

Finally, PV mentions a specific coursebook series which he feels has had a strong influence on subsequent publications, although, by implication, not his own:

> PV: I think the great shame is that because of the – this is not a criticism of *Headway* – the huge success of *Headway* has made people try to clone it ever since.

As we can see, there appears to be a very cyclical process in play. Publishers perceive the existence of norms and expectations and attempt to meet them. The result of this is further coursebooks with broadly the same content, which themselves then reinforce the norms and expectations and act as models for further publications.

An interesting counterpoint to the question of consensus in ELT is offered by JR, who argues that far less of a consensus is typically found with less widely learned languages:

> JR: I think basically books for uncommonly taught languages are based entirely on the intuition of the writers because there's no tradition. The same is true of Cantonese. I did a study when I was in Hong Kong looking at textbooks for the teaching of Cantonese, and we found there was almost no, or very limited overlap in terms of grammar or vocabulary from one book to the other, so they again had no [...] not a convention in terms of publishing materials for Cantonese. So each writer basically made it up on his own or on her own.

To confirm the hypothesis that the level of consensus on grammar tends to increase as a language is more widely taught would require research on grammatical accounts of other languages, obviously outside the scope of this book. However, the claim does not seem unreasonable and ties in with Linn's (2006: 65) assertion that 'grammar-writing in the modern age carries its past with it [...] There is a burden of tradition on anyone writing a grammar, a body of expectation that discourages innovation'. We might speculate that the more (pedagogical) grammar accounts of Cantonese were to be made, the more future grammarians would feel obliged to reflect these existing accounts, and the less variation there would therefore be across titles.

4.3.3 Basic theme: Aspects of the consensus are imperfect or unplanned

A key motivation for carrying out the research presented in this book is that the origins of the grammar canon have not been documented, and nor have decisions made over the years on its content and structure. Indeed, one possibility is that the canon has evolved in an unplanned, organic way (or, to be less charitable, rather by accident). The insights shared by a number of the interviewees in this study certainly suggest as much, particularly in terms of the level system, but also in terms of the choice of grammar points.

In terms of the level system, LS makes it quite clear – as we saw earlier – that the six levels at which the coursebook series *Headway* was eventually published were not originally planned:

> LS: It was never decided that *Headway* would have six levels. It grew to six levels over the years. It evolved. [...] We didn't end up with six levels until the year 2000, in fact. Even though the original two-book series came out in '86.

One might argue that whether or not any particular coursebook series is published at six levels, the choice of six levels might nevertheless be sound from a pedagogical point of view. However, AG suggests that this is not the case, describing several different contexts in which a six-level coursebook series does not appear to match the needs of the teaching programme:

> AG: I remember doing research in Spain and Italy about what do they do and need. Quite a few places use an Upper Intermediate level from one course, and then another Upper Intermediate level from a different course because it's not enough either in level or number of hours to take them to a C1 Advanced level. [...] There are more and more different situations, so, universities in Turkey have got to get from A1 to B2 in 30 weeks, and they use two and a half or three levels of the course during that year, and ideally they'd like something that fits exactly with their needs.

Four interviewees also made reference to situations in which the level system of a coursebook series had to be modified in some way, again indicating that the predominant six-level system found in ELT coursebooks and ELT in general is somewhat ad hoc in nature:

> BU: Louis [Alexander] did it [i.e. established a level system] entirely from his experience teaching in a private secondary school in Greece, with precious little market research. And the result of that was he originally did four books, which took you from *First Principles*, *First Things First*, to [the] Cambridge Proficiency [examination] and beyond. And that was how it was launched. However, within four years of its launch, *First Things First* had been split into two, and *Practice and Progress* had been split into two, so you ended up with a six-year course to [the] Cambridge Lower [examination], which sort of mirrored what was supposed to be going on in secondary schools. So you'd start at 11 and you'd get Lower at 16.

> APP: [W]hat happened, certainly 15, 20 years ago, let's say 20 years ago, was that publishers would go ahead and publish something at non-absolute beginner level, and they would sort of gulp a year or two later, and say, 'Oh dear, people are having difficulty with this level – we need to publish a starter level, or an intro level, or whatever'.

> MS: And in some markets, [...] they just didn't have the class time available and they didn't move at the necessary speed to do anything like getting through one level of the book in one year, which was what I think was originally perceived as what was going to happen. So [...] we did split editions [...] so we had 1A, 1B, 2A, 2B, and if there had been the market for it, the third advanced level might also have turned into 3A, 3B, so we would have ended up, we had potentially a six-level course.

While the six-level system is now well established in major coursebook series, innovation does still appear to be possible. Both AG and DH mention series which have, or will have seven levels:

> **AG:** I think OUP with *English File* in Spain added an extra level to try and bridge that gap [i.e. between Upper Intermediate and Advanced levels]. I think one of the reasons why I think OUP did that with *English File*, to make an extra level in Spain, was because the 'escuelas oficiales', the EOIs, have seven levels in their system and they want something that fits with their system, and they're a big part of the market in Spain.
>
> **DH:** I'm just thinking 'seven' – *Keynote* has got five already and two are coming out. So *Keynote* will have seven. It's got Advanced and Proficiency already, and it's going lower.

However, despite this apparent potential for flexibility, it is worth considering a further comment made by AG when asked whether there was a norm that writers and publishers felt the need to follow in terms of levels.

> **AG:** I think that's what the customers are looking for, but it doesn't fit perfectly and it does give them problems.

It therefore seems that, despite the fact that the current six-level system may not be ideal in many situations, the pressure of conformity to established practice means that six levels are generally maintained.

In terms of the precise grammatical content in a coursebook series, IF and PV, referring to older coursebook series, both note that the content of each series evolved slowly, and was not planned from the beginning.

> **IF:** Right up to *Blueprint* [a coursebook series] and the others, we would do one level at a time and publish that. […] It was very, very much, it happened as we wrote.
>
> **PV:** I don't think we ever sat down and mapped out four levels. We mapped out Level 1, and then we mapped out Level 2. Until we finished Level 2, we didn't start thinking about Level 3. I'm sure we did it a level at a time. And then we would have learnt things, and you would also have tested it.

By comparison, it is revealing that AG refers to current consensus on grammar content as a 'folk syllabus' – with the implication perhaps that its contents may be somewhat arbitrary:

> **AG:** There is this kind of recognised 'folk syllabus' that you teach the present before you teach the past, and you do the conditionals at a certain points and so on.

Other interviewees also hinted at imperfection in terms of the grammar chosen for inclusion, particularly in terms of how certain grammar points are prioritised over others. For example, we already saw LS's about the focus placed on 'have got' in British English courses; conversely, she also discusses areas of grammar that are often ignored in American English versions of coursebooks.

> **LS:** [Interviewer: Did you ever include or exclude any grammar contents that you would have preferred not to?] It usually happens more with the American editions, where they're so kind of hell-bent on saying they don't say this, but in fact, they do. [...] Myths build up within the English Language Teaching world about what isn't used. I remember one big thing – again it was the Upper Intermediate, we were doing this thing of 'bound to happen' as a related verb, modal, you know – and working with the American editor, 'No, we would not say that in American English'. And in fact, amazingly enough, probably because we'd just been using it, he used it a few sentences later. Things like that. [...] You do wonder with certain things in the language whether they're worth spending time on[.]

An alternative perspective on how coursebooks at times erroneously prioritise certain grammar points was offered by PV, in talking about how another author, Robert O'Neill, selected grammar for inclusion in his coursebooks. According to PV, O'Neill prioritised grammar points that had clear learning outcomes in a single lesson – referred to by PV as those that have a 'ding factor' – over others. This, according to this interviewee, leads to certain areas of grammar receiving more attention than they should.

> **PV:** [Robert O'Neill's] selection criteria for [*Kernel Lessons*] *Intermediate* was [...] I used to say it all had a 'ding' factor. [...] It's the ding factor that students go, 'Ah, I've got it'. And all the things in Kernel Lessons Intermediate have a ding factor, where you've done the contrasts between two grammatical points, and then you, 'Ah, that's right – I've got it'. And the ding factor thing that I began to think of in recent years was how comparatives are superlatives is flogged to death in every textbook. And it's flogged to death because it has a major ding factor.

4.4 Organising Theme: Publishers

The second organising theme relates to the role of the publishers in deciding on the content of coursebooks, and the context within which they operate. Two basic themes were identified within this organising theme: 'publisher influence' and 'pressures on publisher'.

4.4.1 Basic theme: Influence of publisher

One extremely common theme to emerge from the interviews was the strong influence that publishers have on content, and the reasons for this. Many comments outline the overall power publishers have in mapping out and deciding on grammatical content for coursebooks. The following excerpts, from two coursebook authors and two publishing professionals, are typical:

> **BU:** It appears that the publishers are the driving force, who put together teams that agree with their ideas.
>
> **APP:** I think generally the publisher decides these days[.]. [...] Publishers control scope and sequence these days, or want control over it.
>
> **ACA:** The publisher has the final say on everything.
>
> **PV:** I think it is much more publisher led now than it ever was. [...] I remember the internet group, 'ELT writers connected'. And you'd listen to authors of a different generation [i.e. authors writing contemporary coursebooks], and they didn't have a choice of how to design a syllabus. They're told to follow Council of Europe levels and this publisher has a very strong idea of the syllabus before they start writing.

In addressing the question of how decisions are made on grading grammatical structures, AG refers to specific programmes at two publishers to standardise the grammar syllabus, putting decisions out of the hand of individuals, whether they be authors or editors.

> **AG:** It depends on the publisher and how they've gone with it, because the attempt at Pearson was to have a standard Pearson syllabus which would be used across all courses, so your variety is in the topic and content and digital configuration and all that, but let's not reinvent the grammar syllabus every time we publish a new course. Here at CUP it's moving in that direction because of things like the EGP, and there's more of a structure there. [...] Publishers are sort of laying out the grid, you need structure and so on[.].

While the role of author is clearly crucial in the production of coursebooks, it appears significant that it was the interviewed authors, not publishing professionals, that primarily commented on the role of the author (which we will see later in this chapter). The main exception was BU, whose involvement in ELT publishing ended in 1979.

4.4.2 Basic theme: Pressures on publishers

One of the key issues raised in Amrani's (2011) account, discussed in Chapter 2, was that while publishers are often portrayed (particularly in accounts by authors) as exerting control over content, they themselves do not feel free of external pressures. The interview data makes it clear that publishers have a range of needs, operate under a range of pressures, and it is these factors that are often the motivation behind their desire to influence the structure and content of the grammar syllabus. The most significant issue appears, unsurprisingly, to be financial in nature: a number of interviewees discussed the need for publishers to avoid commercial risk. APP mentions this several times, in relation to three different aspects of coursebook production.

> APP: [On the selection of grammar points] There's a kind of standard menu these days of grammatical expectations at any one level, and I think people are unwilling in general to risk moving far away from it because I think that might put the series at risk and therefore make nonsense of the investment[.]

> APP: [On the grading of grammar points] I think publishers are unwilling, understandably, to risk doing anything that deviates too much from the norm, because it's too much of a commercial risk.

> APP: [On the possibility of innovation in the grammar syllabus] I also think that, thinking commercially, as you know a course is a massive investment and will inevitably have digital media attached to it these days, often given away free. And publishers are not willing to deviate much from the norm.

The level system adopted for a coursebook series is also said to be a product of commercial considerations. APP points to how financial pressures might affect decisions on how many levels to publish: a publisher will be less likely to want to publish a particular level of a coursebook series if sales are not predicted to be high for that level.

> APP: Publishers, if your sales at top levels, whatever those top levels might be, are 20% of what they are at Pre-Intermediate and Intermediate level, the publisher is going to be reluctant to invest in something for a small number of users.

This practice is confirmed by DH:

> DH: I've certainly come across a number of courses where the publishers will start off with the four core levels, well maybe there are five core levels, I don't know, but they'll start off with four, going from maybe Elementary to Upper Intermediate, because they're the ones that sell most. [...] Then, if the course goes well, they'll start tacking on, they'll put on an Advanced, and possibly a Proficiency, and they'll go down lower and do a starter. And that happened with *Total English*, it happened with *Keynote*, it happened with *Language Leader*, they only did the Advanced later on, so some of it is down to the commercial aspect of sales, what they think will sell.

IF and PV both also explain how commercial factors are likely to be priorities in any decision-making processes on grammar content.

IF: Longman are a commercial enterprise, they want to sell copies, so they don't really decide what is the most teachable route. It's what the markets want, probably more, than what actually is easiest to teach in the classroom.

PV: I think the investment levels now are so huge that no publisher would dare to do it [publish a series] without backing it up with research[.]

JR reflects on a coursebook series, released at approximately the same time as his own, which was both very different from other courses and commercially unsuccessful. The fact that innovation of this kind can be a commercial risk explains, for JR, why publications are unwilling to innovate to any great extent:

JR: That course completely bombed – it just never took off at all. It was trying to do something totally different. So publishers are very cautious about trying to do something that is very different for that reason.

Another key issue is the need to publish multiple levels – typically four out of six – of a coursebook series simultaneously, in order to be able to offer a viable product to the markets. The consequence of this is that syllabus planning needs to be carried out in advance of writing the content, probably by the publisher itself, given that various different authors and authors teams may be working on different levels. PV explains the basic context and result, as he sees it.

PV: The other things is they all want simultaneous introduction of all four levels. [...] But it [...] doesn't let stuff grow when you do that, because you grow a syllabus in a way.

The same basic phenomenon is also described by AG.

AG: That's the thing – you can't have that, Brian [Abbs] and Ingrid [Freebairn] working their way through it [a series of coursebooks]. You've got different pairs working on different levels, you've got to bring out five levels at once, or whatever, so there's no way you can do it [i.e. develop a new grammar syllabus level by level] in that kind of way, because you'll drop things between the levels, or get them in the wrong place. There isn't time to unpick it again, and so 'oh shit, no actually that bit doesn't work, we'd better put it in the level below'. You've got to get your structure right at the beginning and then fill it in.

It is noteworthy that AG presents this practice as inevitable and essential in avoiding problems, rather than lamenting the inability to 'grow a syllabus' discussed by PV. This disagreement is not untypical of the different perspectives held by authors and publishers.

PV also offers a fascinating perspective, admittedly not confirmed by other interviewees, on how a very physical publishing pressure, the fact that print books are made up of 'signatures – 'booklets' typically of 16 or 32 pages – might have a very direct effect on the number of units that can be included within an individual title, and, consequently, on the content of a syllabus:

> **PV:** I have a feeling, knowing how OUP work, that the magic number 96 for profitability on the number of pieces of paper was a major influence in the length. I think the number 96, and multiples of 16 on top of this, might explain a lot about syllabus design. Yeah, I think they wanted 96 pages, with indexes and everything.

4.5 Organising Theme: Institutions

The third organising theme identified in the analysis was 'institutions'. This contains two basic themes and relates to how external institutions can have – or are perceived to have – an influence on grammar content. These two basic themes were:

- schools and ministries;
- exam boards.

4.5.1 Basic theme: Schools and ministries

The influence of schools and ministries of education on content was mentioned by a number of interviewees. APP describes the influence of state school syllabuses in different parts of the world on the makeup of grammatical syllabuses and how that interacts with the expectations of teachers.

> **APP:** [Talking about the influences on selection of grammar points for a coursebook series] Prescriptive syllabuses. I'm thinking really at school level here.

> **APP:** [Talking about how grammar points are assigned to levels] Throughout Latin America, for example, all the school systems have pretty prescriptive syllabuses. In Asia, they don't appear to prescribe, but I think they do prescribe, I think that they definitely determine expectations among teachers.

ACA reports similar influences, this time on the level system, mentioning, like APP, South America, and also the high school system in Italy.

> **ACA:** The decisions come mostly from market research, from how the market is structured. So, for example, the *biennio* [first two years of high school], or the *triennio* [final three years of high school] in Italy.

In other countries, there are also key, large institutions, like university systems. Or large, binational centres in South America. So what you publish reflects their structures. And it also reflects what the Ministries of Education want.

The influence of state institutions does not appear to be a new phenomenon; it was also reported by interviewees when talking about titles from the 1970s and 1980s. IF speaks in detail of the influence of the school system in Italy on the grammatical content of a coursebook series, sometimes putting the influence in a negative light.

> **IF:** And then we went back and did [levels] 1 and 2 [of the *Blueprint* coursebook series], again influenced by the *scuole medie* [middle schools] in Italy because [...] they wanted to build in not only as much grammar as possible, but also as much culture as possible, which didn't really seem to match up with the grammar they'd done. So you might do a little bit of this, that and the other and present continuous and then you'd have a whole section on the Romans in the past tense, so it wouldn't really match up to the language they'd been studying. [...] And the other trouble with Italy at the time was that they always believed that they had to start again when they go into *biennio*. They would start from scratch again – they never seemed to be this sort of progression upwards that one would feel that they had done *Discoveries* before, now let's see if we can use that as the starting point and go upwards. But no, you had to then go back right at the beginning as if they'd never done it before.

IF also describes how different school systems around the world might, unsurprisingly, not always be in total agreement.

> **IF:** You'd always get slight conflicts between what they wanted to cover. [...] What they wanted to cover by the end of Book 1 was always slightly different between the different countries. Some didn't want more than the present tense in Book 1, for instance – you didn't really want any past. Whereas others say, 'No, we've got to cover the present, past tense, past simple' by the end of Book 1. [...] But it might have pleased Poland if they hadn't done it by the end – so to please them, we would probably go with them rather than lose their market. That made sense for us.

A final comment worth noting is made by BU, who again makes a clear the link between coursebook syllabuses and education ministry syllabuses, but also notes that – particularly historically – the creators of both might be the same people.

> **BU:** If you were doing the *Living English for Jordan* in the occupied parts of what is now called Palestine, those books were tied to the Jordanian ministry syllabus, which were pretty explicit about what was

taught at each level. Though that was very often originally written by the people who wrote the courses. So they would be commissioned to work out something for introducing English throughout the secondary school system in Jordan.

In this case, the coursebook series mentioned is not a contemporary title, and it is unclear whether similar situations still occur.

4.5.2 Basic theme: Examinations

As well as schools and ministries of education, examination boards – and the exams they produce – were identified by many interviewees as institutions that have a strong influence on the content of coursebook grammar syllabuses.

Both DH and AG link exams to the likely priorities of end users of coursebooks – teachers and learners. AG argues that changes to the content of coursebook grammar syllabuses are unlikely, as teachers will always want content that is aimed at the exams their students are studying for.

> AG: [Interviewer: In terms of selection of grammar, is there any space for innovation there?] Not while we've got exams, I think, because there'll always be the wash back effect, teachers will want to teach for the exam.

DH makes a similar point, but from the view of learners, suggesting also that the way learners prioritise exams may eventually lead to changes to the contents of coursebooks, perhaps implying that coursebooks do not currently offer the most expedient route to passing the exam.

> DH: It's how these different things work together, what are the exam requirements that they're leading to, because for most students that's the most important thing, they want to get into university, or they can only complete their degree because they've got a certificate that says they're B1, even if they're doing an engineering degree. And then what's the shortest and most effective route to get there. Whether that means that the publishers will start to take all that on board and change their courses – I think it will take time, but it will happen.

APP also makes a similar link between student ambition to pass exams and the grammar syllabus, this time linking exams to the level system – a relationship we speculated on in Chapter 2.

> APP: I think exams and requirements and sort of ambition about exams determines nature of level and number of levels.

In general, though, it is the link between examinations and grammar content – rather than levels – that was mentioned most frequently. APP makes the link between the pressure of exams on the specific content of a grammatical syllabus, arguing that such a pressure will exist even if a particular examination board does not explicitly set out a list of required grammar structures for a particular exam:

> APP: Anything exam orientated [has an influence] because even if Cambridge expresses its grammar in a way which avoids mentioning grammatical terms[2] – 'you need to be able to blah, blah, blah' – there is an implicit, I think, [requirement for] knowledge of a certain level of grammar and I think that coursebooks have managed to tease out of Cambridge exams what grammar points are expected.

DH – a coursebook author – mentions specific exam practice titles that she refers to when deciding on grammatical content for a coursebook series, if it is possible that the series may be used prior to a course that prepares learners for an exam.

> DH: What I refer to are *the Cambridge Grammar for FCE, CAE*, etc. [practice books to prepare candidates for the exams]. I just use those as a reference for what's expected in the exams and therefore if you're producing courses at a particular level, potentially leading to an exams course, these are the structures we need to cover.

In the quotations above, the influence of exams in described in neither positive nor negative terms – exams are simply presented as a factor to take into consideration. However, IF, when discussing areas of grammar that in retrospect she would choose to focus on less, suggests that she and her co-author felt obliged to included reported speech in their coursebooks, purely because it is frequently tested in examinations.

> IF: There are certain things, bits in the syllabus, you think, 'Why did we ever include that?' [...] Reported speech, it's one of those things that we had to include, because it's always there in exams, and of course you listen to young people today, you realise they don't use it at all in speech.

Overall, the experiences presented in this section would suggest that exams have had an influence on the grammatical content of coursebooks. Interestingly, the reverse may also be true; according to APP, successful coursebooks may have potentially fed into exam syllabuses over the years.

> APP: I suppose corpuses and the sort of technical things like the CEFR may have influenced ELT grammar but then the coursebooks and the CEFR and the exams all work in concert with each other anyway [...] Probably books that were published that are established [i.e. have been commercially successful] affected the exams anyway, so I'm sure there was cross fertilisation.

4.6 Organising Theme: Considering the Market and Users

The next organising theme identified in the interview data was 'considering the market and users'. As commercial entities, it is not surprising that publishers are reported to carefully research the market they are selling into, in addition to the end users of their products, and this was reflected in comments in the interviews.

4.6.1 Basic theme: Markets and market research

A knowledge of the target market is clearly a requirement for the development of any product, and that includes the grammar syllabuses of coursebook series. The most common form of market research referred to was reviewers. These are typically teachers or school administrators who comment on manuscripts or parts of manuscripts before the book is published. Publishers often commission reviewers in important markets to produce reports on the manuscript and their feedback is then used to shape the final product. The influence of reports on the writing of one coursebook series is outlined by IF.

> IF: And we were driven by reports early on. For [the coursebook series] *Snapshot*, they would do reports for each level, on the syllabus that we'd produce, and decide whether they'd liked it or not but it wasn't until [the coursebook series] *Sky*, I think, later on, and [the coursebook series] *Upbeat*, that we actually did focus groups, so we'd actually go into the markets and talk to teachers before we actually produced the syllabuses.

APP also confirmed the influence of reviewers – among other influences – in contemporary coursebook production.

> APP: I think the author might, will have input [on the grammatical points to be included in a series], as will reviewers maybe[.]

> APP: [Talking about how it is decided which grammatical points to include at which level] Again, I've got competition, reviews, to some extent syllabuses if they're prescriptive[.]

Not all interviewees presented reviewers in a positive light. PV suggests that publishers rely on too small a group of reviewers, and compares the feedback from reviewers with the apparently more useful and relevant feedback he received from colleagues when writing the original version of a coursebook, in the form of in-house language school materials.

> PV: Publishers going all round the world to ask people over dinner what they thought about it [i.e. a manuscript] [...] [For us] it was actually people who we were sat in the staffroom with us who'd just used it telling us what was wrong. The other problem with it is that publishers

do so-called research and I had to do this 10, 15 years ago, and you go to Spain, and you have lunch with a guy who tells you that he had lunch with Longman last week, and he's having lunch with Cambridge next week, and Macmillan the week after. So they're all researching with the same group of people in different countries.

Later on in the interview, PV neatly summarised his views as follows:

> **PV:** I think the investment levels now are so huge that no publisher would dare to do it without backing it up with [market] research, but the research is dubious.

In terms of the level system used by coursebooks, APP, ACA and JR all mention the markets and market research as having an influence:

> **APP:** I think the number of levels is determined by the competition, to some extent market research, market feedback. [...]
>
> **ACA:** In terms of the six-level system, the markets want six levels. That's the message. [...] When they've suggested adding a level, it's not been a goer. Six levels is what the institutions want.
>
> **JR:** Originally, actually, [*Interchange*] had three levels, and when it came out we realised that there was a demand for a lower level because in some markets what was then level 1 was a bit too high, so I wrote it. [...] A sort of three-stage syllabus was sort of extremely common I think at the time, so I think we were just following what the market suggested.

APP notes an interesting conundrum for publishers. We saw above that publishers may be reluctant to publish a coursebook at a particular level if they do not believe it will be profitable. However, according to APP, in some cases publishing a full range of levels is a requirement for a product to be viable, even if some of those levels are unlikely to sell well.

> **APP:** A publisher would argue, 'Well until you've got an Advanced level, the suite of levels doesn't appear complete'. [...] Without that Advanced level, the earlier levels might not stand up to scrutiny.

4.6.2 Basic theme: Local markets

Some local markets can be large and important enough that their needs are directly reflected in coursebooks. This can take three forms: market specific materials can be produced; global products can be produced with a specific market or markets in mind; and existing global products can be adapted for local markets. In the latter situation, the original global product may nonetheless be influenced by the needs of the local market, in order that the subsequent adaption be as quick and cheap as possible. IF describes writing a coursebook series where this was the case – the requirements of the Italian market influenced the original global product, in ways that the authors were not totally comfortable with.

> IF: When we started with [the coursebook series] *Discoveries*, it was Italy – Italy had been the main market for us all the way through. [...] They've taken each of our courses and adapted them according to what they felt they wanted. So we were quite driven after that by what the markets wanted, and Italy in particular. [...] So we felt very much driven by Italy, and as you probably know, they like to cover a lot of grammar, and they like to do it in groups, group sort of criteria, so they'll do *some* and *any* together, and then they'll do present perfect with *ever*, and then *for* and *since*, and then present perfect continuous, and they would want to do that all together. Whereas our feeling was, 'This isn't how learners will learn it – it's too complicated'. We were much more into wanting to recycle, so there were conflicts. We wanted more a cyclical syllabus, but when it came to them, what they wanted, we were driven slightly by Italy, and so we did group things together that we wouldn't possibly normally have wanted to do. They did their own versions, always slightly different from the global versions, but it did inform the syllabus to a certain extent.

Similarly LS describes how the requirement of a local market led to changes at a global level. However, in this case, the influence is presented more positively – the need for a low-level coursebook for a particular group of users of *Headway* in Germany eventually lead to the introduction of a global Beginner level of the series, and subsequent modification of the syllabus for the previous lowest level, Elementary.

> LS: What happened with Germany was we got news from the *Volkshochschule* in Germany who were using *Headway* that they needed something of a much more low level, because they had a lot [...] of adult students actually who couldn't speak a word of English. So there was somebody out there called Briony Beaven [...] and she put together a kind of thing that was for German use only, a very, very basic beginner book. [...] So when John and I came to actually write a beginners book, which we did with the second editions of the whole series, [...] we would look at what Briony had done and remind ourselves all the time that we were not – now that we'd been writing for quite a while – going to get carried away with showing our brilliant knowledge and skills as trainers and all the rest of it. We would really stick with that. [...] We then went back to the Elementary, and when we did a new edition of the Elementary, we rewrote the first two units of that to reflect the fact that there was now a Beginner *Headway*.

Conversely, when producing a product for a specific market, a publisher and author team may decide to include more generic features than the local market requires, in the hope of also being able to sell the product in other markets. DH describes her experience of this phenomenon as an author: a level system was chosen in the hopes of making sales in a number of different markets, but in doing so it did not reflect the requirements of the main target market.

> **DH:** Thinking back to when I did *Pacesetter* many years ago, which was principally for Turkey, but of course it had to take in other countries as well, it was when Turkey had the system of *Süper Lise*, and they had 28 hours of English teaching a week, [...] we still did four levels, and we still did four levels in four books, but they were all taught in the same year. In reality three ended up being taught in the same year and the fourth one sort of disappeared, but it was just odd that as we were aiming mainly for that market, why didn't we do something a bit more appropriate to that market? Obviously the reason was that this was OUP and they were hedging their bets, and they were expecting it to be able to sell elsewhere, but in the end it did become a bit too Turkey orientated and it didn't do very well elsewhere.

4.6.3 Basic theme: End users

As well as discussing market research, many interviewees talked specifically about how they considered the end users of their books – teachers and learners – when making decisions on grammatical content. Many of these comments also relate to the idea of norms and consensus discussed above, but are distinguished – and analysed separately – in that they contain specific references to users rather than to norms in a more abstract sense.

LS frames the potential influence of considering end users in a generally positive light, and seems happy to include grammar content on the basis that this is what users – in this case higher-level learners – appear to want and enjoy doing.

> **LS:** You do wonder with certain things in the language whether they're worth spending time on, but then going back to those grammar options [optional grammar courses that she taught at International House], that would be exactly the kind of thing that an advanced student would want to know about. You know, what is it about *suggest* that it can go with the gerund, but you can 'suggest that he did', and 'suggest that he do', and all the rest of it. So, that would have been a classic kind of thing you'd have had to hone up for. [Interviewer: So students like that kind of thing.] They love it, yeah. They become, at that level, a lot of the time they're just basically interested in the language and they know a hell of a lot more about it, loads more about it.

AG's description of how teachers are likely to prioritise grammar content over other language areas is similar. However, as we said earlier, his use of the word 'folk' implies that this preference may not necessarily be well founded.

> **AG:** I still think that although if you looked at a coursebook 30 years ago and opened the contents page, it would give you a list of grammar structures. Now you get this great grid of topic, grammar, functional language, pronunciation, whatever else it might be, [but] I still think that the teachers will look first at the grammar syllabus and see if fits their 'folk expectation', and 'Does it have the things that I expect to cover at this level and if it doesn't, I'll use something else'.

In terms of the specifics of a grammar syllabus, PV recalled conversations with his contemporary L.G. Alexander (see also Chapter 3), who, according to PV, made choices on the ordering of elements within a grammatical syllabus considering the context in which the learners were using the books – in this case, school children in a non-English speaking country. The grammar syllabus for such children, the argument goes, can be very different from a syllabus for adult learners in an English speaking country.

> **PV:** Alexander used to say, 'Well, the whole thing about "you need to be able to go out and communicate immediately", is based on language schools in England'. He said, 'If we're teaching abroad, then what's the problem?' He said, 'You should teach logically because immediate communication is not important'. In the first year they're going to get to the present simple whatever you do, so why does it have to come first because it's more frequent?

However, it should be noted that Alexander's titles were written in the 1960s and 1970s. Referring to contemporary times, AG suggests that one group of end users – teachers – can often have very fixed ideas about the content and order of a grammar syllabus.

> **AG:** Certainly from speaking to people in Italy, there is no official ministry grammar syllabus as to what you have to teach, but the teachers there have got a very strong idea what they've to teach, and when, so I think I've seen that quite a lot.

This is echoed in JR's observation that not following teachers' expectations in terms of sequencing grammar items can be problematic:

> **JR:** If you don't sort of follow what teachers expect, then you get some problems. So quite a lot of it had to with getting the idea, well, teachers will expect this in Level 1, or teachers will expect this in Level 2, or not […] save this for Level 3 and so on. So that kind of discussion went on quite a lot.

4.6.4 Basic theme: Learner L1s

One particular characteristic of end users of a language course is their first language, and a number of interviewees mentioned how these are often an important consideration in deciding on grammar syllabuses. It seems uncontroversial to suggest that different L1 groups may find certain aspects of grammar more difficult or easier compared with other L1 groups, and publishers appear to take this into account when possible:

> AG: There are some things that come in a natural sequence, that you're going to teach the present perfect and know they won't get it right for a long time, and at some point later you'll move on to the past perfect. And some things, depending on the nationality, they'll get very easily or they won't.

Similar to IF's comments on how the grammar syllabuses in global coursebooks are influenced by the need to produce subsequent localised versions as easily as possible, DH makes very similar observations in relation to learner L1s.

> DH: I think if you come into market specific materials there might be particular structures that are problematic for particular language speakers and they come in earlier, or they come in later, depending on their approach, like articles in Polish, they obviously always want to see articles addressed because it's one of the issues. So that could have, if you're doing a course that's got some market specific versions but also a global version, that could have an influence on the global version. It's cheaper to bring 'mustn't' in a bit earlier because of German, though we don't really publish for Germany that much, or I suppose, with Spain, because they've got a continuous form, they probably find the continuous easier than French would, for example.

MS suggests that, unsurprisingly, teachers have for a long time been highly knowledgeable of the areas of grammar likely to be priorities or problematic for particular groups of L1 learners, based on their own experience teaching them. He explains that he was able to make use of this mainly in market-specific materials, and his popular grammar title, *Practical English Usage* (Swan, 2016).

> MS: We all knew, us experienced EFL [English as a Foreign Language] teachers in the 60s, we all knew, or lots of us knew, what kind of grammar points mattered for learners of English. A fair number of us knew it on a specific level, in that they had worked in Japan, or Germany, or Italy, or wherever, and they knew what problems, as you certainly know, speakers of that language have. [...] That was something that I wasn't able to exploit very much, except in supervising spin offs of

some of my books for particular national markets. And I was able to get them up to a point in *Practical English Usage*, because there I could put in a fair amount of stuff that was broad-spectrum cross linguistic.

The experiences and views expressed by the interviewees suggest that Swan's design criterion of 'relevance' (see Chapter 2) and the Contrastive Analysis hypothesis appear to be influential to a certain extent in syllabus design.

4.7 Organising Theme: Innovation

The previous two organising themes have identified the role of external factors in perpetuating existing practice and sustaining the consensus on grammar. The issues that emerged from the interviewees' comments generally seem to represent external forces restricting – or at best, informing – decisions on content, in ways that often the interviewees do not agree with. The final organising theme discussed in this chapter is somewhat different: 'innovation'. Here, we will see a variety of views that suggest that, despite the picture painted so far, innovation can nonetheless occur, as result of influences from outside the word of ELT and ELT publishing.

4.7.1 Basic theme: Influence of corpus linguistics

One source of innovation appears to be corpus linguistics. ACA, for example, argues that corpus research has the potential to influence the consensus:

> ACA: Corpora give us the opening to do so [i.e. to influence the grammar syllabus]. We can say, 'This is how this structure is used'.

However, continuing, she argues that any modification will involve adding to the canon rather than changing its contents:

> ACA: But this is addition rather than deletion. There are always some things that are considered essential and must be included. So as an example, if I were sticking close to a syllabus where frequency was the most important thing, I probably wouldn't teach short answers at first, when you first present a tense. But there's an expectation that they'll be there, so you include them.

However, a number of interviewees argued that corpus linguistics does have the potential to modify, rather than simply add to, the consensus. For example, AG notes the potential for corpus evidence on language use in different situations to influence the content of the ELT grammar canon.

AG: You've got to sort of match the situation that people are aiming for. So there is more evidence of corpus-based spoken grammar or conversational strategies and turn taking or how to disagree with somebody or that sort of thing. It started off with situational dialogues twenty years ago of ordering a coffee or buying a stamp and things have moved on, and that affects the grammar to a degree.

AG also notes an increasing awareness of register thanks to corpus-based research. One implication of this is that the monolithic ELT grammar canon may need to be modified to match the needs of different groups of learners in different communicative situations.

AG: I worked with Geoff Leech and Doug Biber on *The Longman Grammar of Spoken and Written English*, where it was using corpus evidence of how language is really used. We picked four genres of speaking: newspapers, fiction and academic prose – and then looked at where did we use this structure, how, why, looking beyond just 'here's the rule', and trying to understand how frequent it is and so on. And then McCarthy has done similar things with Ron Carter, looking at the corpus that they've got. So, that kind of influence of linguistics and evidence has been steadily growing for the last 40 years [...] It depends what your purposes are, if you need to be able to write academic journals then that's very different to somebody who needs a lot of spoken English but hardly needs to write in a foreign language.

Register is also noted by DH as having a potential influence on how individual grammar points are treated.

DH: I suppose in terms of something like the use of *may*, this would probably generally come into a course with *will*, talking about future speculation, whereas actually it's probably more often used in academic English for uncertainty, isn't it? But it's something that I would now want to bring in at a higher level of a course, in its sense, in its use in academic English, and that's something that has only come about through corpus linguistics really. [Interviewer: So, register?] True, yes, because that probably wasn't taken into account in earlier courses.

DH also notes some aspects of the grammar consensus that have already been modified as a result of findings from corpus linguistics.

DH: With the advent of corpora I think there have been some changes that have come about through corpus research. The obvious one is thinking back to the situational approach or whatever, of 'I'm giving you this pen', the fact that going back to books like *Streamline* and those around that time, probably later as well, the very first structure to be taught was always present continuous because it was easy, you could show it in the classroom, and that switched after the advent of corpora and the realisation that we hardly ever use it for the present anyway, that then the present simple became the first structure to be taught. I think the same applies with the use of the future as well, because I think it always used to be that the 'will future' was presented before anything else and I think now we probably tend to use *going to* as the first point of future use.

MS, in personal communication via email after the initial interview, was another to identify research by corpus linguistics as having had an influence on the grammar consensus.

MS: Work on the grammar of speech by discourse analysts and others (Mike McCarthy springs to mind) has given us a lot of useful information which we've been able to incorporate, where appropriate, in teaching and reference materials. The same goes for discourse structure in general.

4.7.2 Basic theme: Influence of real world needs

Another external factor that some interviewees mentioned as potentially leading to innovation are the contexts in which language learners are learning and using English. For AG, increasingly awareness of specific contexts for language use – particularly between non-native speakers – may lead to grammatical content being rethought.

AG: I think there's scope for more focus on the language you really need, and how do you get that, how much do people want to master all English grammar structures, versus, 'actually what I need to do is, I'm a Brazilian, I want to be able to do business with people in Asia, and I want to be able to have a conversation over dinner, and I want to be able to do a Skype meeting where I can contribute and understand what's going on'.

APP, by comparison, makes the connection between real world needs and the level system rather than grammar content in itself. She links the university requirements in many European countries to possible changes in coursebook level systems:

APP: In Spain, and it might be true in other European countries as well, in order to graduate in any subject at university you have to a B1 level in any foreign language, and of course the favourite is English. So that might be making a difference to the number of levels, or perhaps more to the point, where the levels begin. Do they begin at absolute beginner, starter level, or do they begin at post-beginner? And if they begin at post-beginner, it will be interesting to see if, in a couple of years' time, those publishers decide, 'Oh, we are going to produce a beginner or starter level'.

DH refers to a somewhat parallel situation in the past: she recalls predictions that were made on changes to the level system likely to occur as a result of the end of Eastern Block in Europe and an increase across Europe in the teaching of English at primary school.

> DH: A few years ago – I'm probably going back into the 90s, when the Berlin wall fell – suddenly there was this huge market opening up in Eastern Europe etc. [and] it was thought that it wouldn't be necessary for very long to produce starter or elementary levels, because everybody was learning English at primary school. Because English started coming into the school system in Eastern Europe as well as Western Europe, and, yeah, the advent of teaching English at primary school would mean that by the time students got into secondary school, or by the time they started learning as adults in language schools, they'd already have a basic grounding and be able to come into a pre-intermediate level.

However, these predictions, according to DH, did not come to pass.

> DH: But that doesn't seem to have happened! That's been said since the 90s, in 25 years it hasn't happened so I don't think it's going to happen!

As well as changes in policy possibly having effects on the level system, or at least on the relative demand for instruction at particular levels, APP also argues that political events, such as the arrival of refugees, may be similarly influential.

> APP: I remember years and years ago, I lived in a European country where there were a lot of asylum seekers from eastern Europe and Africa, and they needed, from scratch, English, or the language of the country that they were in. So I suppose what's happening in the world could affect the level at which a course begins, and the number of levels, therefore.

4.7.3 Basic theme: Potential of digital products

The final basic theme in this analysis is another potential source for innovation identified by AG: the advent of digital products. Once a print course is published, it is by nature impossible to change without being reprinted. By comparison, courses delivered digitally, for example online, allow for a greater deal of flexibility.

> AG: Once you get into fully digital, then you can have just the first four units for a short course, or the last two units of one level and the first two units of the next, if that's what fits your students' level. It can become much more flexible.

When asked whether such an approach might lead to a rethink on the level system, AG frames the possible effects as being more on matching learners' individual needs. So while the level system is likely to be sustained, it may be that courses delivered digitally will be less constrained by it.

> AG: I think we've got people coming to us asking for different ways of chopping things up, and shorter courses, and if there are different ways of assessing better what students' real level is, and students' strengths and weaknesses, then you can match it more, because having a warehouse full of books is pretty inflexible.

Overall, while it was possible to identify a range of comments relating to the theme of 'innovation', it is important for these ideas to be considered in light of the content of the other themes reported in this chapter. The potential for innovation exists within an 'ecosystem' containing a number of powerful factors that appear most likely to maintain rather than modify the existing consensus. Any innovation is likely, if it happens at all, to be subtle and slow. This point is made by two of the interviewees who themselves identified the potential for innovation elsewhere in the interviews.

> AG: I think a lot of the adult courses like *English File* are still global and that will carry on, and I think people are very nervous about innovating there[.]
>
> ACA: I think you can change market requirements but with baby steps, not huge leaps. If you have too much innovation, you can get a negative reaction. So instead, you need incremental changes. [...] [Y]ou can make small adjustments, for example, in [coursebook series] we delayed the present continuous. We also introduced the continuous for speech reporting, and the past tense for politeness.

According to APP, innovation, while possible in the past, is far less likely to occur in the contemporary context.

> APP: I think that when authors had a lot more influence over courses, when expectations were really being set, there was probably more room for innovation. But I think that there is less room now.

4.8 Summary

The analysis in this chapter has revealed a range of factors that play a role in influencing, and typically sustaining, the existing consensus on pedagogical grammar in ELT. It is clear – and is consistent with the studies on ELT publishing reported in Chapter 2 – that publishers have the final say on over syllabus design, meaning that, particularly at the level of the grammar syllabus, individual authors do not have a free hand in content creation. This control over the syllabus exerted by publishers over the years has led to a standardisation of content across coursebooks.

However, as can be seen from the other themes discussed, it would be overly simplistic to view publishers as the sole actors in this process of standardisation. The existence of norms and expectations within the ELT profession, while not always clearly defined, is frequently mentioned by the interviewees, and these appear to have a life of their own and to be – at least partly – out of the control of publishers. From the accounts given by the interviewees, there does not appear to be any particular attempt among publishers to influence the norms and expectations, but, as commercial organisations, they must do their best to match them, or else risk publishing materials that do not sell. This is entirely in line with Amrani's (2011) account (discussed in Chapter 2), which also talks of the need to match exam syllabuses and meet market expectations.

As we said above, the process of interaction between the publishers and the consensus in the ELT profession appears to be highly cyclical. Publishers investigate norms and expectations by conducting market research and by taking into consideration the views of stakeholders such as schools, ministries of education and examination boards, and then do their best to produce materials that match them. However, in producing materials in this way, they contribute to and reinforce the same consensus they are tapping in to, particularly as the safest strategy for publishers – according to the interviewees in this study – is to produce materials that replicate the content of previously successful titles and avoid the risk of innovation as much as possible.

At this point, I leave the reader with a choice about what to do next. Those who wish to continue exploring the contemporary situation can jump to Chapter 6, where the first part of the analysis of the three case studies is presented, before reading Chapter 5. The case studies in Chapter 6 – which, as we said, examine the treatment of three areas of grammar in five coursebook series and compare this with evidence on learner grammar competence from the English Grammar Profile – remain, like this chapter, firmly rooted in the present and thus triangulate the data presented in the chapter by supplementing it with evidence from primary sources, in other words, the teaching materials in which the canon is manifested.

Alternatively, the reader who wishes to continue reading the analysis of the interview data can proceed to the next chapter, which turns to the past and looks at the question of the evolution and development of the canon, examining the second global theme, 'ELT past and present'. This global theme covers opinions and experiences discussed by the interviewees that relate to differences between the past and present in the ELT profession (and in particular the ELT publishing industry) and to changes they explicitly reported that they had observed taking place.

Notes

(1) Subsequent to the interview, IF clarified that she was referring here to 'the Scope and Sequence followed by the two leading Longman authors at that time: Louis Alexander in *New Concept English* (*First Things First, Practice and Progress, Developing Skills* and *Fluency in English*) and by Robert O'Neill in *Kernel Lessons Intermediate, Kernel Lessons Plus*' (personal communication).

(2) Cambridge English publishes specifications for each level (A2–C2) of its General English examinations. A grammatical inventory is included in the specifications for the A2 (Key) and B1 (Preliminary) exams, but not for exams at B2, C1 and C2.

5 Interviews with Authors and Editors: The Canon in the Past and Present

5.1 Introduction

Chapter 4 presented the methodology used and the thematic network developed for the analysis of the interviews presented in this book. It also discussed the first of our two global themes: 'influences and input'. The discussion in Chapter 4 related primarily to contemporary phenomena which interviewees reported as influencing the grammar content of coursebooks they had written or of which they had been involved in the production. This chapter completes the analysis of the interviews by discussing the second global theme, 'ELT past and present'. As in Chapter 4, we will let the interviewees do the talking for us as much as possible, as it is from their voices that the most interesting insights emerge (see page ix for the list of participants that the abbreviations used in this chapter refer to).

A diagram of the full thematic network can be found in Chapter 4. The part of the thematic relevant to this chapter – that of the global theme 'ELT past and present' – is reproduced in Figure 5.1.

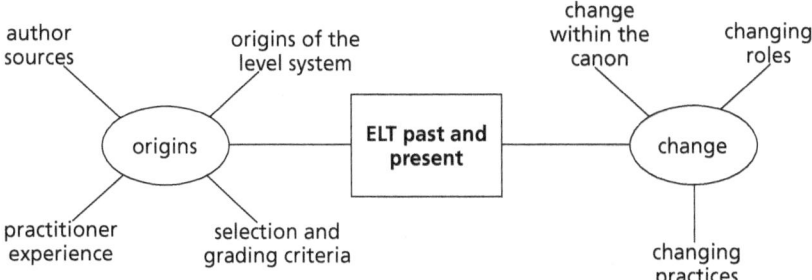

Figure 5.1 'ELT past and present' global theme, with associated organising and basic themes

Two organising themes were identified under this global theme: 'origins' and 'change'. The first relates to the origins of both the content of typical ELT grammar syllabuses, and also to the level system employed by coursebooks. The second organising theme relates to changes over time in practices and roles within the ELT publishing industry reported by the interviewees.

5.2 Organising Theme: Origins

Chapter 4 painted a picture of decisions on grammar content and organisation being largely out of the hands of individual authors – and also out of the hands of the publishers, even if this is perhaps not necessarily the perception of the authors – with grammar syllabuses largely being based on factors such as perceptions of norms, the content of successful competition titles and perceived demands and needs of target markets. However, when talking about older coursebook series, many of the interviewees mentioned quite different sources and influences. This organising theme relates to this topic, and also to the origins of the level system.

5.2.1 Basic theme: Author sources

The first basic theme relates to sources that authors reported using in order to inform the grammar content of their (older) titles. Two grammar reference books were frequently mentioned: Allen's (1947) *Living English Structure* and Alexander *et al.*'s (1975) *English Grammatical Structure* (see Chapter 3 for a description of both). BU, for example, argues that the former was likely to have been a key title in the development of the ELT grammar syllabus for over two decades.

> **BU:** My guess is, this is a guess, is that the Stannard Allen *Living English Structure* is really the sort of key that was used for 20 years plus.

The same title is also mentioned by PV, along with *English Grammatical Structure*; both are said to have played significant roles in his and his co-authors writing of coursebooks:

> **PV:** Now what we discovered at this point [i.e. when starting to write the *Streamline* coursebook series] when we were looking at the syllabus was *English Grammatical Structure*. As Bernie [Harley, his co-author] said, it was a bible, it was brilliant. I suppose we used earlier grammar books as well. [...] Bernie adored *Living English Structure*. And *Living English Speech*. A companion pronunciation one. Bernie adored both books, and would refer to them frequently when we were doing stuff. And he would say it was the first modern ELT book.

MS, IF and JR all recall making reference to a number of different titles in order to inform the grammatical content of their own writing;

again, both *Living English Structure* and *English Grammatical Structure* were among the key titles mentioned:

> **MS:** [When asked to specify the grammar books he reported having consulted] The principal authors were Kruisinga, Curme, I must have read Jespersen, Erades, who wrote together with Kruisinga. [...] The other source of information was, as far as I was concerned, Stannard Allen's book *Living English Structure*. [...] I say this, and it might not be completely literally true, and I do say it – I learnt all my grammar from that book when I was starting out. [...] Student grammars: at some point during my early teaching, the Thompson and Martinet *Practical English Grammar* showed up, and while it's a fairly awful grammar, it did cover the kind of consensus points, the things that my students were getting wrong, were often explained in that grammar. Later, and I don't have a date for this, Alexander's *Longman Student's Grammar* came out, was good. [...] When I was doing my checklists for what was going to go in *Practical English Usage* and subsequently what was going to go in to the *Cambridge English Course*, I was effectively looking at everything there was, supplementing the consensus that was in my head and in the books I'd used by going to other things like the T series. And *English Grammatical Structure* was one of them. [...] Among sources I went to for teaching material and my checklists that went into them, Hornby's *Guide to Patterns and Usage in English* was, I thought, a brilliant book.

> **JR:** Yeah we went through things like that, was it L.G. Alexander? I seem to recall a big chunky Longman book that laid out a syllabus, I think Alexander, R. A. Close [Interviewer: *English Grammatical Structure?*] Yeah, that one, that was one of them, plus, sort of seeing what was in the other books.

> **IF:** [There was] something called *OPEAC*, *Oxford Progressive English Alternative Course*, which did things like 'a', 'and', 'some', 'any' to begin with, and then structurally heavy, globulous, structurally progressive, 'one-bit-at-a-time', and it was linear and everything like that. I didn't use it to teach, but I used it to refer to.

LS's recollections are interesting in that they make clear the passage of expertise (that is, pedagogical grammar content) across 'generations' of authors, as she underlines the significance of Michael Swan's writing (amongst others) on her own:

> **LS:** The basic thing was [...] well, obviously, there are always [...] I love Michael Swan's grammar. I love his *Practical English Grammar*. For me, when I first started teaching, that was the bible, you know? But there are loads of grammar books that you consult all the time actually, to see, but you still have to make the decision out of your own experience as to what it is you feel is worthwhile to put in a coursebook, if you're writing a coursebook. You're consulting all the time, you're reading all the time, you're looking all the time.

Finally, DH reports referring to some specific titles in her role as both coursebook author and editor of contemporary teaching materials.

> **DH:** Exams come into it [...] What I refer to are the *Cambridge Grammar for FCE, CAE*, etc.. I just use those as a reference for what's expected in the exams and therefore if you're producing courses at a particular level, potentially leading to an exams course, these are the structures we need to cover.

In the accounts above, the interviewees refer to their use of sources to inform both older and also relatively recent (in the case of JR) and contemporary (in the case of DH) titles. While the importance of this for contemporary titles may be less important than in the past in shaping an overall syllabus, the interviewees' comments again confirm that one of the roles of coursebook authors in the writing process is, unsurprisingly, to refer to existing grammar accounts in order to inform their own content. It also suggests, again unsurprisingly, that there is, and has long been, available a large body of work on pedagogical grammar for coursebook authors to refer to.

5.2.2 Basic theme: Practitioner experience

Most ELT coursebook authors were teachers themselves at some point, and many of the coursebook authors interviewed made reference to how their own classroom experience informed decisions on grammar content in the material they were writing. For example, BU – the Longman marketing manager – refers to the influence of the teaching experience of the coursebook author Louis Alexander on the level system of the latter's first coursebook series, published in the 1960s.

> **BU:** That [decisions on the level system] was done in sort of general discussion with teachers in private schools around the globe. And Louis [Alexander] did it entirely from his experience teaching in a private secondary school in Greece, with precious little market research. And the result of that was he originally did four books, which took you from *First Principles*, *First Things First*, to Cambridge Proficiency and beyond. And that was how it was launched.

BU also describes a similar process in the matching of grammar points to levels within a coursebook series.

> **BU:** [Interviewer: How did a publisher or author decide at which level to include these grammar points?] They relied much more on the author, who tended to tell the publisher. And that came out of experience.

LS mentions the importance of experience both as a teacher and teacher trainer in driving decisions on which grammar points to cover

– the latter being particularly important in terms of understanding the needs of teachers from different countries:

> **LS:** [Interviewer: How did you decide which grammar points to include in *Headway*?] In general, it is absolutely and utterly based on experience. Right the way through. [...] It *is* from experience [...] [Interviewer: But could you explain what you mean by 'experience'?] Experience as teachers, experience of using other materials, obviously, a whole range of coursebooks, but more than anything, it's your experience in the classroom with students. By that time as well, of course, we were training a lot of foreign teachers, not just native speakers, and it's also what you learn from them, foreign English teachers, about their particular countries and their particular problems and what causes them particular difficulties when they're teaching. It's cumulative, really.

LS also recalls an experience as a teacher at a particular language school which led her and her co-author to believe in the importance of a full and explicit grammar syllabus in a coursebook series.

> **LS:** One of the things that most influenced the whole thing of grammar – although it's come to haunt us because people go on about *Headway* and grammar as if it's the only thing there [...] – was at International House when we worked there, they had, at the end of each morning, they had an hour's what was called an 'hour option'. And they had wonderfully trendy things like 'communicative games', or they had ones focussed on vocabulary. [Interviewer: Sorry, this is for students?] For students, which students did. The students would sign up for these things, and they had discussion groups, conversation groups, and they also had a grammar group. And the one that students stood in queues for was the grammar option.

MS also refers clearly to the role of experience, this time in the allocation of grammar points to level.

> **MS:** [I assigned level to grammar points] on the basis of experience – these seem to be things that it's good to teach to my Elementary students, these are things that I found myself having to teach to my Proficiency students. [...] With beginners [...] you feel that you need to teach a certain number of basic structures for them to be able to communicate. And you know what these structures are – you know you're going to teach present tenses, simple past, and some way of talking about the future, how to make nouns plural, a bit of basic word order. We know what they are. Everybody knows what you teach beginners, pretty much. Higher up, it's a bit up for grabs. You're probably going to run over the main bits of tense use and relative clauses and so on. But it does depend a bit on who you're teaching.

5.2.3 Basic theme: Selection and grading criteria

A further basic theme relates to selection and grading; a number of authors discussed criteria that they have used during the writing process to select and grade grammar points. Again, these mainly refer to older titles; as we have seen, the contemporary canon is sufficiently established that few, if any, decisions of this type actually need to be made for coursebooks today.

'Usefulness' was reported by IF as being the most important criterion at the beginning of her writing career.

> **IF:** Obviously usefulness was our prime one when we started off – this is what we wanted, we definitely wanted to be able to say 'do you like', and 'I like' and 'would you like', so that we decided was useful.

However, later other criteria became more important, because of a growing realisation of teacher preference for what was easiest to teach in the classroom.

> **IF:** It was very much more teachability in the end. Because we didn't do the present continuous in *Starting Strategies* to begin with. We decided it wasn't nice to do the present continuous – who ever uses the present continuous? And it was ridiculed in lectures,[1] 'I am writing on the blackboard', and all that stuff. But eventually it came round that teachers did want, they expected the present continuous to be there because it was very easy to teach. The teachability became one of the criteria that we had to use in terms of determining the grading.

In the interview, IF also discusses referring to frequency data as a criterion for selection, admitting, however, that considering frequency alone can be problematic.

> **IF:** Frequency to a certain extent was a useful criterion that made us make certain decisions. But on the other hand we went wrong, I think, in *Starting Strategies* because we looked at frequency of colours, and 'black' and 'white' were the ones that came up so we always had 'Would you like a coffee? Was it black or white?' And we didn't teach the other colours, but you can't just introduce two colours and not introduce the other colours. So the idea of grouping was important but our first idea was 'we must go with frequency'.

LS also mentions frequency when asked to explain ordering criteria, echoing in some respects IF's discussion of whether present simple or present continuous should be taught first.

> **LS:** The big debate as well is when you bring in the present continuous. In the days of structural syllabuses, right at the beginning, the big

argument was because you taught the verb 'to be' you would then teach the present continuous because it used the verb 'to be'. But of course, in fact, it's not nearly as useful as the present simple, which has a much, much [...] I believe it's the widest used tense in the English language.

Like IF, LS also discusses usefulness, along with the idea of delaying structures that are difficult to 'get your mouth around', implying that complexity is also a key criterion.

> **LS:** So you wouldn't preclude [present perfect continuous] because it's darn useful for somebody way, way down to use, but you're not going to do a big deal, blimey Moses, the level where they need that, they don't also need all the subtleties of use between the present perfect continuous and present perfect simple. [Interviewer: What would make you not want to choose, let's say present perfect continuous, why wouldn't you do that with a beginner group?] Partly because you can't get your bloody mouth around it! [...] Certainly with something like the present perfect continuous [...] [makes sound of somebody stumbling over sounds while trying to speak].

Finally, MS also mentions the same basic criteria – frequency, usefulness, complexity – as being important in choosing content for a grammar syllabus, but noting that these criteria may at times be in conflict with each other.

> **MS:** We all knew more or less that you taught present tenses before unreal past conditionals. That the future perfect progressive didn't come in your first year. [Interviewer: But why? It seems so obvious to say it but why did you know that?] Alright, it seemed because, to take the future perfect progressive as an example, it's rare, and it's complex and it's not very useful. [Complex, meaning?] A structure with several bits. The same way as question formation with lexical verbs is complex. On the other hand, it's not rare and it's useful. So these criteria – off the top of my head, these are the three important ones – useful, frequent, complex – they fight quite often.

These contributions make it clear that, in addition to simply referring to previously published sources, authors are also aware of a number of issues that need to be considered in order to be able to make informed choices on the selection and ordering of grammar points. However, as we have said, the importance of such knowledge appears to be much diminished, as the consensus – and publishers' desire to avoid deviating from it – means that most decisions on selection and grading are effectively out of authors' hands.

Perhaps the most surprising insight to emerge came from PV. In Chapter 4, we saw that 'Student L1s' was identified as a theme and some of the interviewees mentioned that they sometimes take into account the L1s of potential users when writing grammar content. PV, however, goes a step further, suggesting that the overall grammar content found in major coursebook series published in the 1970s and 1980s – many of which first came into existence as in-house teaching materials in private language schools in the UK – are explainable in terms of the student L1 makeup of students at the language schools where the writers worked. PV refers specifically, among others, to the 1970s series *Kernel Lessons*, written by Robert O'Neill, a teacher at the Eurocentres private language school in Bournemouth, UK, and his own *Streamline* series, written in part while he was working at the Anglo Continental School of English (also in Bournemouth).

> **PV:** [I]f you look at *Kernel Lessons*, it is based on the problems of Swiss-German speakers. If you look at the things that are highlighted, they're all things that German speakers find difficult, because Robert [O'Neill]'s main thing was German, with a little bit of French and Italian, because Eurocentres was a Swiss school. So if you took German, French and Italian, that was the problem, those were the languages. At Anglo [Continental School of English], probably our biggest nationalities were Spanish speaking and Portuguese speaking, because we did big deals with Latin America. *Streamline* never took into consideration the problems of Arabs. We sold very well in Japan! But we never took into consideration problems of Arabs – even when we were teaching *Streamline*, all Arab classes when they started did *First Things First* [another coursebook series written by L.G. Alexander]. *Streamline* was too hard for them, if they were zero beginners with non-Roman alphabet. [...] So I think that's a major consideration, that all these things were developed in private [schools] [...] they were all, apart from *Strategies* was Ealing, which is a state college, but *Cambridge English Course* is Swan Schools, which is private, *Kernel* is Eurocentres, which is private, there's loads of stuff from Bell School, which is private, Anglo Continental was private. They were all private language schools. With particular student groups. I think *Streamline* may have been more successful because Anglo Continental had much wider student groups than any of the opposition. [...] [W]e probably had a wider nationality range than the competition. And that might influence us as well of course.

If PV's account is correct, the implications are potentially large. Due to the forces described in Chapter 4, the grammar syllabuses for major coursebook series of the 1970s and 1980s became part of a global ELT grammar consensus. But according to PV, the contents of these coursebooks were initially designed only for specific groups of learners, with specific L1s. They were written with very specific priorities and problems in mind, and – assuming PV is correct – not intended to be used by a wider group of learners or indeed expected to become de facto references for future materials design.

5.2.4 Basic theme: Origins of the level system

The origins of and changes to the level system over the years were also commented on frequently. A number of the interviewees trace the evolution of the competency level system used in ELT coursebooks to the typical number of school years around the world. BU argues that this actually dates back to colonial times.

> BU: I think you actually have to go back to the origins of how the analyses are done, to colonial school publishing. [...] If you look at – and I think I told you – Eckersley was in four books, and then became five. [*The*] *Direct* [*Method English Course*, by E.V.] Gatenby was five [...] I don't know what the original thinking of it was but my guess is that it was seen as sort of 11 to 16. Because language wasn't really taught before the secondary cycle. [Interviewer: So it's all linked to school years?] It's all linked to school years, yeah.

He also confirms the influence of school years during the period – the 1970s – that he was involved in ELT publishing.

> BU: In my day, [the level system of a coursebook series] was entirely built on the market they were trying to go into, which was either a state secondary system, or the parallel private language schools, which tended to teach in parallel year groupings to the secondary schools.

BU makes the same link to school years when talking about L. G. Alexander's 1960s coursebook *New Concept English*. Originally published at four levels, two levels were eventually themselves split into four, creating a six-level publication similar to the modern six-level coursebook system:

> BU: Louis did it entirely from his experience teaching in a private secondary school in Greece, with precious little market research. And the result of that was he originally did four books [...] And that was how it was launched. However, within four years of its launch, *First Things First* had been split into two, and *Practice and Progress* had been split into two, so you ended up with a six-year course to Cambridge Lower, which sort of mirrored what was supposed to be going on in secondary schools. So you'd start at 11 and you'd get Lower at 16.

A six-level system is also mentioned by MS, but with a different origin – the split of each of three broad levels into two. This is remarkably similar – although seemingly unconnected – to the origin of the six levels of the CEFR (see Chapter 2).

> MS: When we started [writing coursebooks], effectively you had three levels in teaching, where I did my teaching – Elementary, Intermediate

and Advanced classes – and you tended to split them into Lower and Higher Elementary, Lower and Higher Intermediate and even two levels of advanced. So the six-level division was actually pretty much inherent in my teaching experience.

DH also discusses the increase in number of levels, noting a shift from a minimum of four levels in older titles, to the specific example of a contemporary coursebook series actually published at seven levels, to reflect seven secondary school years.

> **DH:** I think there are more levels now. Thinking back to the courses I worked on in the 80s, it was definitely four – you didn't think beyond four. And now, four does seem to be the minimum. And I suppose, going back into the school system, thinking of the last secondary course which I worked on, which was *Prepare!* for Cambridge [University Press], that was seven levels, which was specifically to fit into lower and then upper secondary.

She also notes that the number of hours allocated per level matches – by accident or design – the number of hours typically allocated to a subject in a year at secondary school.

> **DH:** I suppose when you think about it, levels are usually worked out in terms of hours, or they're mapped to a certain number of hours, which neatly fall into the numbers of hours accorded to a particular subject in school systems across the world.

In her interview, IF also links levels to school years in the same way. In fact, so close did the relationship between book level and school year appear to be in her eyes that it became apparent during the interview that she was using the term 'book 1' to refer to a school year, something which required clarification.

> **IF:** Some didn't want more than the present tense in book 1, for instance – you didn't really want any past. Others say, 'No, we've got to cover the present, past tense, past simple' by the end of book 1. [...] But it might have pleased Poland if they hadn't done it by the end, so to please them, we would probably go with them rather than lose their market. That made sense for us. [Interviewer: And when you talking about doing something 'by the end of "book 1"', that presumably means by the end of a school year.] Yes.

Beyond the historical interest value, the comments on levels are interesting as they appear to add weight to the idea that the concept of competency levels in language learning is somewhat atheoretical, as discussed in Chapter 2.

5.3 Organising Theme: Change

The second organising theme under the global theme 'ELT Past and Present' relates to change. We will start with content – the fact that the now largely stable content of ELT pedagogical grammar accounts has undergone, historically, a number of changes.

5.3.1 Basic theme: Change within the canon

The presentation of the thematic analysis in Chapter 4 finished with the following comment from APP on the limited scope for innovation in the ELT grammar syllabus compared with the past:

> **APP:** I think that when authors had a lot more influence over courses, when expectations were really being set, there was probably more room for innovation. But I think that there is less room now.

APP's comments appear to confirmed by a number of other interviewees. When older titles were being discussed, the possibility of making changes to the consensus, or innovating in some way was often mentioned. For example, MS (in a contribution provided by email, some days after the original interview) talks about his own role in 'padding out' the content of the grammar canon over the years.

> **MS:** I remember spending a lot of time in the 60s/70s supplementing the standard inventory with additional points that I thought important but which weren't generally covered – this mostly in more advanced teaching and materials production. This stuff got into *Practical English Usage*, which is used quite a bit by materials writers and others, so I may have personally padded out the general consensus a bit.

MS also states that since the 1980s, he and other authors have expanded the consensus further by including coverage of spoken grammar and discourse structure:

> **MS:** And from the 80s onwards, we've all added treatments of points of spoken grammar and discourse structure that didn't figure much in earlier syllabuses. So: I stick to my claim that we still teach what we taught then at pretty much the same levels (with some improvements), and that the most important topics were already pretty well covered; but it needs saying that we now also teach (or may decide to teach) a whole lot more.

One particular area of historical innovation appears to be closely related to – and, given the years of publication of the coursebook series that interviewees refer to, contemporaneous with the emergence of – the idea of functional-notional language and syllabuses. MS, PV and IF all talk about choosing to teach certain grammar structures, such as 'would like', earlier than they might have been taught in older titles, because of their importance in communication:

> **MS:** We swam upstream against some of the consensus in doing the *Cambridge [English] Course* on the basis of usefulness. So a structure which other courses might not bring in till Level 2, whatever that means, we were having students do functional situational communicative things at Level 1, which required at least specific incidences of a kind of structure we weren't going to focus on from a grammatical point of view. To simplify it, we would teach as an idiom or fixed phrase or small item something we looked at it in more detail at a much higher level.

> **PV:** *Streamline* was based on *English Grammatical Structure*, but Bernie [Hartley] and I decided that we would use communicative elements like teaching 'would like' very early, because they're a set phrase and so on. So we changed it, and we added the 'everyday conversations', which were formulas and set expressions. So we deviated in that way, but on the pure logic we followed *English Grammatical Structure*.

> **IF:** I think the first unit of 'white' *Strategies* [the first, single-level edition of the series, with a white cover], it did the present, the verb 'to be', it did 'would you like a', 'would you like to', 'I like', 'So do I', 'Nor do I'. And that was in the first lesson, so, you know, we decided this is what [target uses of the book] wanted to be able to do, to invite people, offer things, invite, that's what we thought was important communicatively.

It should be emphasised that, while the examples presented above are comparatively small in number across the interviews, the titles mentioned were hugely successful and thus influential. It therefore does seem reasonable to view the 1970s and 1980s as a period in which the consensus was expanded significantly, moving closer to its current form.

5.3.2 Basic theme: Changing roles

Another theme related to changes in the roles of the figures involved in ELT publishing. The most common differences referred to by interviewees were changes in the role of authors, and changes in the relationship between publisher and author. We saw in Chapter 4 that control over content generally now lies with the publisher. However, this has not always been the case, with the role of publisher and author in the past being, according to AG, very different:

> **AG:** In days gone by, it used to be the authors who'd have much more control of that [grammar content], and so you got more variety and

individuality. That happens a lot less now because publishers are sort of laying out the grid.

The reason for this, suggests APP, is that this 'variety and individuality' is now a commercial risk.

APP: In the early days of ELT, when it was becoming a business in its own right, I think the authors had a lot of influence, a lot of say. And I think the balance has tipped towards the publisher. And the publishers like to have much more control than, say, forty years ago, over the contents. [...] And since there are so many commercial considerations when a publisher publishes, the publisher is likely to take less risk than at the beginning of ELT, when authors were free to establish, or freer, what the perceived progression and the perceived number of levels of a course should be.

Another explanation for the shift in control, in addition to the financial reasons given by APP, is related to expertise. According to BU, in the past publishers simply did not have the expertise to make decisions on content in house, as the editors who worked for them did not have any teaching experience.

BU: I have also to say, without being rude to my predecessors, because they were all very bright people, very few of the editors had any ELT experience when they started. They were publishing people, so they relied very heavily on people like Bill Allen, Reg Close is another name – these are Longman names – so the editor would work with them.

However, once editors with teaching experience started to work for publishers, the situation began to change.

BU: But gradually the editors in the publishing houses, whether it was Sue [Ullstein] or her original boss Mark Lowe, or others, had their own experience and therefore [...] Sue Jones was another one, who was sort of bringing their own teaching experience and/or marketing experience. [...] There used to be these star authors, like Louis [Alexander], or Robert O'Neill or Brian Abbs or whatever. And they in a way drove what the publishers did, rather than the other way round. Whereas now it appears that the publishers are the driving force, who put together teams that agree with their ideas.

The greater autonomy enjoyed by authors in the past appears to be confirmed by the accounts given by IF and PV, both of whom wrote coursebooks, or started writing coursebooks, in the 1970s.

IF: *Strategies* was still very much 'us', that's Brian [Abbs, co-author] and me deciding what the syllabus would contain, what structures would be at each level[.]

PV: The era I come from, we designed the syllabus. We had no publisher input on the syllabus at all. Nobody at OUP ever said, 'Are you going to do this?', or 'Why haven't you done that?'. Never happened. Nowadays of course authors will be given a syllabus before they start. [...] And that's what authors are complaining about, that the publisher dictates the syllabus. We were in a day when the publisher didn't dictate the syllabus and OUP never [...] I can't remember OUP ever making a syllabus suggestion to us.

PV presents the situation in which current coursebook authors work as being very different.

PV: Nowadays of course authors will be given a syllabus before they start. [...] You listen to authors of a different generation, and they didn't have a choice of how to design a syllabus.

Not all authors portray the influence of publishers and editors in such a negative light, however. JR is clear about the positive influence he felt his editors had on the design of the original syllabus for *Interchange*:

JR: [Speaking about how it was decided at which level to include each grammar point]. We had two very good editors in New York who were quite skilled in [...] had published a lot of courses at other publishers. One of the main ones was Mary Vaughn, who, um, I think she'd been with [the publisher] Prentice Hall, and I'm not sure who else. But she had a remarkable grasp of exactly what went where in different courses, and she worked particularly with me on the Intro level.

In addition, MS presents a somewhat different picture, with very little pressure or influence perceived to be exerted by the publisher, even when he was co-authoring a course published as recently as 2011.

MS: [Interviewer: But did you feel at some point a pressure to include the full aspect of them [i.e. grammar points] within a grammar syllabus?] Scarcely. One of my editors of the recent series that Catherine [Walter] and I did, the *Oxford English Grammar Course*, [...] wanted a bigger list of useful prepositional phrases than I felt, in a purist sort of way, was really required in a grammar book. But it's what teachers are looking for, and if teachers want it and students want it, then we'd better have it. And that's a not-very-serious kind of pressure. I've had very little pressure in any area from any publisher.

These comments, however, are perhaps best seen in the light of the status of MS as an author – and, indeed, co-creator of the consensus – which might somewhat 'insulate' him from the kinds of pressure felt by other authors.

5.3.3 Basic theme: Changing practices

A large number of references were made to how practices within ELT publishing have changed over the decades. One area related to the makeup of the grammar syllabus. In the past, debates on selection and ordering appear to have been common; one such debate was presented above, with both LS and IF discussing potential reasons for teaching present continuous before present simple, or vice versa. The same debate is also mentioned by PV, whose recollection seems to suggest a change in expectations from users of coursebooks, with arguments for changes in sequencing being made because of frequency:

> PV: When I was first going round [doing book promotions], people were starting to say, 'Why are we teaching the present continuous first? The present simple is higher frequency than the present continuous'.

Similarly, MS mentions an example of a specific change to the consensus on grammar that occurred since he started teaching – the teaching of the use of the past tense for distancing. Overall, however, the picture he paints is one of gradual change.

> MS: [T]he consensus was never turned on its head. Things got done better, new uses of structures started getting taught up to a point. [Interviewer: Could you give me an example of that?] Yeah. Use of past tenses for social distancing, or what I call distancing. Like 'Did you want to pay now?' I don't remember that being around in the first teaching materials that I had, I got interested in at and at some point this would have appeared in teaching materials. I would certainly have been teaching it or encouraging the teachers who worked for me to include it in their teaching before it got into print.

IF describes her first coursebook – which was highly commercially successful – as being highly innovative. It is significant that it was successful despite the fact that it was a reaction against – in other words, *intentionally different from* – other available courses at the time. This is in stark contrast to the kind of conformity discussed in Chapter 4, particularly under the basic theme 'Following the competition'.

> IF: *Strategies* was an experiment, and for some reason it was a success. People liked the idea of doing communicative English, it was a reaction against all the other courses that were available, and it took off. [...] [I]t covered everything, you know – we had everything from the first present simple up to, I think, the third conditional in one book, which is unheard of nowadays.

It is interesting to note, in light of the comments discussed above, how rare the kinds of debates described – on selection and ordering – now are. As discussed above, the potential for innovation has been much reduced in recent years, apparently under the weight of norms and consensus.

Another change to publishing practices relates to market research. While clearly authors and publishers are always likely to have considered their target market and target users when developing products, it appears that market research played a much more limited role in the past, as evidenced by the following comment from PV:

> **PV:** We never did research to start with, we just did it. Major difference. That would be true of the Soars [i.e. Liz Soars and her co-author John Soars], that would be true of Abbs and Freebairn, too.

BU provides more detail on the move, in the mid to late 1970s, to market-research-based product design, giving his opinion on the (at least partially negative) consequences of this.

> **BU:** When I moved into the market department – or set up the marketing department, there was no such thing – I very much argued that we should move more to providing what the market wants, away from whatever plopped onto an editor's desk, or he thought there might be a need for. And at the time that I dared to suggest this, I was almost sent to Coventry for writing a paper for a management meeting, based on that idea. And it seems to me now that that idea has been totally adopted and I sort of feel that maybe creativity is crushed.

It is worth recalling at this point IF's description – already discussed in Chapter 4 – of her experiences working on a later coursebook series, *Discoveries* (published in the mid to late 80s) when the influence from a particular market became stronger.

> **IF:** But when we started with *Discoveries* [...] we were quite driven after that by what the markets wanted, and Italy in particular – and Longman are a commercial enterprise, they want to sell copies, so they don't really decide what is the most teachable route, it's what the markets want, probably more, than what actually is easiest to teach in the classroom. There's a bit of a conflict[.] [...] Our feeling was, 'This isn't how learners will learn it – it's too complicated'. We were much more into wanting to recycle – so there were conflicts. We wanted more a cyclical syllabus, but when it came to them, what they wanted, we were driven slightly by Italy, and so we did group things together that we wouldn't possibly normally have wanted to do.

IF's memories, particularly of the shift that occurred between writing her first coursebook and then writing subsequent titles, appears to characterise this period almost as a 'watershed', when the balance of power between author opinion and experience, and market research shifted from the former to the latter. The comments also show – at least from an author's point of view – how the influence of market research can sometimes be unwelcome. In this case, requirements from the market were in conflict with the views and wishes of the authors.

A final shift in practice relates to the question of whether all levels of a new coursebook series are published at once. As we saw in Chapter 4, it is now common practice to publish all levels in a series – or at least four or five levels – simultaneously, so that a whole coursebook series can be adopted by schools. In the past, however, there was no apparent expectation from publishers or users that this should happen, as explained by AG, in general terms, and IF, in reference to specific titles she wrote.

> **AG:** Fifty, twenty years ago, people would start by publishing an intermediate level and then they would work up and down from there, publishing with the same team of authors writing one level a year and eventually five years later you'd have a complete course.
>
> **IF:** Right up to *Blueprint* and the others, we would do one level at a time and publish that.

The reasons why this practice changed are outlined by PV, and essentially revolve around the risk of delays that publishers are unwilling to take.

> **PV:** [T]hey used to say, 'We've got to have all four levels, because schools won't trust that all four levels will be ready unless we publish them on the same day', whereas we said, 'Well, start on Level 1, by the time you get to September we'll have Level 2 out,' you know. 'And by the time you get to September the year after, we'll have Level 3,' and people trusted you. But then of course things went wrong with printing, and people got caught out a couple of times, which is why publishers then said, 'We have to have all four levels out simultaneously'.

The ramifications of this change were discussed in Chapter 4: publishing multiple levels at the same time means working with multiple author teams, and this in turn makes top-down control of syllabus by a publisher more likely, to avoid potential overlaps or omissions. For PV, this is an undesirable outcome:

> **PV:** It also doesn't let stuff grow when you do that, because you grow a syllabus in a way. I don't think we ever sat down and mapped out four levels. We mapped out Level 1, and then we mapped out Level 2. Until we finished Level 2, we didn't start thinking about Level 3. I'm sure we did it a level at a time. And then we would have learnt things, and you would also have tested it.

On the other hand, IF paints exactly the same phenomenon in a slightly more positive light, with the need to consider a whole series at the same time meaning she and her co-authors had to concentrate on planning out all levels.

> **IF:** But it got to something like *Sky* and *Upbeat* [two coursebook series published since 2000], [and] you had to do all four at the same time. They wouldn't accept – the market – that you did one book a year and publish that, so it really made us concentrate on the syllabus and you paid much more attention to it as the courses progressed. And decided in advance exactly what would come into each unit of each course. Which we never did before, it was very, very much, as it happened as we wrote.

5.4 Summary

The first half of the thematic analysis, presented in Chapter 4, largely painted a picture of stagnancy, with only limited opportunity for innovation. Decisions on grammar now appear to be made mainly with reference to perceived norms within the ELT profession, with publishers, rather than authors, largely deciding on grammar content, and these decisions themselves being made on the basis of expectations within the ELT profession and in the markets into which publishers want to sell their products. One particularly important factor in this process is the role of successful competitor titles. Commercially successful books both represent the existing norms and also serve as models for future publications, reinforcing them. This leads to a cycle of homogenous content and few opportunities to step back and review, or attempt to renew, the established canon. The thematic analysis in this chapter has helped to explain what led to this state of affairs, with a shift away from individuality and variation, and a move towards publisher control, meaning, among other things, control over grammar content (although we should remember that publishers may themselves feel just as restricted – due to market demands and expectations – as authors; see Chapters 2 and 4).

The writers who had direct experience of and influence on the initial development of the grammar canon at the beginning of the 20th century are no longer with us. However, the experiences of the interviewees reported here on the development of the canon during their own careers again showed the importance during the writing process of referring to existing titles, some dating from this earlier period. Authors and their work can therefore be seen as mediators, both synchronically and diachronically, of expertise on pedagogical grammar. MS, for example, makes clear the influence of *Living English Structure* on his own development as a teacher and writer, just as LS makes clear the influence of MS' work on her own writing. In Chapter 7 we will see how this process can be manifested at a very basic level, in the way that the wording of certain grammatical explanations and even example sentences used to illustrate these explanations can 'echo' through publications across the centuries.

As positive as the sharing of knowledge in this way is, it is apparent from the interviews that historically this knowledge has often consisted mainly of the personal experience of author-practitioners. While such experience is 'empirical' in one sense, in that it is based on experience of teaching real learners in real classrooms, it nonetheless has the potential to be highly subjective. It is not clear how representative one teacher's classroom experiences – no matter how rich and extensive – are of the needs of learners of English around the world as a whole. This is perhaps most starkly evident in PV's hypothesis that the grammar contents of many highly successful 1970s and 1980s coursebook series, which themselves influenced and helped to establish the current version of the canon, were originally aimed at only very specific groups of learners and not intended, when originally created, to be used more widely. We might also note that the well-established six-level system used by coursebooks appears to originate from the school-year system of secondary schools, rather than from any theoretical base relating to competency levels in language acquisition. None of this need necessarily be a problem if it is understood that any single book represents just one single author or author team's vision of which grammar should be taught, and in which order. However, as we have already seen, the strength of the current consensus means that all books are expected to conform to the consensus view, even though this consensus view appears to be largely an amalgamation of the visions of a comparatively small number of authors.

This chapter completes the analysis of the interview data presented in this study. Chapters 6 and 7 present the three case studies; we begin in Chapter 6 by returning to the contemporary situation through an analysis of the treatment of the three areas of grammar under examination in modern coursebooks and compare this with empirical data in the English Grammar Profile. Having explored the status quo, in Chapter 7 we again attempt to set out how this was arrived at, by analysing the evolution of coverage of the same three areas of grammar across the centuries in 'historical' grammars and coursebooks.

Note

(1) Freebairn reported having studied with David Wilkins at the University of Reading in the late 1960s.

6 Conditionals, Relative Clauses and Future Forms: Contemporary Canon in the Spotlight

6.1 Introduction and Overview of Methodology

In Chapter 4, we saw that there are – according to many of the interviewees – a number of factors that have an influence on, or provide some kind of input into, the structure and content of ELT grammar syllabuses. The totality of these factors has led to a situation in which there is now a very strong consensus within the industry on the grammar that should be taught to learners and on the order in which it should be taught. Consequently, there also exists a consensus among both creators and users of coursebooks and pedagogical grammars on what should be included in such publications and how it should be ordered: that is to say, on the canon of ELT grammar.

What, though, is the precise nature of this consensus, when manifested at the level of the syllabus? And how does it compare with what we know about the grammar that learners are actually able to produce at different levels? This chapter will address these questions through the exploration of the treatment of three areas of grammar (outlined below) in five coursebook series. It sketches out, in the form of these three 'case studies', an overview of coverage of each area of grammar across the five coursebook series, noting areas of convergence and divergence, before comparing them with the descriptors of learner usage in the English Grammar Profile (EGP). This comparison will reveal where the grammatical input in coursebooks appears to be in line with evidence on learner grammatical competence, both in terms of the forms and usage covered and the order in which they are taught, and where it appears to differ.

6.2 Methodology: Exploring Grammar in Contemporary Coursebooks

6.2.1 Choice of areas of grammar

The three areas of grammar under examination – conditionals, relative clauses and future forms – were chosen for three principal reasons. Firstly, all were mentioned explicitly and without prompting by one or more interviewee during the interviews, suggesting that they are significant areas of grammar for those involved in the creation of coursebooks and grammars. Furthermore, they all carry a certain 'weight' within coursebook grammar syllabuses, with each being taught over several lessons at one coursebook level, and each also covered at more than one level. Finally, they each represent slightly different types of grammatical structure: conditionals and relative clauses are essentially syntactic, or syntagmatic, patterns, whereas the collection of future forms taught can be considered as paradigmatic 'items'. They also reflect the distinction discussed in Chapter 2 between 'constitutive' and 'communicative' grammar rules (Williams, 1994): each has structural characteristics that students must simply learn (e.g. verb forms in conditionals and future forms, and choice of relativiser and word order in relative clauses), but also 'choice' elements (the different meanings expressed by the different types of conditional sentence, the difference between defining and non-defining relative clauses, usage differences between the various future forms).

6.2.2 Use of a case study approach

Although case studies are perhaps most commonly associated with studies of people, the approach can be with used with any clearly defined entity (Dörnyei, 2007). As with qualitative research in general, case studies are said to be particularly appropriate when exploring previously unexplored territory' (Hood, 2009: 86). The three case studies presented here combine the aims and elements of what Stake (2003: 136–138) terms 'intrinsic' and 'collective' case studies; the former are typically carried out because 'the researcher wants better understanding of this particular case' and the latter, which involves the analysis of multiple cases simultaneously, 'because it is believed that understanding them will lead to better understanding, perhaps better theorizing, about a still larger collection of cases'. As stated above, the three grammar points chosen play important roles in the canon, and an analysis of their evolution and a comparison of their treatment in coursebooks with empirical evidence on their use in the EGP was felt in itself to be a useful exercise. Furthermore, it was also hoped that an analysis of the three areas of grammar would provide insights that could potentially be generalisable to the grammar canon as a whole, and might reveal something interesting about its evolution and nature.

6.2.3 Selecting the titles for analysis

As already stated, the aim in this study is to examine the canon of grammar used for teaching General English in mainstream contexts. A number of criteria were applied in order to identify coursebook series that could constitute a representative sample of the kinds of teaching materials generally used in this context. Firstly, the titles should all be described as teaching 'General English' and be published by international publishing houses; they should also be commercially successful (judged primarily by the fact that they had been published in two or more editions). They should also be aimed at adult learners, as the Cambridge Learner Corpus, on which the English Grammar Profile (see below) is based, consists of examination scripts produced by candidates sitting examinations aimed at adult learners. Finally, they should be published at the canonical six competency levels (Beginner/Starter, Elementary, Pre-Intermediate, Intermediate, Upper Intermediate and Advanced, typically aligned to CEFR levels A1–C1).

It was also decided to include an 'American English' coursebook series as part of the final selection, in order to investigate whether American English coursebooks might take a different approach to grammar. As Jack Richards had been included as an interviewee for the interviews, it was decided to use his two (co-authored) series, *Interchange* and *Passages*.[1]

The list of coursebooks analysed can be seen in Table 6.1. It should be noted here, however, that, while the coursebooks chosen were felt to be largely representative of the majority of General English coursebooks for adults, they do not necessarily represent all coursebooks. Some coursebook series – for example, the 1980s *Cobuild English Course* and, more recently, *Innovations*, have taken a somewhat different approach to grammar coverage.

One key observation to emerge during the first stages of analysis was that pedagogical grammar explanations found in coursebooks seem

Table 6.1 Coursebooks selected for analysis

Title	Year of publication	Publisher
New English File (2nd edition) (Oxenden & Latham-Koenig, 2006, 2008, 2009, 2010; Oxenden et al., 2004, 2005)	2005–2010	Oxford University Press
face2face (1st edition) (Cunningham et al., 2010; Redston & Cunningham, 2005a,b, 2006, 2007, 2009)	2005–2009	Cambridge University Press
Headway (4th edition) (Soars & Soars, 2009, 2011, 2013a,b, 2014, 2015)	2009–2015	Oxford University Press
New Cutting Edge (1st edition) (Cunningham & Moor, 2002, 2003, 2005a,b,c,d)	2002–2005	Pearson Education (Longman)
Interchange (3rd edition) (Richards et al., 2004, 2005a,b) + *Passages* (2nd edition) (Richards & Chuck, 2008a,b)	2004–2005, 2008	Cambridge University Press

Table 6.2 Micro-level coverage of the macro-level grammar point 'present perfect simple' in *New English File*

Level	Micro-level grammar points
Elementary	past experiences
Pre-Intermediate	past experiences with *ever/never* with *just, yet* and *already* states that started in the past and continue now, with *for* and *since*
Intermediate	past experiences with *ever/never* with *just, yet* and *already*
Upper-Intermediate	past events that are important in the present

to fall into two categories: the macro- and micro-levels. An example of this difference for one grammar point, in one coursebook series, can be found in Table 6.2. In the coursebook series *New English File*, the present perfect simple is taught at four levels; at each level, the coverage involves the teaching of one or more 'details'. These details constitute 'micro-level' grammar points, whereas the overall focus (present perfect simple, in this case) is a 'macro-level' grammar point.

As suggested in the *EAQUALS Core inventory* document (North et al., 2010), there appeared to be broad agreement between coursebooks on the macro-level points to be taught, and the level at which to teach them. At the micro-level, however, the picture was slightly different. While it was relatively uncommon to find disagreement on level assignment (e.g. one micro-level point being taught at one level in one coursebook series, but at a different level in another), it was quite common to see one micro-level grammar point included in one coursebook, but not at all in another. This was interesting as it suggested that the totality of micro-level grammar points could be conceived as a 'pool' from which coursebooks choose when teaching a macro-level grammar point. To use a metaphor, macro-level grammar points are 'dishes', and there is broad consensus within the ELT profession about which dishes should be included (and at which level). However, in the preparation of each dish, coursebook series use different combinations – all potentially valid – of ingredients. Both levels – the macro and the micro – are considered to have inherent value for the research, and this is the case even if a micro-level grammar point is found in just one single publication. For example, only one coursebook series – *Passages* – covers the future perfect continuous, but, this itself seeming remarkable, it is mentioned in the discussion.

6.2.4 Analysing the content

Identifying coverage of grammar points in coursebooks is superficially straightforward: contents pages allow the relevant material to be quickly identified within each book, and it is thus easy to establish

(i) the level at which a given area of grammar is taught at the macro-level, and (ii) the micro-level content of the coverage (e.g. the uses of *will* taught, or the types of conditional sentence taught) and the wording of the rules and explanations given. However, when a more in-depth analysis is attempted, a practical problem emerges. A typical coursebook is between 160 and 184 pages, and is made up of a series of chapters, or 'units', each containing a series of lessons. Many of these lessons have grammar teaching at their heart, with the grammar presented through some kind of written or spoken text, followed by controlled practice activities and then, often, speaking activities. However, most coursebooks also have a grammar reference section at the back of the book (often called 'endmatter' in publishing, a term I will use in this chapter), containing more detailed explanations of the grammar covered in the lessons and, often, extra practice activities for this grammar. Consequently, a particular micro-level grammar point might appear in the main lesson, in the main lesson and the back-of-the-book grammar reference, or only in the grammar reference. Additionally, it might or might not be included in practice activities in the main lesson or grammar reference. For the purposes of analysis, it was decided to separate out coverage in main lesson content and grammar reference sections. If a grammar point was included only in a grammar reference section, it was recorded but this is noted in the discussion.

An additional difficulty is the issue of a grammar point appearing at more than one level. As can be seen by re-examining Table 6.2, repetition across coursebook levels occurs frequently, mainly at the macro level (present perfect simple), but also at the micro level (for example, 'past experiences with *ever/never*'). The difficulty here is how to assign a level for a grammar point that is taught at one level and then revised at a higher level. On the one hand, if something needs to be revised, then it may be the case that the writers or publishers of a coursebook believe it will not be mastered until this higher level. On the other hand, many Upper Intermediate and Advanced level coursebooks include sections that synthesise various areas of grammar covered earlier; for example, the Advanced level of *Cutting Edge* contains a section that reviews and synthesises a number of different uses of perfect forms, including present perfect simple. In the end, it was decided to always record every level at which a grammar point was covered, and to consider this a characteristic of coverage in the canon.

6.2.5 Comparison with the English Grammar Profile

Once the coursebook consensus on the three areas of grammar was established, the comparison with data from the English Grammar Profile (EGP) was carried out. The EGP is a searchable database (freely available online at: www.englishprofile.org/english-grammar-profile) containing over 1000 grammar competency statements across competence levels in English. These statements are based on an analysis of the Cambridge Learner Corpus, a 55.5 million word corpus made up of over 200,000 English language exam scripts written by students taking Cambridge English exams in 215 countries around the world, and are calibrated according to the six levels of the CEFR (see O'Keeffe & Mark, 2017, for an overview).

The statements in the EGP are categorised into 'Supercategories' and 'Subcategories'; for example, the 'present perfect simple' is a Subcategory within the Supercategory 'Past'. When a search is made – either for a Supercategory, a Subcategory, or simply a free search – a list of competency statements is displayed. Figure 6.1 shows the first ten statements for the Subcategory 'present perfect simple'.

The purpose of the comparison with the EGP was twofold. The primary intention was to compare the level assignments in coursebooks with those reported in the EGP: for example, in the case of future forms, at what level do coursebooks typically teach the *going to* future and what level do learners produce it, according to the EGP? In addition, from my basic familiarity with the EGP, I also expected that there would be some uses identified in it that are not typically taught in coursebooks, and that this would form part of the comparison.

One difficulty that arises when comparing the EGP with coursebooks is how to match the levels in the two data sets. Firstly, the B1 level in the CEFR is typically split into two coursebook levels. There is support for such a division in the CEFR document, which suggests that the six

SuperCategory	SubCategory	Level	Can-do statement	Example	Details
PAST	present perfect simple	A2	**FORM/USE:** TIME WITH 'FOR' Can use the negative form with 'for' to talk about a past event or action which hasn't occurred again in the period of time up to now.	Example	Details
PAST	present perfect simple	A2	**FORM/USE:** WITH 'YET' Can use the negative form with 'yet' to talk about events which are expected to be completed at some point in the future.	Example	Details
PAST	present perfect simple	A2	**FORM:** AFFIRMATIVE Can use the affirmative form 'have' + '-ed' with pronouns 'I' and 'we', and with a limited range of verbs.	Example	Details
PAST	present perfect simple	A2	**FORM:** NEGATIVE Can use the negative form 'haven't' + '-ed' with 'I' with a limited range of verbs.	Example	Details
PAST	present perfect simple	A2	**FORM:** QUESTIONS Can use the question form 'have you' + '-ed' with with a limited range of verbs.	Example	Details
PAST	present perfect simple	A2	**FORM:** WITH ADVERBS Can use the present perfect simple with a limited range of adverbs in the normal mid position.	Example	Details
PAST	present perfect simple	A2	**USE:** EXPERIENCES Can use the present perfect simple to talk about experiences up to now.	Example	Details
PAST	present perfect simple	B1	**FORM/USE:** DURATION WITH 'SINCE' Can use the present perfect simple with 'since' to talk about duration.	Example	Details
PAST	present perfect simple	B1	**FORM/USE:** WITH 'ALREADY' Can use the present perfect simple with 'already' to emphasise that something is done, often before the expected time. ▶ adverbs	Example	Details
PAST	present perfect simple	B1	**FORM:** AFFIRMATIVE Can use the affirmative forms with a range of pronouns and nouns and an increasing range of verbs.	Example	Details

Figure 6.1 Competency statements from the EGP for 'present perfect simple'
© Cambridge University Press

main bands can be split (Council of Europe, 2001) including a 'strong threshold B1+' band, but the EGP makes no such distinction as the data in the CLC is aligned only to single CEFR levels. Secondly, coursebook series do not generally attempt to cover the CEFR C2 level, and as a consequence this level needs to be discounted in the comparison. A third problem is that not all coursebook levels are mapped to CEFR levels in a consistent and 'clean' way. For example, the back cover of the Beginner level of *New English File* states that it covers the whole of the A1 level, but the next level, Elementary claims to cover two thirds of the A1 level and all of the A2 level. Similarly, the Intermediate level is said to cover all of the B1 level and a third of the B2 level; the Upper Intermediate level then claims to cover all of B2. The *face2face* series is similar, but with slightly different overlaps and claims of level coverage. On the other hand, *New Cutting Edge* indicates a one-to-one relationship between coursebook level and CEFR level (e.g. Beginner = A1, Elementary = A2 etc.).

One way to overcome this problem would have been to choose only coursebook series with such straightforward coursebook level – CEFR level correspondence, but this would have excluded many best-selling titles. In addition, my own experience in ELT publishing was that the mapping of coursebook to CEFR often comes late in the process, typically *after* a book has been written, and is sometimes little more than a marketing exercise. Private communication with colleagues working within ELT publishing confirmed my experiences, suggesting that claims made by publishers about CEFR levels may not always be reliable. Consequently, for the purposes of the comparison I decided to assume a one-to-one relationship between coursebook and CEFR levels, as set out in Table 6.3. Such an approach is also justifiable if claims made by the coursebooks series about *completion* of levels are considered; for example, since *New English File Elementary* claims to cover two thirds of A1 and all of A2 this means that it aims to help learners achieve competency at the A2 level, and can be matched in this way. Similarly, if *New English File Intermediate* claims to cover all of B1 and a quarter, but not all, of B2, the aim of the book must be to achieve competency at B1. As can be seen in Table 6.3, in order to avoid the somewhat unwieldly ELT level names (and the inconsistency in naming of the lowest level), in the analysis presented here I simply use the numerical labels – from 1 to 6 – to refer to coursebook levels.

The grammar points chosen were examined one by one. The first step was to examine the relevant EGP entries and identify the forms and uses listed and the overall progression of these across CEFR levels. Following this, each coursebook series was examined one by one – across all levels – comparing the coverage with the forms and uses reported in the EGP. The data was recorded on a spreadsheet, with entries colour coded in

Table 6.3 Assumed coursebook–CEFR correspondences

Coursebook level	CEFR level
Level 1 (Beginner/Starter)	A1
Level 2 (Elementary)	A2
Level 3 (Pre-Intermediate)	B1
Level 4 (Intermediate)	
Level 5 (Upper-Intermediate)	B2
Level 6 (Advanced)	C1

order to provide a clear, visual representation of where the canon agreed and disagreed with the EGP, and the nature of any disagreement.

The remainder of this chapter sets out the case studies. In each case, the overall approach used in ELT to describe each grammar point is first outlined, along with relevant previous research. Following this, the coursebook consensus is set out and finally the comparison with the EGP is presented. Unless otherwise stated, example sentences, when provided, have been invented for the purposes of this analysis and discussion.

6.3 Case Study A: Conditionals

6.3.1 Overview and previous research

'Conditional sentences' are here taken to mean sentences containing two clauses, with the event or state contained in the main clause being dependent on the subordinate clause for its realisation. Most typically, these are sentences with the subordinating conjunction *if*, but also included in the analysis are semantically similar or equivalent patterns with inversion (e.g. 'Should you have any questions, …'), words such as *supposing* (e.g. 'Supposing you got lost, …') and also *unless*. However, excluded was the idiomatic *if only*, which, although it contains the word *if*, is not used in the kinds of conditional structures outlined above.

The standard system used in ELT categorises conditional sentences into four types, as follows:

'Zero conditional': *If you heat water to 100 degrees, it boils.* (*if* + present simple, present simple).

'First conditional' (or 'Type 1' conditional): *If it rains, we'll stay at home.* (*if* + present simple, *will* + base form).

'Second conditional' (or 'Type 2' conditional): *If I had more time, I'd do more sport.* (*if* + past simple, *would* + base form).

'Third conditional' (or 'Type 3' conditional): *If you had asked me, I would have helped you.* (*if* + past perfect simple, *would have* + past participle).

We will see in Chapter 7 that the division into three conditional types (first, second and third conditionals) goes back at least as far as Allen's (1947) grammar. Outside of ELT, the fields of semantics and logic often divide conditionals into 'indicative conditionals' (which would include zero and first conditionals), 'counterfactual conditionals' (which would include second and third conditionals) and 'relevance conditionals' (Egre & Cozic, 2016). The latter are also sometimes known as 'biscuit conditionals' after the example sentence, 'There are biscuits on the sideboard if you want them' suggested by the philosopher J.L. Austin. This type of conditional – where the role of the *if* clause is to show the relevance of the content of the main clause rather than set up a conditional meaning – is not typically covered in ELT accounts.

The concept of a 'zero conditional' appears to be more recent than the original three-way distinction. The inspiration for Maule's (1988) study of conditional forms was a student who refused to accept that the sentence, 'If he comes, I go' was correct; in discussing this, Maule does not use the phrase 'zero conditional', and nor does Ur in her (1989) follow-up correspondence, or Fulcher (1991) in his larger study. It was perhaps in response to these, or similar, articles that the term 'zero conditional' was introduced, with the label 'zero' chosen presumably because the numbers 1–3 had already been assigned. A further conditional type often found in ELT materials are so-called 'mixed conditionals', which combine the form found in the *if* clause in a second conditional with that found in the main clause in a third conditional (e.g. 'If I was smarter, I would have passed the exam'), or vice versa (e.g. 'If I had passed the exam, I would have a better job now). As we will see, these are – when covered in coursebooks – seemingly considered an 'advanced' structure, but have been shown to be very rare in native-speaker corpus data, and are in any case an arbitrary selection among many possible tense combinations not described by the canonical ELT categories (Gabrielatos, 2006).

Research going back decades has shown the inadequacy of the ELT system (see, for example, the analysis in Fulcher, 1991; Gabrielatos, 2003, 2006; Maule, 1988; Ur, 1989). In one of the most recent studies of conditionals, Jones and Waller (2011) analysed 196 conditional sentences from the British National Corpus, finding that only 54% of these could fit into the four ELT categories, as a far greater range of tense combinations than those found in the canonical ELT system is attested. Some of these combinations could perhaps be argued to be variations on the ELT categories, for example, the choice of the present continuous instead of the present simple in the *if* clause of a 'first conditional', or the use of *could* rather than *would* in the main clause of a 'second conditional'. However, very different tense combinations can occur, for example, the combination of *going to* and *should* in 'if you're not going to join us, then […] you should let us join you' described in Jones and

Waller (2011: 26). It is not easy to see how the ELT system can account for such forms.

In addition, an entire subtype of conditional sentences is neglected by the four canonical conditional types. As we saw, conditional sentences can be broadly split – ignoring 'biscuit conditionals' – into two types: those that refer to real ('indicative') situations, and those that refer to counterfactual situations. Each of these can have a past or non-past time reference. In the ELT system, zero and first conditionals are both real non-past conditionals, second conditionals are counterfactual non-past conditionals and third conditionals are counterfactual past conditionals. This ignores real past conditionals (for example 'If it rained, the streets flooded'), where the past tense in the *if* clause has a temporal (i.e. referring to the past) rather than modal (i.e. suggesting counterfactuality) sense. This former use is common, accounting for 34.6% of all examples of *if* + past tense in Gabrielatos' (2006) study but, as we have said, is ignored by standard ELT accounts. This is not to say that the structure is unknown to the ELT profession: it is identified in Maule's (1988) study in the ELT Journal, for example, and was also included in Alexander et al.'s (1975) *English Grammatical Structure* (see Chapter 3).

Overall, then, previous research has shown that the ELT system cannot adequately represent the reality of verb forms found in authentic examples of the conditional. The situation is somewhat puzzling; we would not consider, for example, a grammatical account that omitted nearly half of all possible past tense structures to be acceptable, but a descriptive system that accounts for only 54% of conditional forms appears to be considered, by course designers and users, adequate for teaching and learning.

6.3.2 Coursebook consensus

Coverage of the different conditional structures at different levels (1–6) in the chosen coursebooks is summarised in Table 6.4 below; only content in main lessons is shown, as opposed to coverage in the 'endmatter' grammar references.

Table 6.4 Overview of coverage of canonical conditional structures at different coursebook levels (1–6)

Coursebook series	Zero conditional	1st conditional	2nd conditional	3rd conditional
New English File	5	3, 4 (with *unless*), 6	3, 4, 5, 6	4, 5, 6
face2face	4	3, 4 (with *unless*), 6	3, 4, 5, 6	4, 5, 6
Headway		3, 4 (with *unless*), 6	3, 4, 6	4, 5, 6
Interchange/Passages		3, 4 (with *unless*)	3, 4	4, 5
Cutting Edge		3, 4 (with *unless*)	3, 4, 5	4, 5

As can be seen in the table, all five coursebook series examined are in agreement on the teaching of the three main ELT paradigms, even though *Interchange* and *Cutting Edge* do not use the terms 'first conditional', 'second conditional' and 'third conditional'. Coverage is spread across multiple levels, but in no case earlier than Level 3. *Unless* is often taught (for example, in four of the five series at Level 4) as an alternative to *if not* in the first conditional. In terms of grading and progression, the numbering of the conditional system appears to reflect perceptions of difficulty of the structures: first conditionals are taught first, followed by second conditionals and, finally, third conditionals. The exception to this are zero conditionals, taught in only two of the coursebook series examined, and not before the first conditional has already been covered.

A significant characteristic of the coursebook coverage is repetition. First conditionals are covered in the majority of coursebooks at Levels 3, 4 and 6, second conditionals at Levels 3, 4, 5 and 6 and third conditionals at Levels 4, 5 and 6. However, at higher levels there is also a large amount of inconsistency. For example, at Level 5, the only feature in common across all series is coverage of the third conditional; three series repeat the second conditional and one covers the zero conditional. Two of the series at this level also provide a group of alternatives to *if* (e.g. *as long as, imagine, provided* and *supposing*), and a further series covers this at Level 6. At this highest level, *face2face* focuses on additional verb form variations (e.g. *going to*, past perfect continuous and past continuous in the *if* clause), *Interchange* covers inversion with *had, were* and *should* as alternatives to *if* (e.g. *Had I known, ...; Were you to help me, ...; Should you require any information, ...*) and *New English File* teaches *provided, providing, on condition that* and *supposing* as alternatives to *if*, as well as inversion with *had*. *New Cutting Edge* at this level covers no conditional forms at all. The lack of consistency across titles at the top two levels echoes McCarthy's (2015) observation that there is often limited agreement on grammar content in advanced level coursebooks compared with those at lower levels. However, the consistency at lower and intermediate levels appears to confirm the strength of the consensus and the pressure on authors and publishers reported in Chapter 4 to reflect it in teaching materials – Michael Swan's observation that anyone suggesting that there are two main types of conditional rather than three would be considered a 'madman' appears to be borne out by the evidence presented here.

While the dominating patterns across levels and coursebook series are those of the original three-way ELT categorisation system, coursebooks do – as touched on in the previous paragraph – sometimes contain a certain amount of variation on the four canonical patterns, especially in 'endmatter' grammar explanations and at higher levels. In addition to the variations described in the previous paragraph, *face2face Upper Intermediate* presents the use of *might* and *could* instead of *would* in both second and third conditionals and *New English File* and *face2face* include the past perfect continuous – rather than only the past perfect simple – as part of the third conditional paradigm. 'Mixed conditionals' are also sometimes found at the highest two levels, specifically in the main lesson content of one coursebook series at Level 5 and the endmatter grammar explanations in a further two series, and in three coursebooks at Level 6.

6.3.3 Comparison with the EGP

A comparison with the EGP reveals some similarities to the coursebook consensus. The EGP reports that learners are able to produce the first conditional and second conditional – including sentences with both *would* and *could* in the main clause – and the third conditional at B1. This matches the levels at which coursebooks typically teach these patterns, although this comparison is in some ways skewed by the fact that B1 is spread over two coursebook levels: typically, third conditionals are covered at Level 4 for the first time, compared with Level 3 for first and second conditionals. There is also agreement on level assignment between coursebooks and the EGP in the following areas:

- the use of *unless*;
- present simple + *should* combinations (e.g. *If you feel ill, you should see the doctor*), although these are present in only two of the five series examined;
- inversion with *should*.

In terms of differences, the EGP shows that learners are capable of producing zero conditionals at A2, despite the fact that coursebooks do not typically teach any conditional forms before Level 3 (equivalent to the first half of B1), and, as outlined above, the zero conditional is taught only inconsistently across coursebook series. Similarly, the EGP shows that at A2 learners can produce the non-canonical combinations of present simple + *can* (EGP example: 'You can get to my house if you take the number 35 bus') and present simple + imperative (EGP example: 'If you need more information, call me'); these 'variations' are taught in coursebooks only inconsistently. Conversely, some of the coursebooks examined teach third conditionals with *might have* and *could have* in the main clause at Level 5 (equivalent to B2), but the EGP shows that learners do not typically use these forms until C1.

Finally, the EGP identifies a number of further functions and uses that are not taught at all in any of the five coursebook series examined, as follows:

- at A2, the use of 'If you want/like/prefer' as a hedge (in other words, the use of 'biscuit conditionals');
- at B1, the use of ellipted 'If so', and 'If not'; the use of *if* + *would like*;

- at C1, the use of *should* in the *if* clause; the use of ellipted *if* clauses (e.g. *if needed, if requested*);
- at C2, the phrases 'whether or not', 'were it not for', 'if it were not for', 'if it had not been for' and 'had it not been for'.

On the other hand, 'mixed conditionals' are not identified by the EGP at all, mirroring their comparative rarity in native-speaker corpora. This suggests that there may be few situations in which the paradigms are likely to actually be needed.

In summary, there is some degree of agreement between the consensus in coursebooks and the EGP with respect to the sequence in which the 'core' paradigms used in teaching conditional forms – the 'first', 'second' and 'third' conditionals – are taught and produced. However, the EGP also reveals that learners are already able to use a limited number of conditional forms at A2, before they are taught in coursebooks and, across levels, are able to use a large number of conditional forms that do not fit into the standard ELT typology, and make pragmatic uses of conditionals not usually taught. Finally, learners do not seem to use, or need to use, 'mixed conditionals' at any level, calling into question their relevance to teaching.

6.3.4 Discussion of ELT treatment of conditionals

Contemporary ELT treatments primarily involve the prescription of three monolithic sentence paradigms containing *if* clauses, instead of a focus on verb forms. The effect of this is an increase in complexity (two verb forms must be learnt for every conditional 'type'), and a decrease in flexibility (other verb form combinations are seen as variations away from a principal, core form, and either left until higher levels or ignored completely). By contrast, the EGP shows that learners are able to use a far wider variety of verb combinations than the three core paradigms typically taught in coursebooks, and that, in some cases, they start to use them earlier than they are typically taught. On the other hand, mixed conditionals – one of the few variations covered in the ELT system – are not identified by the EGP, echoing Gabrielatos' (2006) findings that this form is attested only rarely in native speaker corpora. We should not forget, however, that written language proficiency exams, of the kind that the data used in the EGP derives from, may not necessarily offer learners the opportunity to use these structures, even if they are known.

6.4 Case Study B: Relative Clauses

6.4.1 Overview and previous research

ELT accounts of relative clauses typically involve the description of two relative clause types – defining and non-defining relative clauses – as follows:

Defining relative clause: *That's the person <u>who I spoke to yesterday</u>.*

Non-defining relative clause: *The Prime Minister, <u>who returned to London last night</u>, is expected to make a statement later today.*

The former are typically said to identify or define the noun phrase which forms their antecedent, whereas the latter are typically said to simply add 'extra information' but do not help identify it. These two relative clause types are, like the three conditional types, canonical in pedagogical treatments.

As we will see in Chapter 7, this binary distinction has not always been followed in grammatical accounts of English, and contemporary accounts also make different distinctions. Huddleston and Pullum (2002: 1033–1034), for example, discuss two categorisation systems: those that distinguish relative clauses by 'formal type' (whether the relative clause uses *that*, *which*, or no relative pronoun) and 'relational type'. The latter involves a four-way distinction, contrasting 'integrated relatives' (equivalent to 'defining' relative clauses), 'supplementary relatives' (equivalent to 'non-defining' relative clauses), 'cleft relatives' (e.g. 'It was Kim who wanted Pat as treasurer') and 'fused relatives' (e.g. 'What you say is quite right'). The latter two, in modern ELT accounts, are typically identified as 'cleft sentences', and not included in analyses of relative clauses.

Unlike conditional sentences, pedagogical descriptions of relative clauses have received comparatively little attention in the literature. Two articles in the *ELT Journal* in the late 1960s (Morris, 1969; Sopher, 1969) discuss the binary distinction outlined above, finding that it is inadequate as many relative clauses appear to fall into neither category, and that the use of commas in written English with relative clauses often represents a stylistic choice rather than signifying whether a clause is defining or non-defining. Since then, however, studies in the same journal on relative clauses have tended to focus on how they should be taught (see, for example, Chiu-ming, 1983; Nakamori, 2002; Pearce, 1975), rather than on how they should be analysed, suggesting that in recent decades, the use of the binary distinction between defining and non-defining as the key categorisation has become strongly fixed in the consensus.

Two studies that do not directly address ELT accounts nonetheless offer insights that would appear to have pedagogical implications. Firstly, Tao and McCarthy's (2001) study examined corpus data on a type of non-defining relative clause sometimes known in ELT accounts as 'comment clauses' – non-defining clauses whose antecedent is the entire previous clause (or indeed, a whole previous stretch of discourse or conversation turn), rather than just a single noun phrase within in it. These clauses typically offer a comment on information given previously, as follows:

We went for a meal last night, <u>which was nice</u>.

This latter type of relative clause is particularly common; McCarthy and Tao's study found that over 70% of non-defining clauses in a sample of the CANCODE and CSAE spoken corpora were 'comment clauses' (or 'continuative', using the terminology preferred by the researchers), and that these often occur across speaker turns in conversation. Their frequency in the corpora examined would suggest that this particular usage – including across speaker turns – is especially useful and would be worth focusing on in pedagogical accounts.

Yamashita's (1994) study provides some useful statistics on relative clause usage as attested in the Lancaster/IBM Spoken English Corpus. Particularly interesting is his observation that 68 of 98 (over 75%) of non-defining clauses found in a sample of 330 relative clauses in the corpus occur in end rather than medial position (1994: 82). For example, sentences such as 'I had a phone call from my sister, who's a doctor', with the relative clause at the end of the sentence (or, indeed, sentences with a 'comment clause', as described above) are more common than sentences such with the relative clause placed in the middle. This suggests that pedagogical accounts would do well to provide learners with comparatively more exposure to end-position non-defining relative clauses than those in medial position, and should give learners opportunities to practice them; as we will see in the next section, this does not in fact occur.

6.4.2 Coursebook consensus

Little appears to have changed since Morris' (1969: 246) assertion that 'standard textbooks […] are apparently in agreement on the need to apply a bipartite classification'. All the coursebooks examined cover both relative clause types explicitly, and use no other system to categorise them. An additional – and key – aspect of the coursebook treatment of relative clauses is the giving of instruction on the choice and selection of relative pronouns and adverbs (for example, *that*, *which*, *where*, *whose*). The coursebooks examined all teach a variety of these across levels, including the 'zero pronoun' – the non-use of a pronoun when it is the object of the relative clause, for example 'That's the man [ ] I met'. Coursebooks do not typically use the term 'zero pronoun', preferring to explain discursively that the relative pronoun can be omitted in certain contexts; as we shall see in Chapter 7, historically the phrase 'contact clause' was often used to describe a relative clause in which the zero pronoun is used. These strong similarities across the coursebook series again point to the need identified by the interviewees in Chapter 4 to follow the norms and expectations within the profession and the example set by previous publications.

One particular aspect of ELT coverage is interesting in light of the data from Yamashita (1994) discussed above. Examples and descriptions in coursebooks of non-defining relative clauses seem to strongly favour relative clauses in medial position. For example, in the two lesson pages dealing with relative clauses in *Headway Upper Intermediate* (pp. 62–63) 10 of the 17 non-defining clauses (59%) are medial position. In the coverage in *face2face Upper Intermediate* (pp. 32–33), medial-position relative clauses make up 10 of 16 (63%) examples. Finally, in *New English File Intermediate* (pp. 92–93, 140–141), the figures are 8 out of 10 (80%). When compared with Yamashita's data, which found that over 75% of non-defining clauses occurred in *final* position (1994: 82), it appears that ELT accounts seriously misrepresent actual usage. It is not clear why such medial-position clauses are favoured in ELT grammar treatments; one possible explanation is simply that with medial-position clauses, the difference between defining and non-defining clauses can be made more obvious by constructing sentence pairs differing only in punctuation to demonstrate the difference. For example, in *Headway Advanced*, learners are asked to discuss the difference between pairs of sentences such as 'My sister, who's a flight attendant, is actually scared of flying', and 'My sister who's a flight attendant is actually scared of flying' (p. 68). Additionally, examples of medial-position non-defining clauses may simply be, and have been historically, more immediately psychologically available to grammarians and materials writers, by nature of their relatively higher frequency in written texts.

Table 6.5 below summarises coverage of relative clause types at levels 1–6. In the five coursebook series examined, there is, as with conditionals, broad agreement that defining relative clauses require repetition across levels, and should be taught before non-defining relative clauses; the former are taught in four of the five series at Level 3, and then again in all series at Levels 4 and 5. By comparison, non-defining clauses are taught in all coursebooks at Level 5, but only inconsistently at other levels. Only two of the five series cover 'comment clauses', and this only in endmatter grammar references; this patchy coverage of a significant area of usage appears to constitute an area of weakness in the ELT account, given the frequency of the structure in spoken language.

In terms of relative pronouns and adverbs, at Level 3 all of the coursebooks that teach defining relative clauses cover the relative

Table 6.5 Overview of coverage of relative clause types at different coursebook levels (1–6)

Coursebook series	Defining	Non-defining	Clauses with 'zero' pronoun
New English File	3, 4, 5	4, 5	4, 5
face2face	3, 4, 5	5	4, 5
Headway	3, 4, 5, 6	5, 6	4, 5, 6
Interchange/Passages	3, 4, 5	4, 5	—
Cutting Edge	4, 5	5	4, 5

pronouns *who*, *that* and *which*, with three also teaching *where*. At Level 4, three of the coursebook series add *whose* as a relative pronoun; the zero pronoun is also covered for the first time at this level in all but one series. At Level 5, there is a degree of variation in the choice of relative pronouns and adverbs included, with, for example, *Headway* and *face2face* teaching only *who* and *which*, while other series also include one or both of *when* and *where*.

One interesting element in the coverage of pronouns concerns the potential choice between *that* and *who* in defining relative clauses with a human antecedent, and between *that* and *which* in those with a non-human antecedent. *New English File* only overtly teaches the use of *who* and *which*, noting only at the back of the book that the pronoun *that* can also be used. In contrast, *face2face* and *Cutting Edge* both state, in their back-of-the-book grammar references, that it is more usual to use *who* and *which*, rather than *that*. This foregrounding of *who* and *which* over *that* seems to constitute an 'echo' of older accounts of relative clauses, which, as we shall see in Chapter 7, often either proscribed the use of *that* or treated it as a less likely, or less desirable, choice. Yet the evidence is that, at least in the context of conversation and fiction, the pronoun *that* is actually used at least as frequently as *who* and *which*.[2] Further coverage of pronouns involves the teaching of *what* as a relative pronoun (e.g. 'This is what you need') in four of the five coursebooks. ELT explanations typically describe this usage by stating that *what* means 'the thing that', but in descriptive accounts, the structure – distinguished from other relative clauses in that it has no overt antecedent – is typically treated separately, and often termed a 'free relative clause' (Aarts *et al.*, 2014).

As with conditionals, the higher levels show a large amount of variation in content. At Level 5, there is somewhat inconsistent coverage of a large number of small details in endmatter grammar sections, with *Headway* mentioning the preference for *that* after *all*, *some*(*thing*), *every*(*thing*), *any*(*thing*), *only* and *It is*, and *face2face* noting that *when* can be omitted 'when the time reference is clear'. At the highest level, coverage fades away, with relative clauses covered in only two of the five series examined. Of these two, *Cutting Edge* adds the use of abstract nouns with relative clauses (e.g. *reason why*, *situations where*, *the way in which*), in a focus that has perhaps more to do with improving lexical, rather than grammatical, competence.

One final peculiarity in the ELT accounts can be found in the endmatter grammar explanations in two coursebook series, *Headway* and *New Cutting Edge*, both of which contrast the use, in non-defining clauses, of phrase-initial prepositions (e.g. 'The privatization of the railways, **to which** the present government is committed, is not universally popular') and phrase-final prepositions (e.g. 'He talked about theories of market forces, which I'd never even heard **of**') (both examples from Soars & Soars, 2014: 149), noting that the latter are associated with a more informal register. What is interesting is that the possibility of using phrase-initial prepositions in defining relative clauses is never mentioned, even though it is of course equally possible. Like the advice on the choice between *that* and *who/which* discussed above, this may again be an echo of coverage in older grammars; as we will see in Chapter 7, Allen's (1947) highly influential *Living English Structure* presents clause-initial prepositions only in the context of non-defining clauses, and it seems that elements of this older account are still, directly or indirectly, influential on contemporary accounts.

6.4.3 Comparison with the EGP

A first comparison of the treatment in the canon with EGP immediately reveals a striking difference. The EGP shows that learners are able to accurately produce both defining and non-defining relative clauses at A2, at least a level earlier than either are typically taught in coursebooks. More specifically, learners at A2 can produce:

- defining relative clauses with *who* as subject, and *which* and *that* as subject and object;
- defining relative clauses with the 'zero pronoun';
- non-defining relative clauses with *who* as subject, and *which* as subject and object.

The non-use of *who* as the object of relative clauses is not easily explainable, beyond speculation over opportunities of use.

At B1, the EGP shows that learners are able to produce defining relative clauses with *when* and *where*. The latter is typically taught in coursebooks at the equivalent level, whereas relative clauses with *when* are only covered in one of the five coursebooks examined at any level. There are two further descriptors at B1 that do not match the coverage at Level 3 or 4 of coursebooks:

- defining clauses with '(the reason) why', covered by one coursebook at Level 5 and one at Level 6, both in endmatter grammar references;
- defining relative clauses with 'the person who/that, the thing that, the (only) one who/that' as a focusing device (EGP example: 'The thing that was great is that the weather was really warm and it didn't rain'), not covered in coursebooks at all.

By contrast, the EGP shows that learners can only use *whose* only in a very limited way at B1 – in the phrase 'whose name' – and that they do not start to use it more generally until B2. Coursebooks, however, generally teach *whose* at Level 4, a level earlier than the EGP suggests learners use it widely.

Finally, the EGP shows that learners at B2 level are able to produce both defining and non-defining clauses with clause-final prepositions, which mirrors the coverage in Level 5 coursebooks. However, while the EGP shows that learners are able to use comment clauses (termed 'evaluative clauses' in the EGP) at B2, we saw above that only two of the five coursebooks examined cover this at all, and this only in endmatter grammar explanations. The EGP shows no further development in the use of relative clauses above B2, even though two Level 6 coursebooks cover them.

Overall, the comparison between the coursebook consensus and evidence from the EGP suggests that coursebooks teach many aspects of relative clauses later than learners appear ready to use them, and indeed – given the range of relative clauses produced by A2 level learners – later than learners apparently *encounter the need* to use them. The one exception to this is the relative pronoun *whose*, which learners use later than it is typically taught. Furthermore, a highly frequent use of non-defining relative clauses – comment clauses – is attested in the production of learners at B2, but covered very inconsistently in coursebooks, typically only in endmatter grammar references.

6.4.4 Discussion of ELT treatment of relative clauses

We have seen that contemporary accounts of relative clauses focus invariably on the binary defining/non-defining distinction, with a strong preference for medial-position relative clauses in non-defining clauses. This preference means that learners receive limited exposure to end-position clauses – particularly comment clauses – and are given few chances to practise them, despite the important role that they appear to play in spoken English (Tao & McCarthy, 2001). This situation is somewhat puzzling, given that descriptions in coursebooks clearly state that medial-position non-defining relative clauses are associated with formal, written contexts – not typically the target language for General English coursebooks.

With the exception of clauses with *whose*, the comparison with the EGP finds principally that learners use relative clauses earlier than they are taught, and that they start to use both defining and non-defining clauses, including medial-position ones, at the same level, whereas these are typically staggered across two different levels in coursebooks. This would suggest that relative clauses are both important and useful, and could be taught earlier than they currently are typically covered in coursebooks, including, of course, end-position non-defining relative clauses.

6.5 Case Study C: Future Forms

6.5.1 Overview and previous research

In this analysis, the term 'future forms' is used to refer to forms that express future time from the perspective of the present (excluding, as a consequence, structures such as *was going to*, sometimes referred to as 'the future in the past'), and that are overtly labelled in ELT accounts as future forms (also excluding, as a consequence, modal verbs such as *may* and *might*, even though they may be used to refer to events in the future). The term 'continuous' will be used in this discussion, even to refer to the content of titles which use the word 'progressive'.

One characteristic of coverage in contemporary ELT materials is that they tend to favour the term 'future form' and/or functional labels such as 'intentions' over the term 'future tense'. As we shall see in Chapter 7, there has been a shift over the years from the idea of English having a 'future tense' – invariably *will* and *shall* – to the idea of it having a number of different forms used to talk about the future in different contexts and for different reasons. The choice of terminology in contemporary coursebooks reflects this shift.

The consensus and agreement that exists on the teaching of future forms appears to have been reached only well into the second half of the 20th century, with articles in the *ELT Journal* in the 1970s and 1980s discussing the uses of different future forms, and attempting to set out what should be taught to learners of English. For example, Close (1970a, 1970b) reviews the coverage in older titles, such as in Jespersen's grammar, and – perhaps inevitably – proposes a pedagogical classification system for futurity. Tregidgo's (1980) article discusses the uses of *will* and *shall* in contemporary English, recommending teaching points up to Intermediate levels. Locke (1986) discusses three different uses of the future continuous (in line with those given, for example, in Allen's (1947) *Living English Structure*), criticising its coverage in many ELT accounts. Beyond this – and in contrast to the other two areas of grammar examined in this title – research on the typical treatment of future forms in pedagogical accounts of English is lacking.

6.5.2 Coursebook consensus

The five coursebooks examined again appear to confirm the existence of a strong consensus: all teach the same five canonical future forms: (1) *will* (and occasionally, *shall*) future, sometimes also called 'simple future', (2) *going to*, (3) the present continuous with future time reference, (4) the future perfect (e.g. 'The train will have left by the time we get there') and (5) the future continuous (e.g. 'I'll be waiting for you at the entrance'). Within these five structures, different uses or functions are generally identified, although not always consistently across titles. In some cases, more than one function is identified for each future form, and these are generally separated out within explanations, or even across lessons. The principal uses and functions associated with the five forms are as follows:

(1) *will*
   - to make predictions;
   - to make offers, promises and requests, and decisions made at the time of speaking;
(2) *be going to*
   - to talk about plans and intentions;
   - to make predictions with present evidence;
(3) present continuous: to talk about arrangements;
(4) future perfect: to talk about an action that is completed before a certain future time;
(5) future continuous (*will* + *be* + *-ing* form)
   - to talk about an action that will be in progress at a certain future time;
   - to talk about an action that will happen 'in the normal course of events'.

The coverage of the five structures at levels 1–6 in the coursebooks under analysis is summarised in Tables 6.6 and 6.7. In addition to the five main future forms, additional structures are sometimes covered, including the present simple (e.g. 'The bus leaves at 6pm'), *to be to* (e.g. 'The prime minister is to make a statement tonight') and other forms such *be due to*, *be about to*, *be likely to* etc. These are covered less consistently across the five series.

Table 6.6 Overview of coverage of *will* and *be going to* at different coursebook levels (1–6)

Coursebook series	will (predictions/ future facts)	will (promises, decisions etc.)	be going to (plans)	be going to (predictions)
New English File	3, 4	3, 4	1, 2, 3, 4	1, 2, 4
face2face	3, 4, 5	4, 5	2, 3, 4, 5	4, 5
Headway	4, 5, 6	3, 5, 6	1, 2, 3, 4, 5, 6	(endmatter only)
Interchange/Passages	3, 4	2	1, 2, 3	3
Cutting Edge	3, 4, 5, 6	5	1, 2, 3, 4, 5	6

Table 6.7 Overview of coverage of present continuous, future perfect and future continuous at different coursebook levels (1–6)

Coursebook series	present continuous	future perfect	future continuous
New English File	3, 4, 6	5	5, 6
face2face	3, 4, 5	5	5
Headway	1, 2, 3, 4, 5, 6	5, 6	5, 6
Interchange/Passages	2	4, 5	4
Cutting Edge	3, 4, 5	5, 6	6

While all five canonical structures are covered in all coursebooks, there is variation in the order in which they are included. The situation is made more complicated by the fact that this area of grammar is one that is taught, in one way or another, at every level of every coursebook series; as a consequence, many of the five forms are taught at more than one level, and in the case of some series, at all six levels. The prevailing consensus therefore appears to be that future forms constitute an area of grammar which needs frequent revision and repetition. However, a more detailed analysis shows that the repetition is also a reflection of the particular approach taken to teach this area of grammar: future forms are typically taught as individual items at lower levels, but then combined with and compared with other future forms at higher levels. For example, at Level 1, *New English File* teaches two different uses of *going to* in two separate lessons, and this approach is repeated at Level 2. At Level 3, *going to* and present continuous are taught in a single lesson, with two separate lessons for two different uses of *will*. Then, at level 4, there is a single lesson in which *going to*, present continuous and *will/ shall* are revised and compared.

The most common future form to teach to beginners is *going to*, which is covered in four of the five coursebooks at the lowest level (to talk about plans and intentions); this confirms Diane Hall's observation (see Chapter 4) that *going to* is now the preferred first future form to teach, when in the past it had been *will*. In addition, *Headway* also teaches the future use of the present continuous, and *English File* also teaches *going to* for predictions. At Level 2, all five series teach *going to* for plans and intentions, while three of the five series add present continuous. A single title – *Interchange* – also covers *will* for requests (for example, 'I'll have a small salad' (Richards *et al.*, 2004: 89)), although this is part of a wider focus with *would* and is not 'signposted' as being a future form.

Content at Levels 3 and 4 is very similar, with three of the five canonical forms (*going to*, present continuous and *will*) covered and often contrasted; coverage of *going to* now typically focuses both on its use to talk about plans and intentions, and also to make predictions with present evidence. It appears, then, that at these learning stages, learners are expected to be familiar with a range of future forms, but to be unsure of exactly when to choose one over another.

The highest two levels see the introduction of the final two canonical forms, the future perfect and future continuous. The former is taught in all five series at Level 5, and the future continuous in four of the five. All four of the coursebook series to teach the future continuous focus on its use to talk about an action in progress at a specific moment in time in the future. Additionally, *face2face* teaches, within the main lesson content, its use to refer to an action that will happen 'in the normal course of events', something also included in three more coursebooks series in endmatter grammar explanations. As we will see in Chapter 7, the use of the phrase 'the normal course of events' as part of explanations of this usage goes back at least 100 years. *Passages* also teaches the future perfect continuous, the only book from the five series examined to do so, at any level. At Level 6, there is further repetition of future forms from previous levels, although the highest level of *Passages* contains no future forms at all. However, as with the other areas of grammar examined at this level, there is only a limited degree of agreement, particularly when the forms covered explicitly within the lessons are considered. The coverage is as follows, with both those titles that teach the form directly in the lesson and those that cover it only in back-of-the-book grammar references given in brackets:

- *will* to express willingness (1/5 in main lesson; 1/5 in endmatter only);
- *will* for predictions (3/5 in main lesson);
- *will* for decisions made at the time of speaking (3/5 in main lesson);
- present continuous (3/5 in main lesson);
- *going to* for intentions (3/5 in main lesson);
- *going to* for predictions with present evidence (1/5 in main lesson; 1/5 in endmatter only);
- future perfect (2/5 in main lesson);
- future continuous (3/5 in endmatter only).

It seems, therefore, that while the coursebooks are in agreement on the need to revise future forms at the highest level, they are not in agreement on which particular forms should be revised.

One oddity in the explanations in the coursebooks is a rule stating that the verb 'go' is not typically used with the *going to* form (so the phrase 'going to go' is said to be impossible or unlikely). This rule is included in the endmatter grammar explanations in Levels 2, 3 and 4 of *face2face*, and also in *New English File* and *Headway* at Level 3. As we shall see in Chapter 7, the rule has a long history, being found in numerous titles going back at least as far Palmer's (1924) grammar. However, Burton (2021) provides a variety of evidence from the British National Corpus and the Corpus of Contemporary American English that the rule is almost certainly not accurate in contemporary English, even though it may have been historically, at least in British English.

6.5.3 Comparison with the EGP

Our comparison with the EGP is by necessity longer than with those of the other two areas of grammar, due to the fact that a larger range of structures and usages are covered under the umbrella term 'future forms' than with conditionals and relative clauses. The comparison is also more problematic; it is hard to compare level allocations in the canon and in the EGP because structures are repeated so frequently across levels in coursebooks. As explained above, *going to*, for example, appears at every level of *Headway* and it is therefore difficult to make direct comparisons with evidence of the development of learners' use of it in the EGP. Equally, many of the EGP entries themselves extend over several levels; for example, the EGP shows that learners are able to use the present continuous at A2 to talk about the future arrangements with a limited range of verbs, at B1 with an increasing range of verbs, and at B2 with a wide range of verbs. Other future forms show development in terms of learners' ability to use them for an increasingly wide range of functions; for example, at A1 learners can use *will* to talk about plans and intentions, at A2 to show willingness and to make requests, and at B1 to make predictions. The canon treatment may therefore be reflective of the fact that future forms seem to be an area of grammar that learners develop competence in slowly and over time. That said, the overall picture in the EGP nonetheless is often markedly different from the treatment of future forms in the canon.

We will again start at the lowest levels. In contrast to the coursebooks examined, which teach *going to* talk about plans at the lowest level, the EGP shows that *will* (in the affirmative) is the future form which learners first start to produce. At A2, there is some agreement between the EGP and the canon – coursebooks at Level 2 generally teach the present continuous and *going to* for plans and intentions, and these are attested in the EGP at A2 (the former, with a limited number of verbs, and the latter, only in affirmative and interrogative questions, however). Yet the EGP also shows that A2 learners are also able to use a number of other future forms beyond *going to* and present continuous, at least a level earlier than that at which they are typically taught, as follows:

- *going to* for predictions, only with the verb *be* (not normally taught until Level 3, the first half of B1);
- questions with *will* and *shall* to make requests (taught in only a single coursebook series, *Interchange*);
- *will*, including in the negative at this point, to talk about plans and intentions, and to express willingness (typically not taught – and even then very inconsistently across titles – until Level 6, equivalent to C1);
- *Shall I …?* and *Shall we …?* to make offers (taught in only a single coursebook series, *New English File*, at Level 4);
- present simple to talk about timetabled events (typically taught at Levels 5 and 6, equivalent to B2 and C1);
- the affirmative form of *shall* in the first person (not found at all in the canon); the two examples given in the EGP ('We shall start tomorrow at 2 o'clock' and 'I shall be free on Sunday at 6 o'clock in the evening') might, however, be regarded as somewhat stilted.

Perhaps most surprising of all at A2 in the EGP is that the learners are also shown to be able to use the future continuous (in the affirmative, to talk about future arrangements), something typically taught at only the highest levels in coursebooks. The EGP addresses this unexpected inclusion in a note: 'Although it is surprising to see this structure at A2, there is a lot of clustering around certain collocations (e.g. 'will be waiting'), and therefore there is enough evidence of its successful use in simple contexts concerning time and place to merit its inclusion at A2'.

The EGP at B1 is in some ways in line with the canon. Learners are reported to be able to use *going to* for predictions (beyond only with the verb *be*, as found at A2), *going to* for intentions (with usage extended, now, to negative forms) and the present continuous. However, these forms and uses are also taught in coursebooks at lower levels, making the agreement less convincing. On the other hand, at B1 learners start to use *will* to make predictions, mirroring its position in the canon, although the use of *will* to talk about 'fixed plans, often with times and dates' attested at this level in the EGP does not feature in the canon at all; in addition, learners at B1 use *shall* to talk about plans and intentions, similarly not present in the canon. Finally at this level, the EGP shows that learners can now use the negative form of the future continuous, something that, as we saw above, is typically taught only at Level 5, equivalent to B2.

The picture at B2 is similar, with convergence between the EGP and the canon at least partly due to the fact that many of the future forms are covered at multiple levels in coursebooks. The EGP shows that learners at this level start to use the future perfect, typically covered at the equivalent coursebook level (Level 5). By contrast, the EGP shows that learners at this level also start to use, with a purely temporal focus, the future perfect continuous (EGP example: 'I will have been working for my company for one year by the end of the June'), something taught only in the *Interchange* series (at the equivalent level). The EGP also shows learners using the future continuous as a polite question form (EGP examples: 'How long will you be staying?'; 'Will you be needing anything else?'), which is only found in coursebooks at Level 6, and even then, only in three endmatter grammar references.

Level C1 in the EGP shows that learners use *going to* with an increasing range of adverbs, the future perfect with adverbs, and *will* to describe habitual actions. In addition, two pragmatic uses of the future perfect are identified: as a politeness strategy (EGP example: 'I hope I will have reassured you') and to make assumptions (EGP example: 'As you will have heard, this year's work experience programme in Britain was in general a success'). Neither of these uses is included in any of the coursebooks examined. However, as we shall see in Chapter 7, the latter was covered in early pedagogical grammars (see also McCarthy, 2015, for a discussion of this use of the future perfect, and how it might be useful to advanced level learners).

The development of learner competence with future forms continues to the C2 level, at which learners are able to use the future perfect in question forms, *going to* with a wide range of adverbs, *shall* for 'long term intentions' (EGP example: 'I shall always remember it as the city of lights') and for predictions in informal contexts, and *will* to express 'willfulness or disapproval'. None of these is covered explicitly at any level of the coursebook series examined. Finally, learners are able to use the future perfect continuous to make assumptions (EGP example: 'I do not think that this aspect is really necessary because it is supossed (sic) that you will be an adult for that moment and you will have been studying very hard to occupy that job'). This is a development beyond the temporal usage of the same structure that learners are shown to use at B2, but the EGP notes the low frequency of the usage in the data.

6.5.4 Discussion of ELT treatment of future forms

The contemporary ELT account of future forms seems relatively advanced and comprehensive – a large number of forms and uses are covered, in stark contrast, for example, to the way conditional sentences are taught. The coverage of future forms is characterised by repeated teaching across levels; this is also the case, to an extent, with the other two areas of grammar examined, but with future forms it is particularly noticeable. This repetition contradicts the oft-levelled criticism (see, for example, Jolly & Bolitho, 1998; Mares, 2003) that coursebooks employing a structural syllabus are based on the (unfounded) premise that a single grammatical form can be acquired in a single lesson, with overall linguistic competence built up, 'brick by brick' in this way. In fact, at least with the grammatical forms examined in this study, it seems that course designers are well aware of the need for a grammatical structure to be practised more than once.

While the fact that future forms are repeated across levels in coursebooks makes a comparison with the EGP more problematic with this area of grammar, there is, nonetheless, clear evidence again of learners being able to use forms before they are typically covered in coursebooks (for example, *going to* for both plans and predictions). Furthermore, the EGP also shows that learners can use *Shall I/we* for offers and suggestions, something which is not typically covered in coursebooks, and that they make various pragmatic uses of future forms not typically taught, for example the use of *will have* to express an assumption, and of the future continuous to ask polite questions. The fact that learners are able to successfully make pragmatic use of these two structures suggests that they could be given more prominence in teaching materials.

6.6 Summary

What, then, can the three case studies presented here tell us about the nature of grammatical content in ELT coursebooks? Considering just the coursebooks alone, and especially at a macro level, there is a high level of agreement in coverage. In all three case studies, the grammatical treatments in the coursebooks largely cover well-established ground with little or no variation: this can be seen in the universal adoption of the three-way conditional system, of the binary distinction between defining and non-defining relative clauses and the teaching of five canonical future forms. There is also strong agreement on ordering: the three canonical conditional forms are always taught in the same order, starting with the first conditional, before moving on to the second and third conditional at higher levels; defining relative clauses are taught before non-defining relative clauses; and the teaching of future forms typically starts with *going to*, with the other forms added as learners progress through levels, and the future perfect and future continuous taught at only the highest levels.

A greater amount of variation in all three areas of grammar is, however, found if we shift our focus to micro- rather than macro-level coverage in coursebooks. As we saw, there is only very inconsistent coverage of the 'zero conditional', and limited agreement on which conditional forms should be revised at the highest two levels, while coverage of relative clauses is inconsistent in terms of the order that different relativisers are taught in and the various 'details' such as comment clauses and clause-initial prepositions that are covered. There is also disagreement on the precise ordering of future forms and on which of them should be revised at the highest levels. The consensus, then, is strong, but not universal – there are disagreements in the details, and particularly on content at higher levels. The primary sources alone cannot tell us why there is such disagreement. However, the most likely explanation seems to be the selective nature of pedagogical grammar, as discussed in Chapter 2. As we saw, pedagogical grammar accounts do not attempt to provide a comprehensive account of a language, but focus on those aspects that are particularly important for language learning. From this already selective account, materials authors must make their own selection, including what feels most expedient considering the expectations of users and the space available in the particular publication.

The comparison with the EGP shows very often that learners are able to use many structures before they are typically taught in coursebooks, and, more generally, that they are able to use a far wider range of structures than are normally covered in coursebooks. For example, learners begin to use conditional forms at A2, a level earlier than they are covered in coursebooks, and show more flexibility in their own usage than that contained in the three-way conditional system presented in teaching materials. The situation is similar with relative clauses: learners start to use them a level earlier than they are taught, and are able, from B2 level, to make use of comment clauses, even though these are only patchily covered by coursebooks. Finally, while a comparison of the teaching of and the use of future forms in coursebooks and the EGP is harder to achieve, we again see learners, in their use of the pragmatic functions of the future continuous and the future perfect, showing more flexibility than would appear to be provided in the pedagogical treatments in coursebook of these forms.

Given the inconsistencies identified between data from the EGP and the 'standard' consensus accounts found in coursebooks, an obvious question is how this information might be acted upon. In other words, what would the ideal relationship be between a resource giving information on learner output across competency levels, like the EGP, and coursebooks? There are a number of different possible implications and questions to answer, for example:

- If the EGP shows that learners can use an aspect of grammar *before* it is typically taught, what does this tell us? That it should be covered earlier in syllabuses? If so, is there room in existing syllabuses to move grammar items earlier than they are currently taught?
- Where the EGP 'agrees' with the current consensus, is this because the consensus is somehow 'correct' in teaching the particular area of grammar at that level, or is this simply a case of learner output reflecting the content of coursebooks? (According to the 'internal syllabus' hypothesis (see Chapter 2), the latter should not really be possible.)
- If the EGP shows that learners use an aspect of grammar *after* it is typically taught, does that mean it is typically taught too early? Or are some grammar points somehow associated with a 'teaching-learning lag', meaning that a certain period of time needs to pass between learners studying the grammar and them actually being able to use it?
- If the EGP shows that learners can use grammar in a way that is not typically taught at all, how did the learners come to develop this competence to start with? (This question also applies to grammar which learners use at an earlier level than it is typically taught at in coursebooks.) And does such evidence show that this language should be added to coursebooks?

These are not questions that can be easily addressed here but some possible answers will be discussed in Chapter 8. However, the fact that such questions are raised by a comparison between the canon accounts and the empirical data offered by the EGP demonstrates the potential for learner corpora, particularly those calibrated for competency level, to bring about a rethink of existing grammar syllabuses.

Having examined in detail the treatment in the canon of conditionals, relative clauses and future forms, and compared this with evidence from the EGP, in Chapter 7 we will attempt to uncover how this consensus was arrived at, by tracking the development of accounts of the same areas of grammar in grammars and coursebooks going back to the 17th century. If you jumped to this current chapter after finishing Chapter 4, I would invite you to read Chapter 5 now in order to see what the interviewees had to say about the evolution of the canon, before reading Chapter 7.

Notes

(1) For American English, it is typical to publish one series covering the four lower levels and another – with a different name – covering the higher two levels; this is the case with the *Interchange* and *Passages* series.

(2) According to Biber *et al.* (1999), the frequency of *that* as pronoun in defining relative clauses is slightly higher than both *which* and *who* combined in conversation, and also in fiction. Given that *that* can be used for both persons and things, this suggests a slight preference for *that* in this context. In news, *that* is slightly less frequent than *which* and *who* individually, suggesting a strong preference for the latter two pronouns; academic writing demonstrates a strong preference for *which*. The findings seem to suggest a preference for *who* and *which* only in formal, written contexts.

7 Conditionals, Relative Clauses and Future Forms: Evolution of the Canon

7.1 Introduction

This chapter completes the case study analysis, and examines how the descriptions of the three areas of grammar we saw in Chapter 6 (namely, conditionals, relative clauses and future forms) have evolved over the centuries, from early descriptive accounts to modern pedagogical ones. It will consider both the overall content and the way explanations and rules are worded; additionally, some examples used in the original texts to illustrate the rules and explanations are analysed. A reader who has arrived at this chapter without first reading Chapter 6 might like to read Section 6.2 for information on why a case study approach was used and why the three areas of grammar under analysis were selected.

There were a number of reasons for carrying out the more 'historical' analysis presented in this chapter. Firstly, the approach throughout this book has to been to attempt to gain as full an understanding of current practice as possible, in order to be able to engage with it successfully. I believe that, in order to fully understand the status quo, it is important to understand where it came from and how it developed. An account of the evolution of the canon based on primary sources can naturally go much further back than the recollections of the interviewees whose views and experiences reported in Chapter 5 can allow – indeed, we will trace the treatment of the three areas of grammar back to the 17th century. Furthermore, as we have said, citations are rare in commercial or educational publications, and in order to understand how grammatical explanations in ELT have evolved over the decades, it is necessary to examine the primary sources in detail. Finally, as Smith (2016) has argued, a careful examination of primary sources allows a researcher to avoid 'presentism' – viewing the past from the perspective of the present – and makes it possible to make robust assertions about past practices with more confidence.

7.2 Methodology: Exploring Grammar in 'Historical' Publications

7.2.1 Selecting the titles for analysis

In order to create this historical overview, a series of key titles was identified for the analysis presented here. This is made up of both grammars and coursebooks and can be divided into four categories, as seen in Table 7.1.

The three titles in the first category – 'historical' grammars – were all described in Chapter 3 and were selected in order to cover both the 'traditional grammar' period and that of the 'Great Tradition'. As we saw in Chapter 3, Murray's grammar was highly successful and was apparently highly influential on titles that followed it, while Jonson's *English Grammar* is chosen for its interest value as a very early pedagogical grammar. Jespersen's *Essentials of English Grammar is a* condensed version of his four-volume Modern English Grammar, and was chosen over the latter because the shorter format made it more suitable for analysis; it is also third in a list of ten grammars in the list of 'useful books for further reference' provided by Allen in his introduction to *Living English Structure*. The second and third categories – historical pedagogical grammars and historical coursebooks – cover a relatively more recent period. Titles were chosen from the 20th century up until the early 1990s. As we have said, the turn of the 20th century roughly represents the beginning of what can be thought of as the 'modern era' of ELT (Howatt & Widdowson, 2004), with the 1990s also being the cut-off point used in this book to separate out references to contemporary titles and publishing practices to historical ones.

The three historical pedagogical grammars chosen for analysis were also described in Chapter 3. As stated, Palmer's grammar is historically significant as perhaps the first modern pedagogical grammar, while the

Table 7.1 Titles chosen for historical analysis in case studies

'Historical' grammars:
- *The English Grammar* (Jonson, 1640)
- *English Grammar: Adapted to the different classes of learners* (Murray, 1795)
- *Essentials of English Grammar* (Jespersen, 1933)

'Historical' pedagogical grammars:
- *A Grammar of Spoken English* (Palmer, 1924)
- *Living English Structure* (Allen, 1947)
- *A Practical English Grammar* (Thomson & Martinet, 1960)

'Historical' coursebooks:
- *Essential English* (Eckersley, 1938, 1940, 1941, 1942)
- *Oxford Progressive English* (Hornby, 1954b, 1955, 1956)

Late 20th-century coursebooks:
- *English Grammatical Structure* (Alexander et al., 1975)
- *Strategies* (Abbs & Freebairn, 1977, 1979, 1980, 1982)
- *Streamline* (Hartley & Viney, 1978, 1979, 1982, 1985)
- *The New Cambridge English Course* (Swan & Walter, 1990a,b, 1992a,b)
- *Headway* (first editions) (Soars & Soars, 1986, 1987, 1989, 1991, 1993; Beaven et al., 1995)

titles by Allen, and Thomson and Martinet, were both commercially very successful and appear – also from the interview data – to occupy a special place in the evolution of accounts of grammar in ELT. As for the coursebook series, these were chosen on the basis of them having been written by well-known figures in ELT, having been published by major international publishing houses, and having seen commercial success. The latter criterion is not always easily established, but can be surmised by the fact that almost all were published in more than one edition and that the authors went on to write other coursebook series. No series earlier than *Essential English* was found to have a clear grammatical syllabus, so this is the oldest of the coursebook series included in the analysis. The reader may recall that *English Grammatical Structure* (also described in Chapter 3) is not, in fact, a coursebook, but is rather a grammatical inventory created for coursebook authors and syllabus designers. Given the fact that the authors were high-profile coursebook authors of the time (in 1977, L.G. Alexander's sales of 4.7m books was recorded in the *Guinness Book of Records* as the greatest number of sales by an individual author in a year) and that it influenced later coursebooks authors, it is likely to be representative of the consensus on grammatical content in mainstream ELT in the period and therefore relevant to the analysis.

7.2.2 Analysing the content

The process of examining the grammatical content of such titles was relatively straightforward. Contents pages or indexes can be used to locate the relevant material within each book. With older titles this can be more problematic because of differences in terminology; for example, Palmer uses the term 'adverbials of condition, supposition, etc.' for what are now known in ELT (and elsewhere) as 'conditionals', while Hornby uses the term *willingness* to refer to a number of uses of *will*. Nevertheless, it was always possible to find the relevant sections for this analysis and, indeed, over the decades the amount of terminological variation decreases, suggesting that a gradual convergence towards a consensus on terminology is a characteristic of the evolution of the grammar canon.

The coverage of each grammar point was analysed in terms of (i) the content of the coverage (e.g. the uses of *will* taught, or the types of conditional sentence taught) and the wording of the rules and explanations given, and (ii) in the case of coursebooks, the level at which it was taught. The account of each of the three grammar points is presented chronologically. As in Chapter 6, each case study is dealt with separately, but we will conclude the chapter with a summary that brings together various overarching characteristics to emerge from the analysis as a whole.

7.3 Case Study A: Conditionals

7.3.1 Historical grammars

Jonson's (1640) grammar covers conditionals only very briefly. He makes a single reference to conditional forms in a section on conjunctions, stating that *if*, *unless* and *except* are conjunctions of 'conditioning'. On the other hand, Murray (1795: 178) discusses conditional sentences in some detail, in part of a discussion of the 'general' requirement of the subjunctive after the words '*if, though, unless, except, whether* &c'. Much of Murray's rules and examples reflect historical differences in English, although he also notes a form of the conditional sometimes found in contemporary pedagogical description: inversion with *were* in place of the *if* clause. Murray gives the example, 'Were there no difference, there would be no choice'. This structure, he argues, exhibits 'a peculiar neatness' (1795: 186). Murray does not discuss the time references of conditional sentences. The examples given include, among others, what could be termed 'second' and 'third' conditionals, but Murray does not attempt to explain the difference in meaning, focusing instead on the form of the verbs.

Like Murray, Jespersen's (1933) focus in mainly on verb form; there is no overall explanation of conditional sentences or an attempt to categorise different patterns. He describes the use of past tenses to refer to hypothetical structures after *if*, a use he calls the 'preterit of imagination' (1933: 255), giving as an example 'If I had money enough, I should pay you' (1933: 254). Jespersen's main observation is that such meanings are contrary to reality: 'In all such cases we deny the reality or possibility of certain suppositions'. Elsewhere, in a section on clauses (1933: 371) Jespersen gives additional examples of non-hypothetical conditional sentences (e.g. 'If he comes back, what are we to do?'), as well as parallel examples which do not make use of *if* (for example, the words and phrases *suppose, supposing, unless, as long as, provided, in case*), as found in contemporary accounts. Finally, like Murray, and many modern coursebooks, Jespersen outlines the use of inversion of subject and *had*, *were* and *should* as an alternative for an *if* clause (1933: 371).

7.3.2 Historical pedagogical grammars

Palmer's (1924) analysis is more comprehensive than those discussed above. He prefers the term 'adverbials of condition, supposition etc.' to describe sentences with *if* and uses a system of categorisation that identifies six kinds of conditional sentence (with two of the six themselves divided into two sub-types). The categorisation system is as follows:

- Type 1: Implying little more than mere Concomitance
  Examples:
  (1a: referring to present time) *If I go to bed early, I get up early the next day.*

(1b: referring to Past time (or in Indirect Speech)) (I said that–) *If I went to bed early, I got up early the next day.*
- Type 2: Implying Simple Condition
Examples:
(2a Referring to Future Tense) *If I go to bed early, I shall get up early tomorrow.*
(2b In Indirect Speech) *I said that if I went to bed early, I should get up early the next day.*
- Type 3: Implying a Higher Degree of Supposition
Example: *If I went to bed early, I should get up early tomorrow.*
- Type 4: Implying a still Higher Degree of Supposition
Example: *If I were to go to bed early, I should get up early tomorrow.*
- Type 5: Implying Contingent or Fortuitous Circumstances
Example: *If you should (happen to) meet him tomorrow, will you tell him to come?*
- Type 6: Implying Circumstances Dependent on Consent
Example: *If it wouldn't be inconvenient to you, I should like you to come before lunch.*

In addition, Palmer notes that the order of clauses can be reversed, in addition to the possibility of using inversion with *should* and *were* instead of *if*, noting that 'this construction is rather literary' (1924: 256). He also notes the use of *provided, providing, supposing, as long as* and *unless* as alternatives to *if* (1924: 254). It is interesting to note that Palmer readily identifies, in his Type 1, the use of past time to refer to the past rather than to hypotheticality, something which – as noted in Chapter 6 – is ignored in the contemporary ELT system. However, in what appears to be an oversight, Palmer does not include conditionals that refer to hypothetical past events (i.e. the 'third conditional' in the modern ELT system).

Allen's (1947) grammar is the earliest examined to use the standard, contemporary ELT typology, noting that 'English can express *three* important ideas with 'if'' (1947: 152). Although here he does not use terms such as 'first conditional' or 'Type 1 conditional', he does offer three example conditional sentences, numbered 1–3, and containing the verb combinations found in any coursebook today. Allen's categorisation system is as follows:

(1) Main clause – future; "if" ... present. (Likely or probable.)
(2) Main clause–conditional; "if" ... past. (Unlikely or improbable; imaginary.)
(3) Main clause–conditional perfect; "if" ... past perfect. (Impossible.)
(1947: 152)

Allen gives examples of the first conditional with both *will* and *shall*, with the preference for *shall* in the first person reflecting norms which elsewhere he describes as 'antiquated' (1947: 117). It is noteworthy that Allen uses the word 'conditional' to refer to the verb form in the main clause (i.e. the combination of *would* + base form) rather than to the overall structure, which he calls 'conditions and unreal past'; this appears to reflect the focus of earlier grammars on verb form rather than overall pattern or paradigm.

Elsewhere, in a later explanation to accompany 'Advanced' exercises, Allen outlines a further four conditional forms, covering equivalents to the 'zero conditional', the use of *should, will* and *would* in an *if* clause, and the use of *were* to, after *if*, and *would, could* or *might* in the main clause to create 'greater improbability in Conditional Types 1 and 2'. Furthermore, like Palmer and Jespersen, he also lists a number of alternatives to *if* (*unless, as if, if only, supposing, suppose, provided, providing, as long as*) and notes the possibility of inversion with *should* and *had*, stating, like Palmer, that it is 'more literary' (1947: 161).

The inclusion of the additional patterns outlined above makes it clear that Allen was aware of the existence of a far greater number of possibilities than those represented by the three-way system he first presents. However, the overall organisation of the section effectively foregrounds the three-way system and presents it as the main 'facts'; anything else is presented as detail, relevant only to 'Advanced' students. If Allen had pedagogical reasons for emphasising the patterns covered by the three-way system over other patterns, he does not explain them.

Thomson and Martinet's (1960) coverage is very similar in that they present a very full picture of conditionals, but again with the three-type model shown first. The opening statement is blunt: 'There are three kinds of conditional sentence: each kind contains a different pair of tenses' (1960: 131). Unlike Allen, they do not include *shall* and *should* as options in the main clauses of first and second conditionals, but, like Allen they describe a large range of alternatives to the three conditional types initially presented, focusing on the use of *will, would* and *should* in *if* clauses (1960: 133). Following this, Thomson and Martinet outline 'possible variations of the tense rules', in which they describe a further *seven* variations of the canonical three-way system. It is somewhat remarkable that, given the number of variations identified, Thomson and Martinet call the three original paradigms 'tense rules' at all, but it appears that by this point, the three-way system had become fixed in practice. In line with the grammars previously discussed, Thomson and Martinet also discuss the use of *unless, provided* (*that*) and *supposing* in place of *if*, and inversion with *had, should* and *were*.

7.3.3 Historical coursebooks

Eckersley covers conditionals only in Book 3 (1941) of the four-level *Essential English* series, as can be seen in Table 7.2.

Table 7.2 Conditionals in *Essential English*

	Book 1	Book 2	Book 3	Book 4
Zero	–	–	–	–
First	–	–	Yes (called 'Open conditions')	–
Second	–	–	Yes (called 'Subjunctive Present Conditionals')	–
Third	–	–	Yes (called 'Subjunctive Past Conditionals')	–
Other	–	–	'Subjunctive Present and Past Conditionals with *should*'	–

Table 7.3 Conditional system in *Essential English*

	Principal Clause	Conditional Clause
OPEN CONDITION	he will learn	if he *works* (*Simple Present*)
SUBJUNCTIVE — PRESENT CONDITIONAL	he would learn	if he *worked* (*Simple Past*)
SUBJUNCTIVE — PAST CONDITIONAL	he would have learned	if he *had worked* (*Past Perfect*)

Eckersley uses the terms 'Open condition' for first conditionals (learners only see the present simple + *will* combination; *shall* is not included), and 'Subjunctive Conditionals' for second and third conditionals. The choice of the term 'subjunctive' is revealing; unlike contemporary treatments, but like the grammars described above, the primary focus remains on the verb form rather than the overall sentence pattern.

In an explanation of the 'subjunctive present conditional' (equivalent to the 'second conditional'), the fictional teacher Mr Priestley, whose scripted dialogues with students the series is structured around, explains that 'The Subjunctive Mood is used in Conditional Clauses implying a negative' (1941: 77). Eckersley goes on to make a distinction between Present Subjunctive Conditionals and Past Subjunctive Conditionals, exactly along the lines of second and third conditionals. The overall system is reproduced in Table 7.3. It is perhaps significant here that, despite Eckersley's primary focus on the verb form in the *if* clause, he chooses to provide this overall summary which includes both the *if* clause and main clause. This is in line with pedagogical grammars like Palmer's (1924), bringing his explanations a little closer to those modern accounts.

In contrast to Eckersley, Hornby includes conditionals at all three levels of *Oxford Progressive English* (Table 7.4). Although his analysis often includes the verb form in the main clause, Hornby uses the term *if* clauses, again suggesting that we have not fully arrived at the contemporary approach of using whole sentences as the unit of analysis and explanation.

Table 7.4 Conditionals in *Oxford Progressive English*

	Book 1	Book 2	Book 3
Zero	Yes	–	–
First	–	Yes (called *if* clauses)	Yes (focus on non-use of *will* in *if* clause)
Second	–	Yes (called *if* clauses)	–
Third	–	Yes (one example)	–
Other	present simple + *can* combinations	–	Requests with *will* and *would* in the *if* clause; *supposed/supposing*

Interestingly, Hornby does not appear to consider the 'third conditional' of much (or any) pedagogical significance; Book 2 contains one example of it, but this is part of a focus on the past perfect and there is no clarification or explanation of meaning and it is not labelled or named. It seems very possible that Hornby was influenced by Palmer's categorisation system, which, as we saw, ignored the third conditional entirely.

Overall, Eckersley and Hornby's treatments can perhaps be seen as something of a bridge between the verb-focused approach associated with older grammars, and the paradigm-focused approach that was to come. While Eckersley refers to 'conditional clauses' (i.e. he appears to be primarily interested only in the verb form in the *if* clause), his coverage essentially revolves around the familiar three-way categorical system, even if he does not number the three sentence paradigms. Similarly, Hornby uses the term *if* clause, but his analysis also considers verbs in the main clause. Hornby does not, however, follow the three-way system closely and, as noted above, does not attempt to explain the meaning of a third conditional when he gives one as an example. This uncertainty and inconsistency was to disappear in the following decades, with a complete shift to a focus on a limited number of sentence paradigms and their meanings.

7.3.4 Late 20th-century coursebooks

English Grammatical Structure (Alexander *et al.*, 1975) covers conditions at three of the six levels, as can be seen in Table 7.5. A variety

Table 7.5 Conditionals in *English Grammatical Structure*

	Level 1	Level 2	Level 3	Level 4	Level 5	Level 6
Zero	–	–	Yes, but not named.	–	–	–
First	–	–	Yes, with *shall*.	–	–	–
Second	–	–	–	–	Yes	–
Third	–	–	–	–	Yes	–
Other	–	–	Past simple + past simple. Variation of first conditional with *going to* and present continuous.	–	Variation of third conditional with *could have*.	21 non-canonical alternatives.

of structures is included, but the primary focus is again the three-way system, with first conditionals, including *shall*, covered at Level 3, second and third conditionals covered at Level 4, and other combinations and 'variations' covered at Level 6.

There is some innovation, however. The section at Level 3 includes, without naming them, both 'zero conditionals' and past simple + past simple combinations with past time reference. The inclusion of zero conditionals at this early point effectively 'promotes' them to a higher position in the hierarchy of structures to be taught, transforming them from an extra detail (cf. Allen, 1947; Thomson & Martinet, 1960) into a more central feature. Also included is a note explaining that *will* is 'replaceable by *going to*' and the present continuous in certain contexts. It seems significant, however, that this observation is framed in terms of 'replacement': *will* is still presented as the standard choice, with other options to be considered variations of this standard.

In addition to the familiar variations on the main paradigms (for example, the use of *provided, providing, on condition that, even if, whether* and *supposing* in first and second conditionals, and the use of *should* in the main clause), the authors include, at Level 6, three sections entitled 'conditional sentences with tense sequences other than those in type 1, 2 and 3', 'conditional sentences with progressive aspect in one of the clauses', and 'variations on the form of *if* clauses' respectively. Across these three sections, a total of 21 conditional sentences are shown, none of which fit into the canonical three-way system. This level of detail is remarkable considering that it predated the emergence of computerised corpus-based analysis by around a decade. Again, however, these forms are presented as advanced 'alternatives' to the main paradigms, left to the highest level, with the three-way categorical system again foregrounded.

The coverage of conditionals in in *Strategies* (Abbs & Freebairn, 1977, 1979, 1980, 1982) is summarised in Table 7.6, and *Streamline* (Hartley & Viney, 1978, 1979, 1982, 1985) in Table 7.7. Both *Streamline* and *Strategies* generally follow the three-way system, with some variations; neither covers the 'zero conditional'.

Coverage in *The New Cambridge English Course* (Swan & Walter, 1990a, 1990b, 1992a, 1992b) includes conditional forms across all four levels, and is summarised in Table 7.8. Perhaps the biggest difference in

Table 7.6 Conditionals in *Strategies*

	Starting	Building	Developing	Studying
Zero	–	–	–	–
First	–	–	Yes	Yes
Second	–	–	Yes	Yes
Third	–	–	Yes	Yes
Other	–	Do you mind if …?	–	–

Table 7.7 Conditionals in *Streamline*

	Departures	Connections	Destinations	Directions
Zero	–	–	–	–
First	–	Yes	Yes, with *unless*	Yes
Second	–	Yes	Yes, with *unless*	Yes
Third	–	–	Yes	Yes
Other	–	–	–	as long as, if ever/ only and in case

Table 7.8 Conditionals in *The New Cambridge English Course*

	1	2	3	4
Zero	–	–	–	–
First	Yes ('conditional structures')	Yes ('*if* clauses (open)')	–	–
Second		Yes ('*if* clauses (hypothetical)'; *If I were you …*)	Yes ('hypothetical *if* clauses with simple past and *would*')	–
Third		Yes ('unfulfilled past conditionals' / 'past conditional tense')	Yes ('past conditionals'), with *would/might/could have*	*if … would have*
Other	*Do you mind if …?*	use of *if* and *when*	–	–

this course is in terminology: Swan and Walter do not use the numbered system for conditionals but favour terms such as 'open', 'hypothetical', 'unfulfilled' and 'past'. However, while the terminology is different, the paradigms are the same and coverage across the four levels follows a now familiar progression from 'open conditionals' at the lowest level, with the addition of 'hypothetical' and '(unfulfilled) past conditionals' at higher levels. Zero conditionals are not included.

Finally, coverage in the first edition of the *Headway* series (Soars & Soars, 1986, 1987, 1989, 1991, 1993; Beaven *et al.*, 1995) is shown in Table 7.9.

Table 7.9 Conditionals in *Headway*

	Beginner	Elementary	Pre-intermediate	Intermediate	Upper-Intermediate	Advanced
Zero	–	–	–	Yes	–	–
First	–	–	Yes	Yes	–	–
Second	–	–	Yes	Yes	–	–
Third	–	–	–	–	Yes	–
Other	–	–	–	–	–	Mixed conditionals

The original two *Headway* books – published at Intermediate and Upper-Intermediate levels – cover the three canonical conditional types and the zero conditional (Intermediate level covers the zero, first and second conditionals; Upper Intermediate the third conditional). As the series expanded, eventually reaching six levels, the coverage was spread out: first and second conditionals were added to Pre-Intermediate, and 'mixed conditionals' were covered at the Advanced level.

7.3.5 Discussion

The evolution of the teaching of conditional forms appears overall to have gone through the following steps, reflecting, as we will see with the other case studies, a general trend of a change in focus from item to pattern:

- a focus, particularly in earlier grammars, only on verb form, particularly that of the verb in the *if* clause when it is a 'subjunctive';
- the development of a categorisation system for conditional sentences, combining a focus on verbs with a focus on longer, overarching patterns;
- the 'fixing' of the three-way paradigmatic analysis first found in Allen's (1947) *Living English Structure*, with any conditional forms that do not conform to one of the three types gradually becoming seen as 'variations' on them;
- the establishment of a teaching sequence of the conditional types across levels, with first and second conditionals taught first, third conditionals next, and, at higher levels, other 'variations' beyond these.

Based on the coverage in Jonson and Murray, conditional forms do not seem historically to have been associated with a large number of prescriptive rules. Rather, it is in ELT that prescriptivism has increased, and this occurred in combination with the change in focus from item (verb form) to pattern (conditional paradigm). As we have seen, contemporary ELT treatments involve the prescription of three monolithic sentence paradigms containing *if* clauses instead of a focus on verb forms. The unfortunate effect of this for the learner is both an increase in complexity (two verb forms must be learnt for every conditional 'type'), and a decrease in flexibility (other verb form combinations are seen as variations from a core form, and either left until higher levels or ignored completely).

7.4 Case Study B: Relative Clauses

7.4.1 Historical grammars

Relative clauses are mentioned only in passing in Jonson's (1640) *English Grammar*, and what limited coverage there is focuses primarily on relative pronouns and adverbs, rather than the relative clause as a whole. Jonson reports the existence of one (and only one, by implication) relative pronoun – *which* (1640: 89) – although he later notes that *that* is also 'used for a relative' (1640: 123). He observes that at times the relative pronoun can be omitted, which he notes was barbarous in Greek and Latin, but that 'the Hebrews notwithstanding use it' (1640: 116). He also gives examples in which '[a]dverbs stand instead of relatives' (for example, *where* in the sentence 'And little worth is fairness in certain in a person, where no virtue is seen' (1640: 135)).

Murray (1795) does not attempt to provide an overarching explanation of relative clauses or to categorise them. As we said in Chapter 3, it was Murray's stated aim to set out guidance particularly in 'cases which custom has left dubious', so it is not a surprise, and is consistent with many other chapters in his grammar, that most of his discussion of relative clauses consists of rules and observations on a large number of small, 'local' points related to syntax. The closest we get to an analysis at a broader level is in a discussion of the difference in use suggested by the use or non-use of a comma before a relative pronoun. This he seems unable to describe with complete clarity, stating only that 'when two members, or phrases, are closely connected by a relative, restraining the general notion of the antecedent to a particular sense, the comma should be omitted' (1795: 238). He also provides some discussion of relativiser choice, explaining the difference in use, for example, between *who, which, that* and *what*, noting the 'declination' of *who* into *whose* and *whom*, and also *which* into *whose* (1795: 55), although the latter is later argued to be not 'generally pleasing' (1795: 138). Further general comments include the explanation that relative pronouns 'serve to connect sentences', and always go before the verb in the relative clause, even if they are the object of the verb (1795: 116).

In terms of the coverage of 'local' points related to syntax, there are far too many to provide a comprehensive account of here, but the list below offers the reader a 'flavour' of the content (some items on the list would not be out of place in a contemporary pedagogical explanation):

- after superlatives, and the word 'same', the preference for *that* over *who* or *which* as a relative pronoun (1795: 136);
- with an antecedent that is both person and thing, it is possible only to use *that*, not *who* or *which* (e.g. The woman, and the estate, *that* became his portion were too much for his moderation' (1795: 136));
- the fact that relative pronouns do not show number, and are therefore sometimes ambiguous, e.g. in the phrase 'the disciples of Christ, whom we imitate', where 'whom' could refer to both 'disciples' and 'Christ' (1795: 138);
- the use of 'where' as a relative adverb in relative clauses, which Murray says is 'an imitation of the French idiom' that 'it would be better to avoid' (1795: 171);

- omission of the relative pronoun, as in 'This is the man they love', compared with 'This is the man *whom* they love' (1795: 190); Murray does not explain exactly when this omission is possible and argues that while it is 'intelligible, and is allowable in conversation and epistolary writing [...] in all writings of a serious and dignified kind, it ought to be avoided' (1795: 275).

Jespersen (1933) covers relative clauses in detail. At times the terminology and analysis is close to that found in modern ELT pedagogical grammar, but at other times there are significant differences. Perhaps the most fundamental difference is the overall categorisation system, which, 'with regard to form', divides relative clauses into three types, as follows (1933: 359):

- clauses with one of the two *wh*-pronouns, *who* and *which*;
- clauses without any connecting word: 'contact clauses';
- clauses with one of the connecting words, *that, as, but*.

This system differs from contemporary ELT treatments in a number of ways. Firstly, relative clauses without a relative pronoun – Jespersen uses the term 'contact clauses' – are treated as a separate type, whereas in modern ELT descriptions this phenomenon is simply framed as a potential feature of defining relative clauses. Secondly, Jespersen conflates relative clauses with *that* with other clauses using the co-ordinators *as* and *but*. Finally, and most notably, Jespersen does not describe defining and non-defining clauses as different types of relative clause. This is not to say that Jespersen does not describe the difference – he does, in detail, but the difference is not described as being a question of form or type. Jespersen's note that in written, non-restrictive clauses 'a comma often comes before a *wh*-clause, especially if it is continuative' (1933: 359), is also interesting; the use of the comma, invariably mandated in ELT materials and in contemporary style guides, is not, in Jespersen's judgement, an absolute requirement, and does not appear to have been so historically (see for example Jonson's (1640: vi–vii) non-use of commas in what appear to be defining clauses). This perhaps explains why he did not consider the difference between defining and non-defining clauses as being a question of form.

A full account of Jespersen's extensive coverage is again beyond the scope of this summary; however, some other noteworthy inclusions are the following:

- an explanation that the belief that the relative pronoun *that* is taking over from *who* and *which* is wrong (Jespersen provides an example from the *Spectator* magazine which 'complains of the injury done recently to the two pronouns *who* and *which* by the 'Jacksprat' *that*'); according

to Jespersen, the historical process was actually the opposite, with *who* and *which* 'gaining ground at the expense of *that*' (1933: 359);
- 'double restriction': the use of a relative clause inside another relative clause (e.g. Can you mention any one that we know who is as talented as he? (1933: 358));
- the high frequency of contact clauses, including when the relative clause begins with *there is* (1933: 361), and when the relative pronoun is, or would be, the predicative in the relative clause (1933: 361);
- the placement of a preposition of place at the end of a relative clause (1933: 365), and situations when this is not possible (1933: 366).

7.4.2 Historical pedagogical grammars

Palmer's (1924: 211) treatment divides relative clauses into two types, which seems to reflect contemporary coverage but with different terminology:

- determinative use (apparently equivalent to 'defining relative clauses');
- parenthetical use (apparently equivalent to 'non-defining relative clauses').

A peculiarity of Palmer's treatment, however, is that he uses brackets, rather than commas, in his examples of 'parenthetical use', for example in the following two sentences:

> The letter wasn't important, but the parcel (which came this morning) was very important.
>
> The school (where I used to teach) is just over there. (1924: 211)

It is unclear whether Palmer is suggesting the use of brackets as the correct punctuation with 'parenthetical' clauses; however, he does not mention the use of commas at any point. The effect of the choice of punctuation, and also the somewhat ambiguous nature of the examples, is such that it is not unambiguously clear whether Palmer's 'parenthetical use' actually equates to a 'non-defining relative clause'.

Palmer identifies three types of 'relative connectives' (i.e. relativisers): relative pronouns (*that, who, which*), the 'relative determinative *whose*' and relative adverbs (*when, where, why, as*). Palmer notes that *that* is the most common of the relative pronouns, but claims that the use of *who* or *which* 'gives greater precision' and is also 'considered more elegant, especially when referring to persons' (1924: 212). No explanation is given as to why *who* and *that* are more precise or are considered more elegant (nor by whom they are considered so), but this comment appears to reflect the suspicion about the use of *that* as a relative pronoun found in prescriptive grammar rules of the time, and that is also mentioned by Jespersen (see above). Curiously, and adding to the confusion outlined above about what exactly Palmer's 'parenthetical use' refers to, Palmer does not explain that the pronoun *that* is not used in non-defining clauses – something that would be unthinkable in a modern pedagogical grammar.

Allen's (1947) coverage of relative clauses more or less aligns with contemporary pedagogical accounts, especially in the way he builds his coverage around the defining vs. non-defining distinction. He states at the start of the section that the best way to approach the 'apparently haphazard system of relatives' is by dividing them 'in their two main groups of defining and non-defining relatives' (1947: 222), arguing that defining relatives should be taught first as they constitute 'by far the greater number of relatives in general use'. Allen's explanation of the difference between the two types of clause will be largely familiar to anyone acquainted with modern pedagogical explanations: he states that a defining clause 'cannot be omitted, since without it we cannot define [the noun it refers to]' (1947: 223), while a non-defining clause 'can be left out without any material damage to the sense' (1947: 227). He also notes the use of the comma, or in speech a pause, before a non-defining clause.

Allen's explanation extends Palmer's treatment by separating out medial-position and clause-final non-defining relative clauses (Palmer focused exclusively on the former). Allen calls these 'parenthetic' and 'connective' clauses respectively, giving the following examples:

parenthetic: My wife, who lives in New York, has just written me a letter.

connective: He has two sisters, who work in the Ministry.

In his discussion of these forms, Allen shows a level of insight not found in other grammars of the time, or in many contemporary accounts (see Chapter 6). He notes that non-defining relative clauses are quite frequent in writing (1947: 227) but are uncommon in speech except as a connective (1947: 233); after giving an example of a parenthetic non-defining clause, he states that 'the above sentence would never occur in spoken English, but is quite a normal written English construction'.

There are some peculiarities, however, in how Allen deals with relative pronouns and relative clauses with prepositions. He presents his system in a format somewhat reminiscent of the grammars of classical languages (1947: 222–223), as shown in Figure 7.1. The pronouns in parentheses are those that can be omitted; those in square brackets are 'acceptable alternatives' which Allen says are '*not* recommended for active teaching' (1947: 222).

Many aspects of this system are puzzling. For example, no rationale is given for why the use of the relativiser *which* as the subject in defining clauses is not recommended for teaching, or why Allen ignores it altogether as object. Similarly, *that* is also not recommended for teaching

		People	Things
A. *Defining Relative.*			
Subject	. .	who, [that]	that, [which]
Object	. .	(that)	(that)
Preposition	.	(that) ... preposition	(that) ... preposition
Possessive	.	whose	of which [whose]
B. *Non-defining Relative.*			
Subject	. .	..., who ...,	..., which ...,
Object	. .	..., whom ...,	..., which ...,
Preposition	.	..., preposition + whom ..., [..., who(m) ... preposition],	..., preposition + which ..., [..., which ... preposition],
Possessive		..., whose ...,	..., of which ..., [..., whose] ...,

Figure 7.1 Allen's system for relativisers

as subject but is allowed as object. Part of the explanation may be found in the more prescriptive accounts of the era: advice to use *that* in defining clauses, and *which* in non-defining clauses (also found in contemporary style guides) goes back at least to Fowler's (1926) *A Dictionary of Modern English Usage*, a title Allen must have been familiar with as he included it in his list of 'some useful books for further reference' (1947: x). This, however, does not explain the recommendation not to teach *that* as subject for human antecedents, advice which seems to reflect a separate prescriptivist notion: the idea that *who* should be preferred over *that*, because the latter – in the words of Fowler – can give the sensation of 'depriving [people] of their humanity' (1926: 716). Indeed Allen himself states that 'custom prefers *who* [over *that*] in the subject for persons' (1947: 223), although here we should perhaps interpret the word 'custom' as meaning 'prescriptive grammar rules'. It still remains unclear, though, why in Allen's system *that* is suggested for human antecedents as objects of a relative clause, and *who* or *whom* are ignored.

In addition to the elements discussed above, Allen's detailed treatment includes – among others – the following points:

- a warning not to move the adverb away from the verb in 'inseparable adverbial phrases' (according to Allen, the sentence 'The courage he faced his enemies with' is impossible as *with* is inseparable from the verb *faced*.) (1947: 240);
- the use of *that* as 'a short cut in clauses of a relative type' (1947: 239), as follows:
  - 'ellipse' (e.g. *He did it in the way (that)* [= in which] *I should have done it myself)*;

- to indicate time (e.g. *by the time (that) you have finished*) and place (e.g. *I'll go anywhere (that) you want me to*);
- in 'forms with introductory "it"', without using the name 'cleft sentence' or identifying the structure as a 'standalone' grammar point;
- the use of relative *as* after *as, same, such*, and *so*;
- the partitive use of *of* (e.g. *I have two friends, both of whom are on holiday at the moment.*) (1947: 240);
- 'double relatives' (1947: 238), equivalent to Jespersen's 'double restriction';
- the need to use *that* (not *who* or *which*), or to omit the pronoun entirely, when it is predicative (e.g. *She's not the woman she was before she married*) (1947: 238);
- the invariable use of *that*, rather than *who* or *which*, before *there is*;
- the use of *that*, rather than *who* or *which*, after *all*;
- the explanation that *wh-* pronouns were originally only used in interrogative clauses, and only later started to be used in relative clauses (1947: 236).

It is noteworthy – and very strong evidence of how much Jespersen's work also influenced Allen – that all of the points in the above list are also included in Jespersen's *Essentials of English Grammar*. In fact, not only are many details shared by both books, but there are even some strikingly similar example phrases and sentences; compare, for example, the example 'It was all he could do to keep from screaming' (1933: 361) in Jespersen's account, with Allen's 'It was all (that) I could do to keep myself from laughing' (1947: 238). Allen also refers to the same *Spectator* article as Jespersen that called *that* a 'Jacksprat'.

Thomson and Martinet's (1960) treatment feels a step closer to modern accounts, while still retaining some aspects of the older descriptions outlined above. The fact that the title of the chapter is 'relative pronouns' rather than 'relative clauses' suggests that the primary focus will be on the individual pronoun, but the authors in fact begin with a definition of defining relative clauses as a whole before discussing relative pronouns.

Relative pronouns are set out in a similar style to that found in Allen (1947), with a strong focus on grammatical case; the authors note that 'accusative' pronouns are often omitted in defining relative clauses (1960: 31). The system is reproduced in Figure 7.2. While the manner of presentation is similar to Allen's, there are some significant departures. Firstly, the idea of 'not actively teaching' nominative *that* and *which* for people and things respectively is not repeated; furthermore, both 'accusative' (to use Thomson and Martinet's choice of terminology) *who* and *whom* are included for people, as is 'accusative' *which* for things, in addition to *whose* as a possessive form for things. The word *what* is also identified as a relative pronoun. These differences seem to suggest a move away from the somewhat prescriptive 'straitjacket' of Allen's system.

[For defining relative clauses]			
For persons:	Nominative:	who that	
	Accusative:	whom who that	
	Possessive:	whose	
For things:	Nominative:	which that	
	Accusative:	which that	
	Possessive:	whose of which	
[For non-defining relative clauses]			
	Nominative	*Accusative*	*Possessive*
a for persons:	who	whom, who	whose
b for things:	which	which	of which, whose

Figure 7.2 Thomson and Martinet's (1960: 31–32) system for relativisers

Thomson and Martinet's descriptions do, however, contain their own prescriptive elements. Learners are told that, as far as the choice between *who*, *whom* and *that* is concerned, *whom* is the 'technically correct accusative form', even though this 'is considered very formal and seldom used in spoken English' (1960: 51). Similarly, it is also argued that 'in technically correct English the preposition is placed before the relative pronoun', with *whom* used, even though 'in informal speech [...] it is more usual to move the preposition to the end of the clause'. In both cases it is the form associated with a formal, written register that is considered 'technically correct', with other forms presented as deviations from this. This is particularly clear in the description of the structure of relative clauses with prepositions, where the authors state that in informal speech, 'it is more usual to *move* the preposition to the end of the clause' (1960: 32, emphasis added), suggesting a default position, which is then modified in spoken language.

Thomson and Martinet's primary focus when discussing non-defining relative clauses is on those in medial-position, as in contemporary accounts. The authors note that 'this construction is fairly formal and more common in written than in spoken English' (1960: 34), but, paradoxically, the examples given often seem to reflect spoken contexts (for example, the word 'this' in the example sentence 'This sherry, which I paid 25/- for, is awful' seems to imply the immediacy of spoken interaction, not written prose). It is unfortunate that Allen's approach to medial- and end-position clauses is not replicated, as it seems that Thomson and Martinet's focus on end-position clauses set the pattern for future accounts.

To finish, the authors offer an emphatic reminder of 'the importance of commas in [non-defining] relative clauses'. This forms an interesting contrast to Jespersen's observation, only half a century earlier, that the comma is 'often' used in this context.

7.4.3 Historical coursebooks

The *Essential English* series (Eckersley, 1938, 1940, 1941, 1942) covers relative clauses as part of a more general focus on subordinate clauses; he refers to them as 'adjective clauses', and they are covered in Book 3 (of four), as illustrated in Table 7.10. With the exception of a single practice exercise, they are not found in Book 4. The focus in Book 3 appears is almost exclusively on defining relative clauses, although they are not named as such. However, one example – 'Joe Marsden who looks after Lucille's car is a very good mechanic' (1941: 56) – appears, despite the punctuation, to be a non-defining clause. Whether the lack of commas suggests that Eckersley did not consider them essential in non-defining clauses (like Jespersen), or that he was not himself familiar with the distinction between defining and non-defining clauses, is unclear.

Book 3 also covers omission of the relative pronoun 'if it is in the objective case' (1941: 57); the reference to grammatical case is in line with the early pedagogical grammars already discussed and places the focus on the individual pronoun rather on the wider clause structure; as we have seen, contemporary explanations typically explain this phenomenon in terms of the pronoun being omitted if it is the object *of a relative clause*. Also present, in large, bold type, is the 'general rule' to 'Put the relative pronoun as near as possible to is antecedent' (1941: 57); this rule, which would not be out of place in a style guide or traditional school grammar, repeats Murray's advice (1795: 266) from 150 years previously but is not typically included in modern pedagogical treatments.

Hornby covers relative clauses in Books 1 and 2 of *Oxford Progressive English* (Hornby, 1954b, 1955, 1956), as shown in Table 7.11; he uses the label 'relative pronouns and clauses'. Hornby's treatment seems to be in part based on Allen's (1947) account, or at least to share a common source: in Book 1, Hornby presents, like Allen, *that* as a the 'default' relative pronoun as subject for 'things' and 'animals', with *which* given in brackets, while *who* is suggested as the default for 'persons', with *that* given in brackets (1954b: 102). Similarly, *that* is presented as the default in all cases (things, animals, persons) when the relative pronoun is the object. An interesting feature of the coverage is

Table 7.10 Relative clauses in *Essential English*

	Book 1	Book 2	Book 3	Book 4
Defining	–	–	No distinction between defining and non-defining clauses.	–
Non-defining	–	–		–
Pronouns	–	–	Use of *which, who, that* and *whom*. Use of *as* as a relative pronoun after 'the same'. Omission of relative pronoun.	–
Other	–	–	Advice to keep relative pronoun as close as possible to antecedent.	–

Table 7.11 Relative clauses in *Oxford Progressive English*

	Book 1	Book 2	Book 3
Defining	Yes	Yes	–
Non-defining	–	Yes	–
Pronouns	that, which, who, whom, whose, where	Use (and omission) of that, which, who, whom, whose and where	–
Other		–	–

that Hornby introduces the grammar focus with the traditional nursery rhyme, 'This is the house that Jack built'; coincidentally, or perhaps not, the title of this rhyme had been used as an example sentence by Eckersley in *Essential English Book 3* (1941: 55). In *Book 2* of Hornby's series, there is a detailed explanation of both defining and non-defining clauses; the exposition runs to four pages, making it one of the longest grammar sections in the book, and suggesting that Hornby considered it an important area of study at the level. The content again matches Allen's (1947) descriptions quite closely, with some minor differences.

7.4.4 Late 20th-century coursebooks

As can be seen in Table 7.12, *English Grammatical Structure* (Alexander *et al.*, 1975) covers relative clauses at Levels 3, 4 and 5 (of 6). Defining relative clauses are taught first, at Levels 3 and 4, with non-defining relative clauses left to Level 5.

The authors appear to largely abandon the pronoun systems adopted in Allen (1947) and in Thomson and Martinet (1960), with *who*, *that* and *which* presented as being equally possible as both the subject and object in defining relative clauses. The 'zero pronoun' (i.e. no pronoun) is presented as the default object form, with *who*, *whom* or *that* presented as alternatives. Level 4 extends the coverage, including defining relative clauses with the relative pronouns *whose*, *whom* and *which*.

Table 7.12 Relative clauses in *English Grammatical Structure*

	Level 1	Level 2	Level 3	Level 4	Level 5	Level 6
Defining	–	–	Yes	Yes	Yes	–
Non-defining	–	–	–	–	Yes, including those that 'refer to the whole previous clause'	–
Pronouns	–	–	that, which, who(m); 'zero'	that, which, 'zero', who(m); whose, when, where, why	as previous levels	–
Other	–	–	clause-final prepositions	the way in which; prepositions before relative pronouns (with note on register); all that	quantifier + of + relative pronoun	–

The pronoun *whom* is noted to be 'more appropriate in formal talk or writing' (1975: 140), as is the use of a preposition before *whom*. Finally, like Allen, and Jespersen before him, the authors state that the pronoun *that*, rather than *which*, should be used after *all*. Level 5 recapitulates the previous coverage, adding non-defining relative clauses, including comment (continuative) clauses; Alexander *et al.* do not name these, but simply note that they 'refer to the whole previous clause'.

Overall, *English Grammatical Structure* appears to represent a departure from the approach in Eckersley and Hornby. It splits coverage across levels, covering defining clauses first, and non-defining clauses at later levels, and also dividing relative pronouns and adverbs into groups, each dealt with separately. As we saw in Chapter 6, this is an approach that endures in the current consensus.

There are a number of similarities in the coverage in *Streamline* (Hartley & Viney, 1978, 1979, 1982, 1985), *Strategies* (Abbs & Freebairn, 1977, 1979, 1980, 1982) and *The New Cambridge English Course* (Swan & Walter, 1990a, 1990b, 1992a, 1992b), as can be seen in Tables 7.13–7.15. Common to all three is the overall sequencing: all three ignore relative clauses at the lowest level, teach defining relative clauses at the second level and then non-defining clauses later. At the highest level, all three series teach both defining and non-defining relative clauses. *Streamline* and *Strategies* also cover a larger number of relative pronouns, but these are less prominent in *The Cambridge English Course*.

Table 7.13 Relative clauses in *Strategies*

	Starting	Building	Developing	Studying
Defining	–	Yes	Yes	Yes
Non-defining	–	–	–	Yes
Pronouns	–	who and which	who, whose, where	who, which, that, whose, where
Other				

Table 7.14 Relative clauses in *Streamline*

	Departures	Connections	Destinations	Directions
Defining	–	Yes	Yes	Yes
Non-defining	–	–	Yes	Yes (included in exercises)
Pronouns	–	that, omission of relative pronoun	who, which, that where, whose, whom	where, whom, which, when, who
Other	–	–	use of *with* and *-ing* instead of relative clause	preposition + *whom/which*; *of which, of whom three, many of whom*

Table 7.15 Relative clauses in *The New Cambridge English Course*

	Book 1	Book 2	Book 3	Book 4
Defining	–	Yes	Yes	Yes ('identifying')
Non-defining	–	–	–	Yes ('non-identifying')
Pronouns	–	that, who, where, zero	that, zero	zero, whose, who(m), which
Other	–	end position of pronoun	end position of prepositions in relative clauses	reduced relative clauses

Table 7.16 Relative clauses in *Headway*

	Beginner	Elementary	Pre-intermediate	Intermediate	Upper-Intermediate	Advanced
Defining	–	–	–	–	Yes	Yes
Non-defining	–	–	–	–	Yes (only in endmatter)	Yes
Pronouns	–	–	–	–	who, that, whom, which, whose, what, why, when, where, zero	–
Other	–	–	–	–	end position of prepositions	–

The first editions of *Headway* (Soars & Soars, 1986, 1987, 1989, 1991, 1993; Beaven *et al.*, 1995) cover relative clauses only at the highest two levels, as illustrated in Table 7.16. Coverage in the endmatter is interesting in that learners are told that, when subject of a defining relative clause, the relativisers *that* for a human antecedent and *which* for a non-human antecedent are not as common as *who* and *that* respectively (1986: 118). This is exactly in line with Allen's coverage from some 40 years earlier: the relativisers suggested by *Headway* as being less common are those that Allen, as we saw earlier, recommended should not be 'actively taught'.

7.4.5 Discussion

The gradual evolution of pedagogical descriptions of relative clauses has involved the adoption of a binary distinction between defining and non-defining relative clauses as the main categorisation principle, despite the fact that historically different divisions were made. The use of commas – one of the key features of non-defining clauses in contemporary accounts – does not seem to have always been universally accepted or seen as important but gradually became so. However, Allen's (1947: 222) assertion that relative clauses are 'best approached by teaching them from the beginning in their two main groups of *defining* and *non-defining* relatives' seems to have signalled the beginning of a new approach, one which endures in contemporary accounts.

As with conditional forms, it is again possible to observe a shift in focus in coverage over the years from item to pattern, with older grammars focusing mainly on the correct choice of relative pronoun, and almost completely ignoring different types of relative clause and their functions. This is perhaps epitomised in Murray's treatment, which – as is often the case in his work – focuses on a large range of very specific details on usage, such as which relativiser to use with antecedent consisting of both a person and a thing, without any attempt to provide an overall account of relative clauses. As the 20th century unfolded, however, pedagogical grammars progressively took a more balanced approach, focusing equally on clause and choice of relativiser.

At times, older prescriptive attitudes or a preference for written standards appear to emerge even in relatively more recent accounts, such as in Thomson and Martinet's assertion that the 'technically correct' position of a preposition in a relative clause is before the relative pronoun. In general, though, through the decades the prescriptive style found in older treatments gradually disappears. Finally, and as in all three case studies discussed in this chapter, it is at times possible to find examples of the direct influence of one title on another. This can be seen, for instance, in content and example sentences given by Jespersen and subsequently repeated in Allen's title; a similar instance is an example sentence found in the work of Eckersley and Hornby. Equally, there are indications that *English Grammatical Structure* was a key title in defining how coverage of relative clauses can be divided across levels, influencing titles up to the present; this appears to confirm the characterisations made by many interviewees reported in the analysis in Chapter 5 of the title as being highly influential.

7.5 Case Study C: Future Forms

7.5.1 Historical grammars

Both Jonson and Murray focus almost exclusively on *will* and *shall*. Jonson (1640: 91) uses the term 'times' to refer to tense, identifying three times possible with English finite verbs: present, past and future. The 'futures', he states, 'are declared by the *infinitive*, and the *verb shall*, or *will*' (1640: 132). He also (1640: 133) gives examples of the future perfect, which he does not name, but explains as 'taking the nature of two divers[e] *times*; that is, of the *future* and the *time past*'.

Like Jonson, Murray (1795: 75) identifies two main future forms, which he calls the 'first future' and the 'second future', as follows:

- **first future**: *the sun will rise to-morrow;*
- **second future**: *I shall have dined at one o'clock.*

Perhaps surprisingly, Murray also briefly mentions *going to*, stating that – despite suggestions to the contrary in other publications at the time – 'nothing can be more obvious, than "[...] I am going to write," is a future tense'. However, he does not discuss this use elsewhere or in any more detail.

Jespersen's (1933) grammar devotes a whole chapter to *will* and *shall*, stating that *will* is used 'primarily' (1933: 271) to denote volition. Jespersen's account identifies the following uses of *will* as a future form:

- in the first person, a 'volition-coloured future', and additionally 'certainty of fulfilment, and often implies promise or threat' (e.g. 'I'll tell you some other day' (1933: 272));
- particularly in the second and third person, the 'pure future' (e.g. 'Look out, or you will be run over' (1933: 273));
- 'requests and invitations' (e.g. 'Will you come for a walk this afternoon?' (1933: 273));
- 'a mere supposition' (e.g. 'This, I think, will be the key' (1933: 275)).

All of these uses can be – or have been – found in ELT explanations.

As for *shall*, Jespersen notes the following main uses:

- in the first person, 'mere futurity' (1933: 274);
- 'fatal obligation or necessity, independent of human will' (e.g. 'Death is certaine to all, all shall dye' (1933: 276));
- promise or threat in the second and third person (e.g. 'He shall pay dearly for this affront' (1933: 272));
- 'obligation due to human will' (e.g. 'I am determined she shall have no cause to complain' (1933: 276).

The future perfect is covered in a brief note, in which he states that '*will* with the perfect infinitive' expresses the 'before-future' (1933: 275).

At the end of the chapter, Jespersen notes – almost in passing – 'the tendency to use *will* everywhere' (1933: 281). This tendency is said to be 'counteracted by the desire for clearness', leading to, among other the things, the 'growing' use of *going to*, the only reference he makes to that particular future form. Jespersen's explanations largely reflect what might be described as 'mainstream thinking' at the time (and more recently) on the differences in use between *will* and *shall*, particularly as they relate to grammatical person.[1]

In his (separate) chapter on tense, Jespersen only mentions the future briefly, noting that the present tense is sometimes used to refer to future time, 'chiefly when something is settled as part of a programme or agreement' (1933: 239). He also outlines the difference in usage of *will*, present continuous and future continuous (or 'expanded future', to use Jespersen's choice of terminology) in the following way:

- 'people will come' speaks only vaguely of the future;
- 'people are coming' speaks of the immediate future;
- 'people will be coming' refers to the coming as near, though not exactly immediate (1933: 267).

However, no additional guidance is given on what exactly would constitute an event in 'the immediate future' compared with one that is 'near, though not exactly immediate', or on what speaking 'only vaguely of the future' means in practice.

7.5.2 Historical pedagogical grammars

Palmer's (1924) detailed account of English tenses recognises four finite tenses: the present, the preterite, the future and the future preterite (1924: 146–148). In his discussion of the future and future preterite, he identifies 13 different structures (although he does not state this number explicitly). This account will focus on what he presents as the 'future tense' – structures involving *will* and *shall* – in addition to some other forms, such as present continuous and *going to*, which Palmer also discusses.

The 'future tense', for Palmer, is 'used to express actions about to take place or associated with an adverbial of future time' (1924: 147). All examples given of the 'future tense' contain either *will* or *shall* and there is no suggestion that these two modal verbs are among a number of options for talking about the future – they are simply presented as the default way of talking about future time. Palmer runs through the differences in use between the two, roughly along the lines of the account in Jespersen (1933).

Palmer also discusses the use of the future perfect and future continuous. The former is said to denote 'an action already completed before a moment or period expressed by an adverbial or future time' (e.g. 'I shall have finished my letter by the time you come back' (1924: 150)). The latter, for Palmer, is used (a) to express an action begun before and concluding after a given moment in the future'; (b) when speaking of a future action which will happen in the ordinary course of events, or which is already decided upon or anticipated' (e.g. 'I needn't write to him tonight, because I shall be seeing him tomorrow') (1924: 154–155). The phrase 'the ordinary course of events', or variants of it, is one that has been used again and again to describe this structure and is a formulation that endures, as we saw in the previous chapter, in contemporary coursebook accounts. Finally, Palmer also covers the future perfect progressive, which he describes as 'an action [...] or a state commencing before and continuing up to (and possibly beyond) the future moment or period with which it is associated' (1924: 282).

In addition to structures based around *will* and *shall*, Palmer discusses the use of:

- *going to* for 'an action [...] or a state associated with future time and implying a decision or an arrangement[2] made (or an intention already formed)', stating that the verbs *come* and *go* are 'generally excluded' from this structure (1924: 280; see Chapter 6 for more on this claimed 'exclusion');
- present continuous, which Palmer notes 'is sometimes used as a future tense, more especially with such verbs as *go, come, stay*' (1924: 154);
- the present simple to refer to the future in the case of a 'formal programme of movements or events' (1924: 281).

Although Palmer's main focus is on *will* and *shall*, his more detailed coverage of these additional future forms certainly represents an innovation. However, compared with contemporary ELT treatments it is noticeable how little assistance is to the learner on when to choose or prefer one future form over another. For example, it is unclear how useful Palmer's statement that the present continuous 'is sometimes used as a future tense' would be, or how exactly a term such as 'immediate future' should be understood. This again recalls the distinction between 'constitutive' and 'communicative' grammar rules (Williams, 1994); Palmer provides details on form here, but does not provide the reader with enough information on how to choose one form over the other (with the exception of the traditional rules on *will* and *shall*). This criticism can also be levelled at Jespersen's account, but, as we shall see, it is apparent that as the 20th century progressed, pedagogical grammars started to be more effective in aiding learners in this area.

As with the other two areas of grammar discussed in this chapter, Allen's (1947) account of future forms appears to represent a significant step towards contemporary descriptions, and offers many improvements on the older grammars. Describing the problem of choosing between tenses as 'a very vexing one' (1947: 117), he acknowledges that the traditional rules for *will* and *shall* are 'already antiquated', but despite this he nonetheless dedicates a large amount of space to differences in use between them. The explanations revolve partly around the question of which forms should be considered 'pure future'. He calls *will* and *shall* the 'normal pure (or colourless) future', stating that they are used for future actions that 'depend upon some external factors' (1947: 119), and 'not on any person's will or intention' (1947: 121). The exception to this is their use in the first person, in which context it is said that *will* 'colours the future with the speaker's intention or promise' (1947: 121). In contrast, *shall* is said to 'colour' the future with 'promise, compulsion or (in negative) restraint' (1947: 130), for example in the sentences 'You shall have it back tomorrow' and 'He shall never come here again'.

Compared with modern accounts, perhaps the biggest difference in Allen's explanations is the lack of reference to the use of *will* to make predictions.

Allen describes *going to* as 'increasingly popular', an affirmation confirmed by modern studies (see, for example, Leech *et al.*, 2009), but states that it sometimes sounds 'out of place', although without explaining why or when (1947: 117). His advice to the reader is to use *will* 'when in doubt' and to 'beware of the innocent-looking "going to" form' (Allen, 1947: 117). Nevertheless, the latter receives far more attention than in previous titles. Allen states that its 'fundamental meaning' is, with a human as subject, 'intention and certainty' (e.g. 'He's going to give me a new one tomorrow'), and with a non-human as subject, 'probability and inevitability *in the mind of the speaker*' (e.g. 'Look out! The tram's going to overturn!') (1947: 124). These two descriptions appear to be in line with modern treatments, with the latter equivalent to 'predictions with president evidence'.

In addition, Allen describes the use of the present continuous as a future form, the future perfect and also the future continuous. The latter is contrasted with both *going to* and *will*. In the comparison with *going to*, Allen states that *going to* shows 'the present intentions of the actors', compared with the future continuous, which 'tells of the *results* of the intention, but by-passes the intention itself' (1947: 128). In the contrast with *will*, the following distinction is made:

Will you come again tomorrow? (invitation)

Will you be coming again tomorrow? (in the ordinary course of events) (1947: 134)

Finally, in a separate section, Allen also describes an alternative use of the future perfect: the 'future of assumption' (e.g. 'You'll have noticed from my lecture how complicated this subject really is' (1947: 144)). As McCarthy (2015) notes, this use (although not strictly a 'future form', as defined here) is not typically covered in modern pedagogical explanations despite its apparent usefulness. Overall, what stands out most in Allen's account is his attempt to explain differences in use (beyond the traditional explanations of the differences between *will* and *shall*) between the various English future forms; despite the ambivalence in some of the explanations, this is quite a development and would presumably have been welcomed by teachers and learners.

On first encountering Thompson and Martinet's (1960) chapter on the future, the reader has the initial impression that the contents will follow familiar themes, as they state from the outset that 'the future tense in English is **shall/will**' (1960: 118). However, the authors immediately go on to say that 'this tense is not used nearly so often as students naturally expect', and consequently deal with other future forms before looking at *will* and *shall* – a not inconsiderable innovation.

Thompson and Martinet's coverage starts with the use of the present simple, 'for a planned future action or a serious of actions' (1960: 118), before moving on to the present continuous, described as being used for a 'definite future arrangement', with 'little or no idea of intention' (1960: 118–119). The *going to* future is then said to (a) show the speaker's 'intention to perform a certain future action […] the intention is always premeditated', and (b) to 'express the speaker's feeling of certainty'. Like Palmer, Thomson and Martinet state that 'it is not very usual to put the verbs **go** and **come** into the **going to** form'.

When they arrive at *will* and *shall*, Thomson and Martinet's account returns to the familiar discussions on the differences in use relating to grammatical person, although there is far less detail than in the older titles examined. The modal *shall* is said to be the 'grammatically correct form' in the first person, although the authors do not explain what exactly they mean by 'grammatically correct'. They do, however, note that 'many people avoid **shall** except in the interrogative', and that – almost in the exact words of Allen – learners 'should therefore use **will** when in doubt' (1960: 121). A number of specific uses of the 'future tense' (i.e. *will* and *shall*) are identified (1960: 201–202), before the authors move on to the future continuous and future perfect. In a separate section, they also note, like Allen, that *will*, including the future perfect, can be used to introduce an assumption (1960: 140).

Thomson and Martinet's chapter, like Allen's, has a number of sections that attempt to explain differences in usage between future forms. As we have said, this is a major difference between these two later grammars and, for example, Palmer's grammar, and seems to reflect a growing understanding of the need to provide this kind of information to teachers and learners. Thomson and Martinet's discussion is particularly detailed, covering the difference between *going to* and *will* (1960: 123); the present continuous and the future continuous (the future continuous is said to be used for an action that – again echoing the words of Palmer – 'will occur in the normal course of events' (1960: 207)); and *will* and the future continuous (1960: 207).

7.5.3 Historical coursebooks

Eckersley (1938, 1940, 1941, 1942) covers future forms only in the first two levels of four ('future in the past' is covered in Book 3, and will not be discussed), as can be seen in Table 7.17. Book 1 covers *will/shall*, *going to* and present continuous. The main focus is on *will* and *shall*, which Eckersley calls the 'future tense'. The difference between *will* and *shall* is not discussed, with a note simply stating that in the first person 'we sometimes use "shall" and sometimes "will"' and a footnote promising that this will be explained at the following level (1938: 130). Eckersley also explains that 'we sometimes express a future meaning using the present

Table 7.17 Future forms in *Essential English*

	Book 1	Book 2	Book 3	Book 4
***will* (+ *shall*)**	Yes (the 'future tense')	Yes – *will* + *shall* with discussion of differences.	–	–
going to	Yes – 'another way of expressing the future'	Yes – 'intention' and 'strong probability'	–	–
present continuous	Yes	–	–	–
future perfect	–	Yes	–	–
future continuous	–	Yes	–	–
other	–	Future passive	Future in the past	–

continuous, often with a word or phrase like *to-morrow*, *next week* etc.' (1938: 132), and learners also see examples of *going to*, described as 'another way of expressing the future' (1938: 144). The use of the three future forms is not contrasted in any way.

In Book 2, Eckersley fulfils his earlier promise and explains the difference between *will* and *shall* along familiar lines, noting differences between Scottish and English speakers, and among English speakers, on their use (1940: 82–84). Book 2 also repeats *going to*, which – in something of a departure from other titles of the era – is described as the 'commonest and easiest way of expressing the future' (1940: 86). Eckersley states that it shows intention (1940: 86) and strong probability (1940: 87), but it cannot be used for 'simple futurity'. As an example of strong probability, Eckersley gives the sentence, 'I think it's going to rain' (1940: 87), but does not mention the idea of prediction with present evidence (as in contemporary explanations). 'Simple futurity' is not defined, but Eckersley states that the sentence, 'I'm going to be 12 years old tomorrow' is not possible (1940: 86). Book 2 also contains explanations of the future continuous and the future perfect.

Coverage of future forms in *Oxford Progressive English* (Hornby, 1954b, 1955, 1956) is comparatively light, as can be seen in Table 7.18 below. Book 1 covers *will/shall*, which Hornby calls the 'pure future' (perhaps under influence of Allen) and *going to*. In the examples presented, *shall* is used in the first person, and *will* in the second and third person, but this is not explained. A number of functions of *will/shall* are covered and subsequently revised at the beginning of Book 2. Following this, Book 3 revises *going to*, and adds the future continuous and present continuous. From a modern perspective, it is a surprise to see the future use of the present continuous taught only at the highest level.

Hornby describes the future progressive as 'a polite way of asking about the future' (e.g. 'Shall (or Will) you being staying here long?' (1956: 64)), rather than as being used to refer to an action in progress at

Table 7.18 Future forms in *Oxford Progressive English*

	Book 1	Book 2	Book 3
will (+ shall)	Yes ('pure future' + promises, polite requests, offers of service, suggestions and obligation)	Yes (revision)	Yes (as part of future continuous focus)
going to	Yes	Yes (revision)	Yes (as part of future continuous focus)
present continuous	–	–	Yes (as part of future continuous focus)
future perfect	–	–	–
future continuous	–	–	Yes
Other	–	–	–

a particular future time. This is interesting as in modern coursebooks, the focus is typically on the temporal reference of the future continuous, with its potential pragmatic use given as an additional detail. Book 3 also contains a section comparing *will/shall*, present continuous, *going to* and future continuous. The comparison is similar to that offered by Allen, but with somewhat different interpretations. Finally, Hornby describes the difference between *going to* and future continuous in a way that touches on Allen's idea of something happening 'in the ordinary course of events'. The future perfect is not covered at all.

7.5.4 Late 20th-century coursebooks

English Grammatical Structure (Alexander *et al.*, 1975) is somewhat unusual in its coverage, in that future forms are covered at only three out of six levels, as seen in Table 7.19. At Level 2, *will* with a 'simple future reference' (1975: 48) in included, perhaps analogous to the idea of 'pure

Table 7.19 Future forms in *English Grammatical Structure*

	Level 1	Level 2	Level 3	Level 4	Level 5	Level 6
will (+ shall)	–	Yes, including *shall*.	–	–	Yes (immediate future)	–
going to	–	Yes (intentions and predictions)	–	–	Yes (predictions)	–
present continuous	–	–	–	–	Yes (present intention or plan)	–
future perfect	–	–	–	Yes	–	–
future continuous	–	–	–	Yes	Yes	–
other	–	–	–	future perfect continuous	present simple; *be to …*; *be just about to* (immediate future)	–

future' in older grammars; the use of *will* as a feature of formal style is also covered. The modal *shall* is mentioned simply as 'an optional replacement for *will* after *I* or *we*', a clear move away from the old prescriptive rules. Level 2 also includes the use of *going to* as a future showing intention and for making predictions with 'present signs'; like Palmer, Alexander *et al.* also include 'just going to' (1975: 48).

Level 4 introduces future perfect, future continuous and future perfect continuous. All three are described simply as having future time reference (1975: 129); no reference is made to uses parallel to Allen's 'future of supposition'. Perhaps the biggest surprise is that the use of the present continuous is introduced for the first time only at Level 5, in contrast with modern coursebook series, which invariably cover it at the earliest levels. Level 5 also includes the use of *will* to refer to 'immediate future' (e.g. 'I'll post your letter now' (1975: 159)), perhaps analogous to the use of *will* for promises generally identified in contemporary materials.

Level 5 also repeats the future continuous 'as an alternative to [the present continuous], with less emphasis on present plan and more on future action' (1975: 159). Yet another interpretation of the future continuous, this is nevertheless similar to Allen's description of it as focusing on the results of an intention, but 'by-passing' the intention itself. Finally, the use of the present simple for events 'fixed by schedule' or on a 'fixed date' is included, as well as *be to* and *be just about to* (1975: 159).

As can be seen in Tables 7.20–7.22, the coverage in *Strategies* (Abbs & Freebairn, 1977, 1979, 1980, 1982), *Streamline* (Hartley & Viney, 1978, 1979, 1982, 1985) and *The New Cambridge English Course* (Swan & Walter, 1990a, 1990b, 1992a, 1992b) seems to suggest a growing consensus on which future forms should be included; all cover the five canonical future forms, and in approximately the same sequence, with lower levels covering some or all of *will*, *going to* and present continuous, before future perfect and future continuous are covered at higher levels; *shall* is largely abandoned.

Coverage in *Streamline* and *The Cambridge English Course* is very similar in terms of content and sequencing. The lowest levels of both

Table 7.20 Future forms in *Strategies*

	Starting Strategies	Building Strategies	Developing Strategies	Studying Strategies
will (+ *shall*)	–	Yes (arrangement, prediction)	Yes (future definite predictions)	Yes
going to	–	Yes	–	–
present continuous	–	–	Yes	–
future perfect	–	–	–	Yes
future continuous	–	–	–	Yes
other	–	–	–	–

Table 7.21 Future forms in *Streamline*

	Departures	Connections	Destinations	Directions
will (+ shall)	Yes, in questions only (including *Shall I/we ...?*)	Yes ('simple future')	Yes ('simple future')	Yes ('simple future')
going to	Yes	–	–	Yes
present continuous	Yes	–	–	–
future perfect	–	–	Yes	Yes
future continuous	–	–	Yes	Yes
other	–	–	–	Future perfect continuous

Table 7.22 Future forms in *The New Cambridge English Course*

	Book 1	Book 2	Book 3	Book 4
will (+ shall)	Yes (predictions)	Yes (predictions; agreeing and offering)	Yes (*will have to; won't* for refusals; predictions)	Yes (making offers; predictions); also *shall* in 1st person
going to	Yes (plans, predictions)	Yes (plans and intentions, predictions)	–	–
present continuous	Yes	Yes	–	–
future perfect	–	–	–	Yes
future continuous	–	–	–	Yes
other	–	*may*	–	–

cover *going to*, present continuous and *will*. Both also cover *will* at Levels 2 and 3, while *Streamline* adds the future perfect and future continuous. At the highest level, *Streamline* adds the future perfect continuous – the only series to cover this form. The highest level of *The Cambridge English Course* also covers the future perfect and future continuous. In both series, the focus of explanations of the future perfect and continuous in is on their temporal reference – no mention is made of the more pragmatic uses identified in the earlier pedagogical grammars, for example Allen's 'future of assumption'. Unusually for books in this period, *shall* in the first person in affirmative sentences is also in *The Cambridge English Course*, possibly because it features in a poem included as a text in the lesson.

Strategies does not cover future forms at the lowest level. At the second level, *will* and *going to* are taught, with *will* revised at the third level and present continuous added. This comparatively late coverage of the present continuous is a significant difference from *Streamline* and the *New Cambridge English Course*, and also from the current canon, but reflects the relatively late position it is given in Hornby's *Oxford Progressive English*, and also in *English Grammatical*

Table 7.23 Future forms in *Headway*

	Beginner	Elementary	Pre-intermediate	Intermediate	Upper-Intermediate	Advanced
will (+ *shall*)	–	–	Yes	Yes	Yes	
going to	–	Yes	Yes	Yes	Yes	
present continuous	–	–	–	Yes	Yes	
future perfect	–	–	–	–	Yes	'review of tenses'
future continuous	–	–	–	–	Yes	
other	–			future possibility (*might/could*)		

Structure. In personal communication, Ingrid Freebairn, the co-author of *Strategies*, stated that 'at the time, [the future use of the present continuous] was considered by our markets as being a more sophisticated way of expressing the future, although I wouldn't agree with that in retrospect'. Finally, like *Streamline* and the *New Cambridge English Course*, the future perfect and future continuous are covered at the highest level, again with a focus on their temporal reference than pragmatic functions.

Finally, the original two levels – Intermediate and Upper Intermediate – of *Headway* (Soars & Soars, 1986, 1987, 1989, 1991, 1993; Beaven *et al.*, 1995) also cover the five canonical future forms, as shown in Table 7.23. Intermediate level teaches *will* (for predictions, future facts, and intentions/decisions made at moment of speaking), *going to* (for future intentions, plans or decisions thought about before the moment of speaking) and present continuous (for future arrangements); at Upper Intermediate, these are all revised, and the future perfect and continuous are added, with the focus of the latter two on time reference only. Upper Intermediate also adds the predictive use of *going to*. The first edition of Elementary covers only *going to*, with both *going to* and *will* (for predictions and promises) taught at Pre-Intermediate. The original Beginner level book did not include future forms. The Advanced level contains revision of all the future forms covered.

7.5.5 Discussion

The analysis of coverage of future forms paints a picture that is somewhat different compared with the first two case studies. It is possible to observe through the 20th century a notable increase in complexity of content but also a relatively recent convergence towards a consensus on what should be taught. The accounts in Jonson, Murray and Jespersen (outside of the discussion on *will* and *shall*) are relatively brief, especially when one considers the frequency with which future forms are used, and compared with the other two areas of grammar analysed in this chapter. One reason for this comparative brevity may be related to the question of tense choice. Choosing between future forms arguably causes few or no problems for native speakers, unlike relative clauses and conditionals with their potential for syntactic complexity. As a consequence, they appear to represent an area of grammar that had simply received little attention from English grammarians over the centuries. Whatever the explanation, apart from detailed explanations of the 'traditional' rules on *will* and *shall*, the early 20th-century writers of pedagogical grammars and coursebooks had relatively little to work with when producing their own accounts. Evidence of this can be found in Allen's description of the English tense system as 'vexing' (1947: 117).

The fact that descriptions of English future forms were rather 'immature' at the beginning of the 20th century is reflected by the amount of disagreement, both diachronically and synchronically, that can be found between the descriptions in different titles, and sometimes even within titles. One clear example of this is the lack of consistency that can be found across the titles examined on whether or not the present continuous is used to talk about the 'immediate future' or not, with Jespersen (1933), Allen (1947), Thomson and Martinet (1960), Palmer (1924) and Alexander *et al.* (1975) all expressing somewhat different views on this. There is also, as has been described, disagreement historically on the order that future forms should be taught. In older titles, the initial focus tended to be on *will* and *shall*, with *going to* sometimes briefly covered; the present continuous was left until higher levels in many titles. By contrast, in contemporary titles the present continuous tends to be one of the first future forms that learners see, with *will* left until later.

Another development that has taken place over the last century is a change in understanding of what exactly, if anything, constitutes the 'future tense' in English. Older titles present *will* or *shall* as 'the' future tense, with other future forms such as *going to* and present continuous mentioned, if at all, only in passing. The dominance of *will* and *shall* endured until at least the middle of the 20th century, with terms such as 'pure future' and 'future simple' perpetuating the idea of the existence of one standard future form, leaving other future forms to be covered briefly only later (and in spite of the fact that there is nothing particularly 'simple' about the uses associated with *will*). ELT accounts from the second half of the 20th century clearly represent an improvement in this respect, in that they typically talk of future *forms* rather than identifying a single 'future tense', and place structures such as the present continuous and *going to* on an equal footing to *will*. On the other hand, contemporary coursebooks tend to ignore the pragmatic uses of the future continuous (to make polite enquiries) and the future perfect (to talk about assumptions about the past), which, especially in the case of the future continuous, were readily identified in older accounts. This appears to deprive learners of some useful additional functions of the grammar they are studying.

It is again possible to observe how certain choices of words and phrases in descriptions appear to 'echo' through time and across publications. For example, Palmer's use of the phrase 'in the ordinary course of events' (which may not have originated with Palmer himself), or variations of it, appeared in publications across the 20th century and is still the preferred wording in contemporary accounts of the future continuous; similarly, the word 'coloured', chosen by Jespersen in descriptions of the usage *will*, and by Allen to talk about both *will* and *going to*, is also found in explanations of the future continuous in the latest edition of *Headway Upper Intermediate* (2014: 145). A further echo can be seen in the employment of an example sentence about clouds and rain to help explain the use of *going to* make predictions, typically along the lines of 'Look at the clouds – it's going to rain'. Examples of this can be found in Eckersley's *Essential English* (Level 2), Alexander *et al.*'s *English Grammatical Structure* (Stage 2), Swan and Walter's *New Cambridge English Course* (Book 1), Soars and Soars' *Headway* (Upper Intermediate, first edition)) and Oxenden *et al.*'s *English File* (Intermediate level). Another example of this phenomenon is the rule prohibiting the use of 'going to go' and 'going to come', which has appeared again and again in ELT accounts for nearly a century. The rule is repeated, uncritically, in title after title, apparently considered 'correct' by the virtue of the fact that it has appeared in print elsewhere.

7.6 Summary

Looking across the three case studies, a number of general phenomena related to the evolution of accounts of ELT pedagogical grammar emerge. One of the most obvious relates to the unit of analysis, with a shift in emphasis from item to pattern. This can be seen both in the descriptions of conditional forms, with a change in focus from a consideration of only the verb form in the *if* clause to the use of numbered categorisation system for entire sentences, and in the descriptions of relative clauses, with a shift in focus from the relativiser to the use and function of the relative clause as a whole. A similar change in approach can also be found in the way future forms are described, with the pedagogical accounts examined gradually moving away from the idea of English having a 'future tense' (i.e. *will/shall*), to considering a wider range of forms used to express futurity, eventually putting *going to*, the present continuous and other future forms on an equal footing. This change is perhaps reflective of a wider change in approach to describing language; as we saw in Chapter 3, the work of influential teacher-authors like Harold Palmer and A.S. Hornby placed an increasingly greater emphasis on identifying and teaching wider patterns over individual items. This change appears to have brought both advantages and disadvantages: there are clear benefits for learners in basing analysis and examples around whole structures, but it can be problematic if a whole structure or paradigm eventually becomes the 'rule' itself. As we saw with conditionals, this can lead to an increased learning load for learners, and a decrease in flexibility in the language they practise and produce.

A second tendency revealed from the analysis is the gradual abandonment of prescriptivist rules and advice. Modern pedagogical treatments contain nothing in the style of Murray's instruction to avoid the use of the relative adverb 'where' because it is 'an imitation of the French idiom', or of Samuel Jonson's opinion that the use of the zero relative clause is 'barbarous'. But this change has been gradual, with grammatical treatments in the early- to mid-20th century at times retaining elements of a prescriptivist approach. We saw this, for example, in Palmer's assertion that the use of *which* or *who* instead of *that* offers 'greater precision' in relative clauses, or in Thomson and Martinet's claim that the use of *whom* over *who* is the 'technically correct' option. However, we should avoid taking an overly 'progressivist' perspective here, as the ELT profession has not certainly not been immune to creating its own prescriptivist – and inaccurate – rules, for example the instruction to avoid *go* and *come* after *going to*, or the unrepresentative categorisation system used to describe conditionals. The latter is particularly interesting, since – as we saw – conditional forms historically seem to have attracted very little interest or attempts at regulation from grammarians. The much-maligned three-way paradigm used in ELT appears to have developed no earlier than the mid-20th century, and certainly cannot be blamed on 'traditional' school grammars.

A third observation to emerge from the historical analysis of the case studies emphasises the collaborative nature of the evolution of the canon, with writers building on each other's work, and elements of grammar coverage 'echoing' through the decades from publication to publication. We saw, for example, how individual wordings within explanations, or even whole example sentences, repeated in later publications. On the other hand, and we also saw how even the inaccurate '*going to* rule' proscribing the use of 'go' after 'going to', first found in Palmer's (1924) grammar, is still repeated in contemporary coursebooks. Similarly, Palmer's possibly accidental omission of past hypothetical forms in his coverage of conditionals was largely replicated in Hornby's *Oxford Progressive English* series. Authors are naturally influenced by the works of those before them, but in the case of ELT publishing, where there is no requirement for citations or references to empirical evidence, this influence may not always lead to the repetition of accurate or relevant grammatical descriptions, but rather to the repetition of unfounded assertions. It seems that once critical mass has been reached, in the form of publication in multiple titles, any one grammar point, rule, or choice of wording or terminology becomes accepted as part of the canon and can be sustained indefinitely, regardless of its merit or accuracy.

Finally, it is possible to observe in the three case studies a development in the way that learners are helped to make choices between different grammatical options, recalling Williams' (1994) 'communicative', as opposed to 'constitutive', grammar rules, and Carter and McCarthy's (2006) 'grammar as choice'. As we said in Chapter 2, creating accounts of grammar that provide learners with information of predictive value is particularly important for pedagogical grammar but represents a challenge. Although rightly criticised, the categorical system used for conditionals does at least potentially equip learners with the skills to express a range of different meanings (for example, real vs. hypothetical situations in the present; hypothetical situations in the present vs. in the past), while a focus exclusively on verb forms, as found, for example, in Jespersen (1933), does not. Similarly, explaining relative clauses through a distinction between defining and non-defining clauses appears to be designed to equip learners with the ability to choose one type of clause over the other in order to express different meanings. Again, this cannot be said for the older, non-pedagogical grammars, which focused primarily on relativisers. Finally, as we saw, grammatical descriptions of the future in English tended to focus almost exclusively on *will* and *shall* – often repeating prescriptive rules which possibly never actually reflected usage – with other future forms either ignored or mentioned in passing. Gradually, the focus expanded to cover a range of future forms and, crucially, provide advice on how to choose between them.

In all three case studies, it is Allen's (1947) grammar in particular which appears to offer a breath of fresh air in this respect, containing descriptions and explanations that do far more than older grammars to 'demarcate' the area of grammar so that, in the words of Swan, 'a learner will know when to use the form and when not to' (1994: 47). As much as we might lament the accuracy and representativeness of some of the contents of the ELT grammar canon, we should not overlook the importance of the 'predictive value' that ELT pedagogical grammarians have been able to impart into their explanations over the decades and the benefits that learners have presumably drawn from them. I would argue that explanations of this kind are a natural (and positive) outcome of practitioners creating pedagogical materials, born from their own experiences and their own perceptions of the needs of learners, even if, as we have seen, the results of such a process are not always necessarily perfect.

Notes

(1) According to the OED, 'since the middle of the 17th century the general rule (subject to various exceptions) has been that mere futurity is expressed in the first person by *shall*, in the second and third by *will*' (OED Online, 2022), and vice versa when modality is expressed. Yet 'it is unlikely that this rule has ever had any consistent basis in actual usage' (Butterfield, 2016: 547).
(2) It is interesting that Palmer choses the word 'arrangement', since in modern treatments of future forms it is typically the present continuous that is described as being used for talking about arrangements.

8 Conclusion

To conclude, we will begin by returning to the three questions posed in Chapter 1, and review how they have been answered in this book.

8.1 How, When and Where did the Consensus on the ELT Grammar 'Canon' Develop?

We have approached this question from several different angles. Firstly, the broad analysis of historical pedagogical grammars and the overall historical context presented in Chapter 3 suggest that ELT pedagogical grammar – as represented in contemporary mainstream ELT publications – is a relatively recent phenomenon. Although it has its origins in work at the beginning of the 20th century, it only really began to take a familiar shape in the middle of the century. There appears to have been a strong interaction between the grammatical accounts being developed in ELT and 'background' events such the 'Reform Movement', methodological developments and more generally research into language teaching and acquisition, such as Palmer and Hornby's work on patterns, the Contrastive Analysis hypothesis, and the notion of 'communicative competence' to name but a few.

However, while providing a general account of the development of ELT grammar is relatively straightforward, tracing its exact path is more challenging, due to the lack of any 'official' documents setting out policy and mandating syllabuses for ELT. Research using primary sources – that is to say, published ELT materials – can tell us a great deal and, as we saw in the previous chapter, it is possible to note a number of phenomena which appear to reveal changes in underlying beliefs and practices. One tendency we saw in all three case studies was the shift in focus from item to pattern, seemingly reflecting wider beliefs about what the most useful unit of analysis and exemplification is for pedagogical grammar accounts. We can speculate that it also reflects wider developments in linguistics, for example the development of structuralist theory, with its focus both on the underlying system but also on utterances as a whole. A further tendency is the gradual abandonment of prescriptivist rules, even though pedagogical accounts tend to be by nature normative in character. Again, the move away from normative grammar accounts is associated with structuralism (see, for example, the account in Levin, 1960) but also, of course, modern linguistics in general. A separate development seems to have been the growing realisation that learners – unlike users of reference grammars aimed at native speakers – need assistance in choosing *between* different forms and this is increasingly reflected in the content of ELT pedagogical grammar accounts. We might link this to the notion of 'choice' in Hallidayan Systemic Functional Linguistics, but the change was gradual and it seems equally likely to be the result of the classroom experience of the teacher-authors who wrote ELT grammar descriptions in the 20th century.

However, while fruitful, the analysis of primary sources is limited by the fact that such publications do not typically contain citations and lists of references. For this reason, the genesis of apparently key titles such as Allen's (1947) *Living English Structure* – which the eminent Michael Swan recalls having learnt all his grammar from at the beginning of his career – remains somewhat mysterious. In terms of references, Allen provided no more than a list of 'some useful books for further reference', although as we saw in Chapter 7, it is at times possible to trace apparent lineage across titles, for example in the influence of Jespersen on Allen's explanations and even example sentences, and then, subsequently, from Allen's work on the later books.

Overall the development of a consensus on ELT grammar in the first half of the 20th century seems to have been largely an organic, bottom-up process, driven by the work of individual teachers and teacher-authors, in disparate parts of the world. Their activities appear to meet Wenger's (1998) three criteria for a 'community of practice' – 'mutual engagement', 'joint enterprise' and 'shared repertoire'. 'Mutual engagement' was achieved through the creation of research groups such as IRET in Japan (see Chapter 2), and facilitated more generally by publications such as the *ELT Journal* (we saw, for example, pedagogical grammar knowledge being shared through the regular 'Question Box' feature). The 'joint enterprise' appears clear: these professionals were working together to develop ideas on how to best teach English, including the question of what to teach. Finally, the pedagogical grammar that they developed constitutes part of their 'shared repertoire'. The professionals involved in this were also supported to a great extent by the substantial body of work known as the 'Great Tradition' – the new, scientific grammars produced around the turn of the 20th century. The fact that these grammars were mainly written by non-native speakers seems to have meant their content was often particularly relevant for the development of pedagogical grammar accounts.

In the second half of the century, the focus appears to have shifted to UK-based teacher-authors, often working for private language schools, but also, as we have said, influenced to an extent by developments in research in linguistics and education. This period of time is 'accessible' from the data collected during the interviews. As we saw, those interviewees who had been involved in coursebook production in the 1960s, 70s and 80s recalled having, or there being, a great deal of freedom in terms of content, with publishers leaving choice of grammar content and organisation to the individual author. This also meant that the developing consensus was relatively fluid, with innovation possible in terms of the ordering of grammatical elements (for example, the foregrounding of communicative elements such as *would like* under the influence of the functional-notional approach) or the addition to the canon of new grammatical elements as a result of research into discourse. At some point, however, this started to change. Ingrid Freebairn's account is particularly interesting from this point of view, as her memories as a coursebook author over the decades reveal the gradually increasing influence of market research and the need to match user expectations, resulting in more homogeneity in content.

8.2 What is the Nature of the Canon Today, and the Consensus that Perpetuates and Sustains It?

The relatively broad consensus found in contemporary coursebooks in the case studies appears to confirm one of the premises of the research presented in this book, and claims made elsewhere (for example, Ellis, R., 2006; O'Keeffe & Mark, 2017; Thornbury, 2013), that it is easier and less risky for a new coursebook series to imitate, at the level of grammatical content, previously successful titles, meaning that there is very little variety in the grammar content of contemporary ELT teaching materials. However, as we saw in Chapter 6 the consensus on grammar content works somewhat differently at the macro and micro levels. The greatest level of convergence occurs at the macro level, with all coursebooks adopting the same approach to the teaching of three areas of grammar examined in the case studies (i.e. the standard three-way conditional system; the treatment of relative clauses based on a binary distinction between defining and non-defining; the five canonical future forms) and their ordering within a multiple-level syllabus. However, at the micro level, the pool of details associated with these areas of grammar can be seen as a list of ingredients from which materials designers choose in order to create their dishes, meaning that not all books teach exactly the same things, particularly in main-lesson content. The greatest level of variation – both at macro and micro levels – between coursebooks was found at the highest levels, echoing McCarthy's (2015) observations.

The homogeneity of coursebook grammar content has often been presented negatively in the literature, seen as an example of the hegemony of publishers in an increasingly capitalist and commodified world. Thornbury (2013: 216), for example, links the 'endless reproduction of what is essentially the same grammar syllabus' to the 'commodification' of language learning, an approach that allows 'a model of production, consumption and regulation that not only avoids threatening the status quo, but underpins a lucrative global marketing strategy'. While the data in this study cannot answer directly to Thornbury's criticisms, it certainly does point to the existence of a circle (whether vicious or virtuous), whereby publishers provide their customers with the kind of teaching materials that they are asking for, and their customers continue to ask for the same kinds of teaching materials as they feel that what they have seen before represents the norms they should be following. However, the interview data suggests that publishers may simply be part of this cycle rather than the creators of it. Some interviewees seemed to echo Amrani's (2011: 268) observation that publishers also feel themselves to be operating under significant restrictions, having 'less of a free hand than previously' because of market expectations. Publishers perhaps do have the power to break the cycle, but there would be commercial risks associated with doing so and this is likely to make them reluctant. The data collected in this study does not suggest that publishers have any kind of agenda beyond this.

The current situation appears to be in stark contrast to the situation in the 1970s described by coursebook authors such as Ingrid Freebairn and Peter Viney; there is now little space for innovation in syllabus content as the priority appears to be to meet the expectations of markets. This situation, however, was not reported in universally negative terms. A number of interviewees reported understanding the need for meeting the requirements of the target audience, and reluctance to innovate that publishers seem to have. The investment costs in producing coursebooks are high, and many interviewees seemed to be accepting and understanding of the fact that this means that risk needs to be eliminated as far as possible. In the words of Jack Richards, reported in Chapter 4, 'common practice was probably a good way to go, because if you depart too much from it, you're likely to lose your target audience'. These, of course, are mainly commercial considerations, but they cannot be ignored.

8.3 Does the Canon Reflect Empirical Evidence on how Grammatical Competence Develops in English Language Learners?

The comparison of this consensus with the data from the English Grammar Profile produced mixed results. There were significant areas of agreement in terms of content and level assignments, but also significant divergences. The latter consist most frequently of (i) individual uses identified in the EGP but not typically taught, or taught at all, in the coursebooks examined or covered in their grammar explanations, and

(ii) structures or uses of structures which the EGP indicates that learners are able to produce at least a level earlier than they are typically taught in coursebooks. In addition to this, there are (iii) a much smaller number of incidences of structures or uses of structures that the EGP indicates that learners are only able to use later than the level at which they are typically taught.

In terms of the first two types of divergence, the obvious question is how learners are able to produce the language if they have not been taught it. It may be that learners are able to use the grammar they are taught as 'building blocks', meaning that as part of the acquisition process learners are able to extrapolate from the limited input they receive and exemplars they are exposed to in pedagogical accounts, which, one could speculate, resonates with usage-based models of learning (Ellis *et al.*, 2016; Tomasello, 2005). Additionally, the evidence from the EGP may also suggest that learners are able to produce language that they encounter, or perhaps seek out, outside the context of the coursebook, whether that is inside or outside of the classroom.

Only three incidences of the third type of divergence were identified, as follows:

- the use of *might have* and *could have* in conditional sentences (typically taught at Level 5, but at C1 in EGP);
- the use of *whose* is defining and non-defining relative clauses (typically taught at Level 4, but at B2 in EGP);
- the use of *going to* talk about plans and intentions, in affirmative sentences and in questions (typically taught first at Level 1, but at A2 in EGP).

In such cases, it is possible to speculate about some kind of lag between learning and production, or it might simply be the case that learners are not developmentally ready to use these structures at the level at which they are typically taught. Such explanations would perhaps need to be explained by underlying acquisition processes. The question of 'opportunity of use' (Buttery & Caines, 2012) is also important; the EGP is based on data from written exams, and the exam questions might simply not provide learners with the opportunity to use certain structures.

8.4 Discussion

What, overall, can we take from this study? Firstly, its limitations must be acknowledged. This study has a wide focus – investigating a posited consensus on grammar within the mainstream ELT profession – and such a broad approach by nature does not consider all contexts. For example, global coursebooks teaching General English were considered to be those most likely to clearly represent the consensus in mainstream ELT, but they are nevertheless a subset of all coursebooks published. Similarly, only a comparatively small number of books were chosen for the historical analysis; these were chosen to be representative of the periods under consideration, but it is possible that an analysis of a wider range of, or just different, titles might produce different results. In terms of the interview data, only a comparatively small group of people were interviewed, and it must be acknowledged that their views may not be representative of those of everyone working in the field. Having said that, the writers and editors of coursebooks work in a highly specialised field and the group of informants in this study have produced, over decades, materials that have been used around the world by thousands of teachers and learners over several decades.

Despite these limitations, I believe that the research presented here fills a number of gaps in our understanding of the pedagogical grammar used in mainstream ELT accounts. In terms of the investigation into the evolution of the ELT grammar canon, I believe that one of the most important outcomes of the analysis I have presented is to show that while its development has generally been driven by highly competent professionals – the product of the 'chalkface' experience of practitioners – its evolution has been largely unplanned, and has taken place without any kind of oversight. That the canon developed in this organic way, from the bottom up, responding to needs identified by practitioners, is not in itself a negative point. However, if the initial development of pedagogical accounts of English grammar can be conceived of as a shared repertoire, one element of a community of practice within the ELT profession, the interviews presented in Chapter 4 suggest that the current consensus seems to have more in common with the concept of 'best practice'. In Edge and Richards' (1998) critique of the concept, 'best practice' is said to rest on the assumption that 'there exists, at any one time, a best way of achieving clearly identifiable ends and that this best way can be made generally available' (1998: 570). In the ELT profession, 'best practice' often involves, in part, the uncritical use of a well-established catalogue of grammar points to create syllabuses, with an assumption that this one-size-fits-all grammar canon, with its associated content and ordering across levels, represents the best way to achieve the aims of ELT. Unfortunately, as Edge and Richards (1998: 571) note, best practice is 'not open to challenge', something that, in the context of grammar content selection and ordering, is confirmed by the interviews. As we saw, those designing courses and producing mainstream ELT materials are bound by the norms and needs (of the profession, of schools, of ministries and examination boards, and of markets and users), but the expectations underlying these appear to be based mainly on simply what has come before. The role of successful competitor titles appears to be crucial in this; those books that have found commercial success serve as models for future publications, leading to a self-perpetuating cycle of homogenous content and limited opportunities to review the established canon or innovate from it.

The current stagnancy makes the origins of the canon, in my opinion, problematic. That is not to say that I believe that the ELT grammar canon is all wrong – far from it – but I do believe that it is wrong to think that it is all right. The canon should be open for critical analysis, both in terms of the overall catalogue of grammar points that it contains (and those that it does *not* contain), and the order in which the grammar is typically taught. As Sheehan (2015: 92) argues, in a comment piece responding to Edge and Richards' (1998) article, 'best practice' can become a more useful concept if practitioners are 'given the opportunity to initiate sharing their own good practices and leaving the concept of "better" and "best" to the discretion of the individual teacher who may determine, in an exploratory way, its relevance and efficacy for a particular group of learners'. In my opinion, an individual practitioner will be more empowered to make innovative decisions on grammar content if they understand where the consensus view on content and ordering actually originates.

I am certainly not the first to point out inaccuracies in grammatical explanations used in mainstream ELT publications. However, as I have stated several times, I do believe it is necessary for researchers to engage with practitioners (whether teachers, publishers or materials writers) if there is any hope to bring about change. Given the reluctance of publishers to produce innovative materials that might be considered 'deficient' (to use the word chosen by the anonymous coursebook author interviewed) in some way, the most likely way for change to occur would seem to be some kind of bottom-up demand for it, from users. I believe that by fully understanding how ELT pedagogical grammar has evolved, and acknowledging its positive aspects as well as weaknesses, calls for such change can be stronger.

Quasi-longitudinal learner corpora and resources based on them such as the EGP may represent one source of renewal. Having readily and freely available information on how learners actually use grammar at different competency levels – in other words, evidence grounded in practice – may be enough to persuade publishers and end users that innovation is both possible and desirable. Admittedly, it is not always easy to ascertain how a materials designer should respond to findings in the EGP. For example, how should an author – given a free hand – respond to findings from the EGP that learners are able to use grammar earlier than it is typically taught in coursebooks, or grammar that is not typically taught at all? One possible response would be to suggest changes to existing syllabuses, by either adding extra grammar coverage, or reordering the grammar that is already taught. Neither response is unproblematic. Current coursebook syllabuses are already 'full'; adding new grammar to a level – whether by adding completely new elements, or by teaching earlier elements that are currently covered in later levels – would necessitate either increasing the total amount of grammar taught at a level, eliminating other grammar points, or making space for the new grammar by postponing other grammatical points, which might as a consequence themselves be taught 'too late'. However, at the level of individual grammar points, empirical data from learner corpora certainly have the potential to improve existing accounts. For example, Burton (2022) proposes a modified system for categorising and teaching conditionals, which takes into account empirical evidence from the EGP but also respects the apparent need within the ELT profession to provide teachers and learners with a workable categorisation system that can be employed across multi-level teaching materials and courses. There would seem to be potential for similar learner-corpus-based studies on other major areas of grammar, which could help to update aspects of the existing canon without seeking to reject them entirely (an endeavour which in any case would be doomed to failure, for the reasons discussed in this book).

Finally, I also feel that there are implications from the historical research I have presented here for the 'stories' we tell about the history of ELT methods and approaches. As Smith (2016: 75) notes, historical narratives on ELT 'tend to stereotype and demonize the past in a "progressivist" manner, serving to assert the supposed superiority of current conceptions'. In the case of the role of grammar in language teaching, there is often a tendency to refer to 'traditional grammar' or 'traditional syllabuses' in ELT, without explaining exactly which 'tradition' is being referred to. Referring to foreign language teaching in general, McLelland neatly summarises this phenomenon as follows:

> We might summarize a layperson's view of how foreign language teaching and learning has changed over time as follows: in the (imprecisely defined) Old Days, language teaching was all about grammar and translation, but nowadays things are "better", and people learn to speak the language. (2019: 85)

Examples of this kind of imprecision in historical accounts of ELT grammar teaching are not hard to find. For example, McDonough and Shaw (2003: 16) state that, in the mid-20th century, the prevailing methodology meant that 'language learners were required, above all, to manipulate grammatical forms accurately', and that '[a] glance at many of the tables of contents of teaching materials published in the 1950s and 1960s will confirm this focus'. An almost identical claim is made in an article on the 'one stop english' website, a resource site for teachers run by Macmillan Education: 'a quick look at foreign language course books from the 1950s and 1960s, for example, will soon reveal the non-communicative nature of the language used' (Bowen, 2006). My own archive work, however, did not confirm such assertions. In fact, one of the difficulties in researching the grammar content of older titles is precisely that they often do not explicitly state their grammatical content. As we saw in Chapter 3, research on methodology in ELT in the first half of the 20th century focused on the teaching of vocabulary and phraseology, rather than grammar.

The reality is that a comparison of the table of contents of a modern coursebook with the grammar content of coursebooks from the first half of the 20th century would show that there is in fact far more extensive and detailed coverage of grammar now compared with the past. With the increase in the number of levels that coursebooks are published at, there is simply more space than ever before for grammar content. The modern, detailed accounts of ELT grammar are therefore far from a legacy of the distant past, but a modern invention. It should be possible to engage with them and update them in a way that both validates their origins routed in practice, and the work of the teachers, materials authors and others who shape or have shaped them, but that also takes advantage of recent research in and insights from applied linguistics.

References

Aarts, F.G.A.M. (1988) A comprehensive grammar of the English language: The great tradition continued. *English Studies* 69 (2), 163–173.
Aarts, B., Chalker, S. and Weiner, E.S.C. (2014) *The Oxford Dictionary of English Grammar* (2nd edn). Oxford: Oxford University Press.
Abbs, B., Ayton, A. and Freebairn, I. (1975) *Strategies*. Harlow: Longman.
Abbs, B. and Freebairn, I. (1977) *Starting Strategies*. Harlow: Longman.
Abbs, B. and Freebairn, I. (1979) *Building Strategies*. Harlow: Longman.
Abbs, B. and Freebairn, I. (1980) *Developing Strategies*. Harlow: Longman.
Abbs, B. and Freebairn, I. (1982) *Studying Strategies*. Harlow: Longman.
Alexander, L.G., Allen, W.S., Close, R.A. and O'Neill, R.J. (1975) *English Grammatical Structure: A General Syllabus for Teachers*. London: Longman.
Allen, W.S. (1947) *Living English Structure*. London: Longman.
Allen, J.P.B. and Widdowson, H.G. (1974) Teaching the communicative use of English. *IRAL – International Review of Applied Linguistics in Language Teaching* 12 (1–4), 1–22.
Amrani, F. (2011) The process of evaluation: A publisher's view. In B. Tomlinson (ed.) *Materials Development in Language Teaching* (2nd edn) (pp. 267–295). Cambridge: Cambridge University Press.
Attride-Stirling, J. (2001) Thematic networks: An analytic tool for qualitative research. *Qualitative Research* 1 (3), 385–405.
Barbieri, F. and Eckhardt, S.E.B. (2007) Applying corpus-based findings to form-focused instruction: The case of reported speech. *Language Teaching Research* 11 (3), 319–346.
Beaven, B., Falla, T., Soars, J. and Soars, L. (1995) *Headstart: Beginner Student's Book*. Oxford: Oxford University Press.
Bell, J. and Gower, R. (1998) Writing course materials for the world: A great compromise. In B. Tomlinson (ed.) *Materials Development in Language Teaching* (pp. 116–129). Cambridge: Cambridge University Press.
Bell, J. and Gower, R. (2011) Writing course materials for the world: A great compromise. In B. Tomlinson (ed.) *Materials Development in Language Teaching* (2nd edn) (pp. 135–151). Cambridge: Cambridge University Press.
Bialystok, E. (1991) Achieving proficiency in a second language: A processing description. In R. Phillipson, P.C. Keller, L. Selinker, M. Sherwood Smith and M. Swain (eds) *Foreign/Second Language Pedagogy Research: A Commemorative Volume for Claus Færch* (pp. 63–78). Clevedon: Multilingual Matters.
Biber, D. and Reppen, R. (2002) What does frequency have to do with grammar teaching? *Studies in Second Language Acquisition* 24 (2), 199–208.
Biber, D., Johansson, S., Leech, G., Conrad, S. and Finegan, E. (1999) *Longman Grammar of Spoken and Written English*. Harlow: Longman.
Block, D. (2000) Revisiting the gap between SLA researchers and language teachers. *Links & Letters* (7), 129–143.
'Book reviews' (1949) *ELT Journal* 4 (2), 52–56.
'Book reviews' (1959) *ELT Journal* 13 (2), 84–85.

Bowen, T. (2006) Teaching approaches: The grammar-translation method. See https://www.onestopenglish.com/methodology-the-world-of-elt/teaching-approaches-the-grammar-translation-method/146493.article (accessed January 2022).

Braun, V. and Clarke, V. (2006) Using thematic analysis in psychology. *Qualitative Research in Psychology* 3 (2), 77–101.

Brindley, G. (1999) Describing language development? Rating scales and SLA. In L.F. Bachman and A.D. Cohen (eds) *Interfaces between Second Language Acquisition and Language Testing Research* (pp. 112–140). Cambridge: Cambridge University Press.

Burton, G. (2012) Corpora and coursebooks: Destined to be strangers forever? *Corpora* 7 (1), 91–108.

Burton, G. (2021) 'Are you going to go?' Putting a pedagogical grammar rule under the corpus spotlight. *Glottodidactica. An International Journal of Applied Linguistics* 48 (1), 7–26.

Burton, G. (2022) Rehabilitating the ELT conditional system. *ELT Journal* 76 (3), 338–347.

Butterfield, J. (ed.) (2016) *Fowler's Concise Dictionary of Modern English Usage* (3rd edn). Oxford: Oxford University Press.

Buttery, P. and Caines, A. (2012) Normalising frequency counts to account for 'opportunity of use' in learner corpora. In Y. Tono, Y. Kawaguchi and M. Minegishi (eds) *Developmental and Crosslinguistic Perspectives in Learner Corpus Research* (pp. 187–204). Amsterdam: John Benjamins.

Cambridge University Press (2021) *English grammar in use fifth edition*. See https://www.cambridge.org/gb/cambridgeenglish/catalog/grammar-vocabulary-and-pronunciation/english-grammar-use-5th-edition (accessed November 2021).

Campion, G.C. (2016) 'The learning never ends': Exploring teachers' views on the transition from General English to EAP. *Journal of English for Academic Purposes* 23, 59–70.

Candlin, C.N. (1994) General editor's preface. In M. Bygate, A. Tonkyn and E. Williams (eds) *Grammar and the Language Teacher* (pp. vii–viii). Harlow: Longman.

Carter, R. (1998) Orders of reality: CANCODE, communication, and culture. *ELT Journal* 52 (1), 43–56.

Carter, R. and McCarthy, M. (1995) Grammar and the spoken language. *Applied Linguistics* 16 (2), 141–158.

Carter, R. and McCarthy, M. (2006) *Cambridge Grammar of English: A Comprehensive Guide: Spoken and Written English Grammar and Usage*. Cambridge: Cambridge University Press.

Carter, R. and McCarthy, M. (2017) Spoken grammar: Where are we and where are we going? *Applied Linguistics* 38 (1), 1–20.

Chalhoub-Deville, M. (2014) Content validity considerations in language testing contexts. In R.W. Lissitz (ed.) *The Concept of Validity: Revisions, New Directions and Applications* (pp. 241–263). Charlotte, NC: Information Age Publishing.

Chalker, S. (1994) Pedagogical grammar: Principles and problems. In M. Bygate, A. Tonkyn and E. Williams (eds) *Grammar and the Language Teacher* (pp. 31–44). Harlow: Longman.

Chalker, S., Aarts, B. and Weiner, E.S.C. (2014) *The Oxford Dictionary of English Grammar* (2nd edn). Oxford: Oxford University Press.

Chiu-ming, L. (1983) A four-step technique for teaching relative clauses. *ELT Journal* 37 (1), 88–88.

Chomsky, N. (1959) Review: Verbal behavior by B. F. Skinner. *Language* 35 (1), 26–58.

Close, R.A. (1970a) Problems of the Future Tense (1). *ELT Journal* 24 (3), 225–232.

Close, R.A. (1970b) Problems of the Future Tense (2). *ELT Journal* 25 (1), 43–49.

Conrad, S. (2004) Corpus linguistics, language variation, and language teaching. In J.M. Sinclair (ed.) *How to Use Corpora in Language Teaching* (pp. 67–85). Amsterdam: John Benjamins.

Cook, G. (1998) The uses of reality: A reply to Ronald Carter. *ELT Journal* 52 (1), 57–63.

Copley, K. (2018) Neoliberalism and ELT coursebook content. *Critical Inquiry in Language Studies* 15 (1), 43–62.

Corder, S.P. (1975) Applied linguistics and language teaching. In J.P.B. Allen and S.P. Corder (eds) *The Edinburgh Course in Applied Linguistics* (Vol. 2) (pp. 1–15). Oxford: Oxford University Press.
Council of Europe (2001) *Common European Framework of Reference for Languages: Learning, Teaching, Assessment.* Cambridge: Cambridge University Press.
Council of Europe (2017) *Common European Framework of Reference for Languages: Learning, Teaching, Assessment. Companion Volume with New Descriptors.* Strasbourg: Council of Europe.
Crystal, D. (2017) English grammar in the UK: A political history (Supplementary material to *Making Sense: The Glamorous Story of English Grammar*). See http://www.davidcrystal.com/?fileid=-5247 (accessed June 2019).
Cunningham, S. and Moor, P. (2002) *New Cutting Edge Starter Student's Book.* Harlow: Longman.
Cunningham, S. and Moor, P. (2003) *New Cutting Edge Advanced Student's Book.* Harlow: Longman.
Cunningham, S. and Moor, P. (2005a) *New Cutting Edge Elementary Student's Book.* Harlow: Longman.
Cunningham, S. and Moor, P. (2005b) *New Cutting Edge Pre-Intermediate Student's Book.* Harlow: Longman.
Cunningham, S. and Moor, P. (2005c) *New Cutting Edge Intermediate Student's Book.* Harlow: Longman.
Cunningham, S. and Moor, P. (2005d) *New Cutting Edge Upper Intermediate Student's Book.* Harlow: Longman.
Cunningham, G., Bell, J. and Redston, C. (2010) *face2face Advanced Student's Book.* Cambridge: Cambridge University Press.
DeKeyser, R. (2014) Skill acquisition theory. In B. VanPatten and J. Williams (eds) *Theories in Second Language Acquisition* (2nd edn) (pp. 94–112). Abingdon: Routledge.
Dörnyei, Z. (2007) *Research Methods in Applied Linguistics: Quantitative, Qualitative, and Mixed Methodologies.* Oxford: Oxford University Press.
Dulay, H.C. and Burt, M.K. (1974) Natural sequences in child second language acquisition. *Language Learning* 24 (1), 37–53.
EAQUALS (2021) Our members. See https://www.eaquals.org/our-members/ (accessed November 2021).
Eckersley, C.E. (1938) *Essential English for Foreign Students: Book 1.* Sofia: Foreign Languages Press.
Eckersley, C.E. (1940) *Essential English for Foreign Students: Book 2.* Sofia: Foreign Languages Press.
Eckersley, C.E. (1941) *Essential English for Foreign Students: Book 3.* Sofia: Foreign Languages Press.
Eckersley, C.E. (1942) *Essential English for Foreign Students: Book 4.* Sofia: Foreign Languages Press.
Edge, J. and Richards, K. (1998) Why best practice is not good enough. *TESOL Quarterly* 32 (3), 569–576.
Educational Testing Service (2014) A guide to understanding TOEFL IBT scores. See https://www.ets.org/s/toefl/pdf/performance_feedback_ brochure.pdf (accessed May 2019).
Egre, P. and Cozic, M. (2016) Conditionals. In M. Aloni and P.J.E. Dekker (eds) *The Cambridge Handbook of Formal Semantics* (pp. 490–524). Cambridge: Cambridge University Press.
van Ek, J.A. (1976) *The Threshold Level in a European Unit/Credit System for Modern Language Learning by Adults.* Strasbourg: The Council of Europe.
Ellis, N.C. (2006) Language acquisition as rational contingency learning. *Applied Linguistics* 27 (1), 1–24.
Ellis, N.C., Römer, U. and O'Donnell, M.B. (eds) (2016) *Usage-Based Approaches to Language Acquisition and Processing: Cognitive and Corpus Investigations of Construction Grammar.* Chichester: Wiley.

Ellis, R. (2006) Current issues in the teaching of grammar: An SLA perspective. *TESOL Quarterly* 40 (1), 83–107.
Fowler, W.F. (1926) *A Dictionary of Modern English Usage*. Oxford: Oxford University Press.
Fries, C.C. (1945) *Teaching and Learning English as a Foreign Language*. Ann Arbour: University of Michigan Press.
Fries, C.C. (1952) *The Structure of English*. New York: Harcourt, Brace & World.
Fries, C.C. (1959) Preparation of teaching materials, practical grammars, and dictionaries, especially for foreign languages. *Language Learning* 9 (1–2), 43–50.
Fulcher, G. (1991) Conditionals revisited. *ELT Journal* 45 (2), 164–168.
Gabrielatos, C. (2003) Conditional sentences: ELT typology and corpus evidence, 36th Annual BAAL Meeting. 4 September. See http://eprints.lancs.ac.uk/140 (accessed September 2020).
Gabrielatos, C. (2006) Corpus-based evaluation of pedagogical materials: If-conditionals in ELT coursebooks and the BNC, 7th Teaching and Language Corpora Conference. 1 July. See http://eprints.lancs.ac.uk/882/1/TALC_2006-CG.pdf (accessed September 2020).
Goldberg, A.E. (2019) *Explain Me This: Creativity, Competition, and the Partial Productivity of Constructions*. Princeton, NJ: Princeton University Press.
Granger, S. (2002) A bird's-eye view of learner corpus research. In S. Granger (ed.) *Computer Learner Corpora, Second Language Acquisition and Foreign Language Teaching* (pp. 3–33). Amsterdam: John Benjamins.
Gray, J. (2002) The global coursebook in English language teaching. In D. Block and D. Cameron (eds) *Globalization and Language Teaching* (pp. 151–167). Abingdon: Routledge.
Greenbaum, S. (1987) Reference grammars and pedagogical grammars. *World Englishes* 6 (3), 191–197.
Halliday, M.A.K. and Hasan, R. (1976) *Cohesion in English*. London: Routledge.
Hanks, P. (2008) Lexical patterns: From Hornby to Hunston and beyond. In *Proceedings of the XIII Euralex International Congress* (pp. 89–129). Universitat Pompeu Fabra, Barcelona.
Hartley, B. and Viney, P. (1978) *Streamline English: Departures*. Oxford: Oxford University Press.
Hartley, B. and Viney, P. (1979) *Streamline English: Connections*. Oxford: Oxford University Press.
Hartley, B. and Viney, P. (1982) *Streamline English: Destinations*. Oxford: Oxford University Press.
Hartley, B. and Viney, P. (1985) *Streamline English: Directions*. Oxford: Oxford University Press.
Harwood, N. (2014) Content, consumption, and production: Three levels of textbook research. In N. Harwood (ed.) *English Language Teaching Textbooks: Content, Consumption, Production* (pp. 1–45). New York: Palgrave Macmillan.
Hinkel, E. (2017) Prioritizing grammar to teach or not to teach: A research perspective. In E. Hinkel (ed.) *Handbook of Research in Second Language Teaching and Learning* (Vol. 3) (pp. 369–383). Abingdon: Routledge.
Holmes, J. (1988) Doubt and certainty in ESL textbooks. *Applied Linguistics* 9 (1), 21–44.
Hood, M. (2009) Case study. In J. Heigham and R.A. Croker (eds) *Qualitative Research in Applied Linguistics: A Practical Introduction* (pp. 66–90). Basingstoke: Palgrave Macmillan.
Hornby, A.S. (1951) The Question Box. *ELT Journal* 6 (1), 30–33.
Hornby, A.S. (1953a) The Question Box. *ELT Journal* 7 (4), 138–141.
Hornby, A.S. (1953b) The Question Box. *ELT Journal* 8 (1), 25–27.
Hornby, A.S. (1954a) *A Guide to Patterns and Use in English*. Oxford: Oxford University Press.

Hornby, A.S. (1954b) *Oxford Progressive English for Adult Learners: Book One*. Oxford: Oxford University Press.
Hornby, A.S. (1955) *Oxford Progressive English for Adult Learners: Book Two*. Oxford: Oxford University Press.
Hornby, A.S. (1956) *Oxford Progressive English for Adult Learners: Book Three*. Oxford: Oxford University Press.
Hornby, A.S. (1959) *The Teaching of Structural Words and Sentence Patterns: Stage One*. Cambridge: Cambridge University Press.
Hornby, A.S. (1966) Looking back. *ELT Journal* 11 (1), 3–6.
Howatt, A. and Smith, R. (2014) The kistory of teaching English as a foreign language, from a British and European perspective. *Language & History* 57 (1), 75–95.
Howatt, A. and Widdowson, H.G. (2004) *A History of English Language Teaching* (2nd edn). Oxford: Oxford University Press.
Huddleston, R.D. and Pullum, G.K. (2002) *The Cambridge Grammar of the English Language*. Cambridge: Cambridge University Press.
Hulstijn, J.H. (2007) The shaky ground beneath the CEFR: Quantitative and qualitative dimensions of language proficiency. *The Modern Language Journal* 91 (4), 663–667.
Hulstijn, J.H. (2014) The Common European Framework of reference for languages: A challenge for applied linguistics. *International Journal of Applied Linguistics* 165 (1), 3–18.
Hunston, S. and Francis, G. (2000) *Pattern Grammar: A Corpus-Driven Approach to the Lexical Grammar of English*. Amsterdam: John Benjamins.
Hunston, S., Francis, G. and Manning, E. (1997) Grammar and vocabulary: Showing the connections. *ELT Journal* 51 (3), 208–216.
Hymes, D. (1972) On communicative competence. In J.B. Pride and J. Holmes (eds) *Sociolinguistics: Selected Readings* (pp. 269–293). Harmondsworth: Penguin.
Interagency Language Roundtable (2011) Introduction: Descriptions of proficiency levels. See https://www.govtilr.org/Skills/ILRscale1.htm (accessed May 2019).
International House World Organisation (2011). See ihjournal.com/an-interview-with-liz-and-john-soars-2 (accessed November 2021).
James, C. (1994) Explaining grammar to its learners. In M. Bygate, A. Tonkyn and E. Williams (eds) *Grammar and the Language Teacher* (pp. 203–214). Harlow: Longman.
Jespersen, O. (1909) *A Modern English Grammar on Historical Principles*. London: George Allen & Unwin Ltd.
Jespersen, O. (1933) *Essentials of English Grammar*. London: George Allen and Unwin Ltd.
Johnson, K. (1994) Teaching declarative and procedural knowledge. In M. Bygate, A. Tonkyn and E. Williams (eds) *Grammar and the Language Teacher* (pp. 121–131). Harlow: Longman.
Johnson, K. (2001) *An Introduction to Foreign Language Learning and Teaching*. Harlow: Longman.
Jolly, D. and Bolitho, R. (1998) A framework for materials writing. In B. Tomlinson (ed.) *Materials Development in Language Teaching* (pp. 90–115). Cambridge: Cambridge University Press.
Jones, C. and Waller, D. (2011) If only it were true: The problem with the four conditionals. *ELT Journal* 65 (1), 24–32.
Jones, L. (1981) *Functions of English*. Cambridge: Cambridge University Press
Jonson, B. (1640) *The English Grammar*. New York: Sturgis and Walton Company.
Joseph, J.E. (2016) Structural linguistics. In K. Allan (ed.) *The Routledge Handbook of Linguistics* (pp. 431–466). Abingdon: Routledge.
Kellerman, E. (1978) Giving learners a break: Native language intuitions as a source of prediction about transferability. *Working Papers on Bilingualism* (15), 59–92.
King, H.V. (1959) Oral grammar drills. *ELT Journal* 14 (1), 13–18.
Kramsch, C. (1986) From language proficiency to interactional competence. *The Modern Language Journal* 70 (4), 366–372.

Kumaravadivelu, B. (2006) *Understanding Language Teaching: From Method to Post-Method*. Mahwah, NJ: Lawrence Erlbaum Associates.

Lado, R. (1957) *Linguistics Across Cultures: Applied Linguistics for Language Teachers*. Ann Arbor: University of Michigan Press.

Leech, G. (1994) Students' grammar - teachers' grammar - learners' grammar. In M. Bygate, A. Tonkyn and E. Williams (eds) *Grammar and the Language Teacher* (pp. 17–30). Harlow: Longman.

Leech, G.N. (1997) Teaching and language corpora: A convergence. In A. Wichmann, S. Fligelstone, T. McEnery and G. Knowles (eds) *Teaching and Language Corpora* (pp. 1–23). London: Routledge.

Leech, G. and Svartvik, J. (1975) *A Communicative Grammar of English*. London: Longman.

Leech, G.N., Hundt, M., Mair, C. and Smith, N. (2009) *Change in Contemporary English a Grammatical Study*. Cambridge: Cambridge University Press.

Levin, S.R. (1960) Comparing traditional and structural grammar. *College English* 21 (5), 260–265.

Linn, A. (2006) English grammar writing. In B. Aarts and A.M.S. McMahon (eds) *The Handbook of English Linguistics* (pp. 72–92). Oxford: Blackwell.

Little, D. (1994) Words and their properties: Arguments for a lexical approach to pedagogical grammar. In T. Odlin (ed.) *Perspectives on Pedagogical Grammar* (pp. 99–122). Cambridge: Cambridge University Press.

Littlejohn, A. (1992) Why are English language teaching materials the way they are? Unpublished PhD thesis, University of Lancaster. See www.andrewlittlejohn.net/website/books/phd.html.

Littlejohn, A. (2012) Language teaching materials and the (very) big picture. *Electronic Journal of Foreign Language Teaching* 9 (1), 283–297.

Locke, M. (1986) The future progressive. *ELT Journal* 40 (4), 323–325.

Long, M.H. (2011) Methodological principles for language teaching. In M.H. Long and C.J. Doughty (eds) *The Handbook of Language Teaching* (pp. 373–394). Chichester: Wiley-Blackwell.

Long, M.H. (2015) *Second Language Acquisition and Task-Based Language Teaching*. Chichester: Wiley-Blackwell.

Luk, Z.P. and Shirai, Y. (2009) Is the acquisition order of grammatical morphemes impervious to L1 knowledge? Evidence from the acquisition of plural *-s*, articles, and possessive *'s*. *Language Learning* 59 (4), 721–754.

Maley, A. (2003) Creative approaches to writing materials. In B. Tomlinson (ed.) *Developing Materials for Language Teaching* (pp. 167–187). London: Continuum.

Mares, C. (2003) Writing a coursebook. In B. Tomlinson (ed.) *Developing Materials for Language Teaching* (pp. 130–140). London: Continuum.

Marlina, R. (2018) *Teaching English as an International Language: Implementing, Reviewing, and Re-envisioning World Englishes in Language Education*. Abingdon: Routledge.

Maule, D. (1988) 'Sorry, but if he comes, I go': Teaching conditionals. *ELT Journal* 42 (2), 117–123.

McCarthy, M. (2015) The role of corpus research in the design of advanced-level grammar instruction. In M. Christison, D. Christian, P.A. Duff and N. Spada (eds) *Teaching and Learning English Grammar: Research Findings and Future Directions* (pp. 87–102). Abingdon: Routledge.

McCarthy, M. (2021) *Innovations and Challenges in Grammar*. Abingdon: Routledge.

McCarthy, M. and Carter, R. (2002) Ten criteria for a spoken grammar. In E. Hinkel and S. Fotos (eds) *New Perspectives on Grammar Teaching in Second Language Classrooms* (pp. 51–75). Mahwah, NJ: L. Erlbaum Associates.

McCarthy, M., McCarten, J. and Sandiford, H. (2005a) *Touchstone Level 1 Student's Book*. Cambridge: Cambridge University Press.

McCarthy, M., McCarten, J. and Sandiford, H. (2005b) *Touchstone Level 2 Student's Book*. Cambridge: Cambridge University Press.

McCarthy, M., McCarten, J. and Sandiford, H. (2005c) *Touchstone Level 3 Student's Book*. Cambridge: Cambridge University Press.

McCarthy, M., McCarten, J. and Sandiford, H. (2005d) *Touchstone Level 4 Student's Book*. Cambridge: Cambridge University Press.

McCullagh, M. (2010) Initial valuation of the effectiveness of a set of published materials for medical English. In B. Tomlinson and H. Masuhara (eds) *Research for Materials Development in Language Learning: Evidence for Best Practice* (pp. 381–393). London: Continuum.

McDonough, J. and Shaw, C. (2003) *Materials and Methods in ELT: A Teacher's Guide* (2nd edn). Malden, MA: Blackwell.

McGrath, I. (2013) *Teaching Materials and the Roles of EFL/ESL Teachers: Practice and Theory*. London: Continuum.

McLelland, N. (2019) *Teaching and Learning Foreign Languages: A History of Language Education, Assessment and Policy in Britain*. Abingdon: Routledge.

Michael, I. (1970) *English Grammatical Categories and the Tradition to 1800*. Cambridge: Cambridge University Press.

Michael, I. (1987) *The Teaching of English: From the Sixteenth Century to 1870*. Cambridge: Cambridge University Press.

Michael, I. (1991) More than enough English grammars. In G. Leitner (ed.) *English Traditional Grammars: An International Perspective* (pp. 11–26). Amsterdam: John Benjamins.

Morris, I. (1969) The relative clause in broad perspective. *ELT Journal* 23 (3), 246–253.

Murakami, A. and Alexopoulou, T. (2016) L1 influence on the acquisition order of English grammatical morphemes: A learner corpus study. *Studies in Second Language Acquisition* 38 (3), 365–401.

Murray, L. (1795) *English Grammar: Adapted to the Different Classes of Learners*. Hallowell, ME: Goodale, Glazier and co.

Murray, N. and Muller, A. (2019) Some key terms in ELT and why we need to disambiguate them. *ELT Journal* 73 (3), 257–264.

Nakamori, T. (2002) Teaching relative clauses: How to handle a bitter lemon for Japanese learners and English teachers. *ELT Journal* 56 (1), 29–40.

Nassaji, H. (2012) The relationship between SLA research and language pedagogy: Teachers' perspectives. *Language Teaching Research* 16 (3), 337–365.

Negishi, M. (2022) The impact of the CEFR in Japan. In D. Little and N. Figueras (eds) *Reflecting on the Common European Framework of Reference for Languages and its Companion Volume* (pp. 10–22). Bristol: Multilingual Matters.

Newby, D. (2000) Pedagogical grammar. In M. Byram (ed.) *Routledge Encyclopedia of Language Teaching and Learning* (pp. 459–461). Abingdon: Routledge.

North, B. (2010) A CEFR core curriculum. *EL Gazette* (371), 6.

North, B. and Schneider, G. (1998) Scaling descriptors for language proficiency scales. *Language Testing* 15 (2), 217–263.

North, B., Ortega, A. and Sheehan, S. (2010) *British Council – EAQUALS Core Inventory for General English*. London: British Council / EAQUALS.

Nunan, D. (1988) *Syllabus Design*. Oxford: Oxford University Press.

Odlin, T. (1994) Introduction. In T. Odlin (ed.) *Perspectives on Pedagogical Grammar* (pp. 1–22). Cambridge: Cambridge University Press.

OED Online (2021a) canon, *n*.1. In *OED Online*. Oxford: Oxford University Press. See https://www.oed.com/view/Entry/149226 (accessed November 2021).

OED Online (2021b) practice, *n*. In *OED Online*. Oxford: Oxford University Press. See https://www.oed.com/view/Entry/27148 (accessed November 2021).

OED Online (2022) shall, *v*. In *OED Online*. Oxford: Oxford University Press. See https://www.oed.com/view/Entry/177350 (accessed January 2022).

O'Keeffe, A. and Mark, G. (2017) The English grammar profile of learner competence: Methodology and key findings. *International Journal of Corpus Linguistics* 22 (4), 457–489.

Oxenden, C. and Latham-Koenig, C. (2006) *New English File Intermediate Student's Book*. Oxford: Oxford University Press.
Oxenden, C. and Latham-Koenig, C. (2008) *New English File Upper-intermediate Student's Book*. Oxford: Oxford University Press.
Oxenden, C. and Latham-Koenig, C. (2009) *New English File Beginner Student's Book*. Oxford: Oxford University Press.
Oxenden, C. and Latham-Koenig, C. (2010) *New English File Advanced Student's Book*. Oxford: Oxford University Press.
Oxenden, C., Latham-Koenig, C. and Seligson, P. (2004) *New English File Elementary Student's Book*. Oxford: Oxford University Press.
Oxenden, C., Latham-Koenig, C. and Seligson, P. (2005) *New English File Pre-Intermediate Student's Book*. Oxford: Oxford University Press.
Palmer, H. (1916) *Colloquial English. Part 1: 100 Substitution Tables*. Cambridge: W. Heffer & Sons Ltd.
Palmer, H. (1921) *The Principles of Language-Study*. New York: World Book Company.
Palmer, H. (1924) *A Grammar of Spoken English on a Strictly Phonetic Basis*. Cambridge: W. Heffer & Sons Ltd.
Palmer, H. (1938) *A Grammar of English Words*. London: Longman, Greens and co.
Pearce, R.A. (1975) Teaching conditional and related clauses. *ELT Journal* 229 (3), 206–213.
Pearson (2021) *Azar-Hagen grammar series*. See https://www.pearson.com/english/catalogue/english-skills/azar-hagen-grammar-series.html (accessed November 2021).
Phan, N.L.H. (2020) *The Place of English as an International Language in English Language Teaching: Teacher's Reflections*. New York: Routledge.
Pienemann, M. (1989) Is language teachable? Psycholinguistic experiments and hypotheses. *Applied Linguistics* 10 (1), 52–79.
Pike, K.L. (1967) *Etic and Emic Standpoints for the Description of Behavior* (2nd edn). The Hague: Mouton & Co.
Prodromou, L. (2003) In search of the successful user of English. *Modern English Teacher* 12 (2), 5–14.
'Question Box' (1948) *ELT Journal* 3 (1), 25–26.
Quirk, R. (1957) From descriptive to prescriptive: An example. *ELT Journal* 12 (1), 9–13.
Quirk, R., Leech, G. and Greenbaum, S. (1985) *A Comprehensive Grammar of the English Language*. London: Longman.
Quirk, R., Greenbaum, S., Leech, G. and Svartvik, J. (1972) *A Grammar of Contemporary English*. London: Longman.
'Readers' Letters' (1972) *ELT Journal* 26 (2), 202–203.
Redston, C. and Cunningham, G. (2005a) *face2face Elementary Student's Book*. Cambridge: Cambridge University Press.
Redston, C. and Cunningham, G. (2005b) *face2face Pre-intermediate Student's Book*. Cambridge: Cambridge University Press.
Redston, C. and Cunningham, G. (2006) *face2face Intermediate Student's Book*. Cambridge: Cambridge University Press.
Redston, C. and Cunningham, G. (2007) *face2face Upper Intermediate Student's Book*. Cambridge: Cambridge University Press.
Redston, C. and Cunningham, G. (2009) *face2face Starter Student's Book*. Cambridge: Cambridge University Press.
Richards, J.C. (2001) *Curriculum Development in Language Teaching*. Cambridge: Cambridge University Press.
Richards, J.C. (2017) Curriculum approaches in language teaching. In E. Hinkel (ed.) *Handbook of Research in Second Language Teaching and Learning* (Vol. 3) (pp. 117–131). Abingdon: Routledge.
Richards, J.C. and Chuck, S. (2008a) *Passages 1 Student's Book* (2nd edn). Cambridge: Cambridge University Press.

Richards, J.C. and Chuck, S. (2008b) *Passages 2 Student's Book* (2nd edn). Cambridge: Cambridge University Press.
Richards, J.C. and Rodgers, T.S. (2001) *Approaches and Methods in Language Teaching* (2nd edn). Cambridge: Cambridge University Press.
Richards, J.C. and Schmidt, R.W. (eds) (2007) *Longman Dictionary of Language Teaching and Applied Linguistics* (3rd edn). Harlow: Longman.
Richards, J.C., Hull, J. and Proctor, S. (2004) *Interchange 2 Student's Book* (3rd edn). Cambridge: Cambridge University Press.
Richards, J.C., Hull, J. and Proctor, S. (2005a) *Interchange 1 Student's Book* (3rd edn). Cambridge: Cambridge University Press.
Richards, J.C., Hull, J. and Proctor, S. (2005b) *Interchange 3 Student's Book* (3rd edn). Cambridge: Cambridge University Press.
Römer, U. (2005) *Progressives, Patterns. Pedagogy: A Corpus-Driven Approach to English Progressive Forms, Functions, Contexts, and Didactics.* Amsterdam: John Benjamins.
Rose, H., Syrbe, M., Montakantiwong, A. and Funada, N. (2020) *Global TESOL for the 21st Century: Teaching English in a Changing World.* Bristol: Multilingual Matters.
Ryan, G.W. and Bernard, H.R. (2003) Techniques to identify themes. *Field Methods* 15 (1), 85–109.
Savignon, S.J. (1985) Evaluation of communicative competence: The ACTFL provisional proficiency guidelines. *The Modern Language Journal* 69 (2), 129–134.
Sharifian, F. (ed.) (2009) *English as an International Language: Perspectives and Pedagogical Issues.* Bristol: Multilingual Matters.
Sheehan, R. (2015) Problems with best practice. *ELT Journal* 69 (1), 90–92.
Sheen, R. (2003) A response to Thornbury (2001). 'The unbearable lightness of EFL'. *ELT Journal* 57 (1), 60–63.
Shortall, T. (2007) The L2 syllabus: Corpus or contrivance? *Corpora* 2 (2), 157–185.
Sinclair, J.M. (1985) Selected issues. In R. Quirk and H.G. Widdowson (eds) *English in the World: Teaching and Learning the Language and Literatures* (pp. 248–254). Cambridge: Cambridge University Press.
Smith, R. (2004) An investigation into the roots of ELT, with a particular focus on the career and legacy of Harold E. Palmer (1877–1949). Unpublished PhD thesis, University of Edinburgh.
Smith, R. (ed.) (2005) *Teaching English as a Foreign Language, 1936-1961: Foundations of ELT.* Abingdon: Routledge.
Smith, R. (2007) The origins of ELT journal. See https://academic.oup.com/DocumentLibrary/ELTJ/The-origins-of-elt-journal.pdf (accessed August 2022).
Smith, R. (2016) Building 'applied linguistic historiography': Rationale, scope, and methods. *Applied Linguistics* 37 (1), 71–87.
Soars, J. and Soars, L. (1986) *Headway: Intermediate Student's Book.* Oxford: Oxford University Press.
Soars, J. and Soars, L. (1987) *Headway: Upper-Intermediate Student's Book.* Oxford: Oxford University Press.
Soars, J. and Soars, L. (1989) *Headway: Advanced Student's Book.* Oxford: Oxford University Press.
Soars, J. and Soars, L. (1991) *Headway: Pre-Intermediate Student's Book.* Oxford: Oxford University Press.
Soars, J. and Soars, L. (1993) *Headway: Elementary Student's Book.* Oxford: Oxford University Press.
Soars, J. and Soars, L. (2009) *New Headway Intermediate Student's Book* (4th edn). Oxford: Oxford University Press.
Soars, J. and Soars, L. (2011) *New Headway Elementary Student's Book* (4th edn). Oxford: Oxford University Press.
Soars, J. and Soars, L. (2013a) *New Headway Beginner Student's Book* (4th edn). Oxford: Oxford University Press.

Soars, J. and Soars, L. (2013b) *New Headway Pre-Intermediate Student's Book* (4th edn). Oxford: Oxford University Press.
Soars, J. and Soars, L. (2014) *New Headway Upper-Intermediate Student's Book* (4th edn). Oxford: Oxford University Press.
Soars, J. and Soars, L. (2015) *New Headway. Advanced Student's Book* (4th edn). Oxford: Oxford University Press.
Sopher, H. (1969) The classification of relative clauses. *ELT Journal* 23 (3), 254–257.
Stake, R.E. (2003) Case studies. In N.K. Denzin and Y.S. Lincoln (eds) *Strategies of Qualitative Inquiry* (2nd edn) (pp. 136–164). Thousand Oaks, CA: Sage.
Stranks, J. (2003) Materials for the teaching of grammar. In B. Tomlinson (ed.) *Developing Materials for Language Teaching* (pp. 329–339). London: Continuum.
Swan, M. (1994) Design criteria for pedagogic language rules. In M. Bygate, A. Tonkyn and E. Williams (eds) *Grammar and the Language Teacher* (pp. 44–55). Harlow: Longman.
Swan, M. (2007) Follow-up to Claire Kramsch's 'classic book' review of Lado, 1957, Linguistics across cultures: History is not what happened: The case of contrastive analysis. *International Journal of Applied Linguistics* 17 (3), 414–419.
Swan, M. (2011) Grammar. In J. Simpson (ed.) *The Routledge Handbook of Applied Linguistics* (pp. 557–570). Abingdon: Routledge.
Swan, M. (2016) *Practical English Usage* (4th edn). Oxford: Oxford University Press.
Swan, M. and Walter, C. (1990a) *The New Cambridge English Course: 1*. Cambridge: Cambridge University Press.
Swan, M. and Walter, C. (1990b) *The New Cambridge English Course: 2*. Cambridge: Cambridge University Press.
Swan, M. and Walter, C. (1992a) *The New Cambridge English Course: 3*. Cambridge: Cambridge University Press.
Swan, M. and Walter, C. (1992b) *The New Cambridge English Course: 4*. Cambridge: Cambridge University Press.
Sweet, H. (1892) *A New English Grammar, Logical And Historical*. (Vol. I Introduction: Phonology, and Accidence). Oxford: Oxford University Press.
Swender, E., Conrad, D. and Vicars, R. (2012) *ACTFL Proficiency Guidelines*. Alexandria, VA: ACTFL.
Tao, H. and McCarthy, M.J. (2001) Understanding non-restrictive which-clauses in spoken English, which is not an easy thing. *Language Sciences* 23 (6), 651–677.
'The Question Box' (1947) *ELT Journal* 1 (4), 111–112.
Thomson, A.J. and Martinet, A.V. (1960) *A Practical English Grammar*. Oxford: Oxford University Press.
Thornbury, S. (2013) Resisting coursebooks. In J. Gray (ed.) *Critical Perspectives on Language Teaching Materials* (pp. 204–233). New York: Palgrave Macmillan.
Timmis, I. (2014) Writing materials for publication: Questions raised and lessons learned. In N. Harwood (ed.) *English Language Teaching Textbooks: Content, Consumption, Production* (pp. 241–261). New York: Palgrave Macmillan.
Timmis, I. (2015) *Corpus Linguistics for ELT: Research and Practice*. Abingdon: Routledge.
Tomasello, M. (2005) *Constructing a Language: A Usage-Based Theory of Language Acquisition*. Cambridge, MA: Harvard University Press.
Tomlinson, B. (2011) Conclusions. In B. Tomlinson (ed.) *Materials Development in Language Teaching* (2nd edn) (pp. 437–442). Cambridge: Cambridge University Press.
Towell, R. (2016) Design of a pedagogic grammar. See https://www.llas.ac.uk//resources/gpg/410.html (accessed September 2020).
Tregidgo, P.S. (1980) 'Shall', 'will', and the future. *ELT Journal* 34 (4), 265–269.
Trim, J.L.M. (2012) The Common European Framework of Reference for Languages and its background: A case study of cultural politics and educational influences. In M. Byram and L. Parmenter (eds) *The Common European Framework of Reference:*

The Globalisation of Language Education Policy (pp. 14–34). Bristol: Multilingual Matters.

Ur, P. (1989) Correspondence. *ELT Journal* 43 (1), 73–74.

Weir, C.J. (2013) Measured constructs: A history of Cambridge English language examinations 1913 - 2012. *Research Notes* 51, 2–10.

Weir, C.J., Vidakovič, I. and Galaczi, E.D. (2013) *Measured Constructs: A History of Cambridge English Language Examinations 1913-2012.* Cambridge: Cambridge University Press.

Wenger, E. (1998) *Communities of Practice: Learning, Meaning and Identity.* Cambridge: Cambridge University Press.

Wilkins, D.A. (1976) *Notional Syllabuses.* Oxford: Oxford University Press.

Williams, E. (1994) English grammar and the views of English teachers. In M. Bygate, A. Tonkyn and E. Williams (eds) *Grammar and the Language Teacher* (pp. 105–118). Harlow: Longman.

Willis, J. and Willis, D. (1988a) *Collins COBUILD English Course. Student's Book 2.* London: Collins ELT.

Willis, J. and Willis, D. (1988b) *Collins COBUILD English Course. Student's Book 1.* London: Collins ELT.

Willis, J., Willis, D. and Davids, J. (1988) *Collins COBUILD English Course. Student's Book 3.* London: Collins ELT.

Yamashita, J. (1994) An analysis of relative clauses in the Lancaster/IBM spoken English corpus. *English Studies* 75 (1), 73–84.

Zandvoort, R.W. (1945) *A Handbook of English Grammar.* Groningen: Wolters-Noordhoff.

Zhou, Y. (1991) The effect of explicit instruction on the acquisition of English grammatical structures by Chinese learners. In C. James and P. Garrett (eds) *Language Awareness in the Classroom* (pp. 254–277). Harlow: Longman.

Index

n.b. References to authors as interviewees in Chapters 4 and 5 are not included in this index; similarly, references to their works when they form an integral part of the case studies presented in Chapters 6 and 7 are also not included.

Abbs, B. 26, 51, 69, 99, 102
Alexander, L. G. 26, 41, 46–48, 64, 78, 86n, 88, 89, 90, 94, 99
Allen, W.S. 41, 43–45, 46, 88, 89, 99, 171, 174
American Council on the Teaching of Foreign Languages (ACTFL) 19, 20, 22
articles 29, 31, 36, 42, 43, 45, 51n, 79
audiolingual approach 38–39, 46, 51n

behaviourist theory 46, 51n
Biber, D. 25, 40, 81
British Council 4, 44
Bullokar, W. 8, 30–31

Cambridge English examinations 2, 18–19, 86n, 111
Cambridge Learner Corpus 108, 111
Carter, R. 2, 13, 25, 40, 81, 171
Chomskyan linguistics 39
cleft sentences 119, 151
Common European Framework for Languages 19–20, 21, 26n, 28, 73, 95, 108, 111–113
Communicative competence 1, 173
comparatives and superlatives 31, 32, 45, 66, 146
competency levels. See 'level system'
conditional forms 25, 29, 32, 60, 65, 93, 101, 107, 113–118, 132, 138–145, 168, 169, 170, 175, 177, 180
constitutive and communicative grammar rules 13, 107, 160, 171
contrastive analysis hypothesis 39, 80, 173
corpus frequency data 16, 25, 40, 80, 92, 93, 101, 120, 121, 134n
corpus-informed critiques of ELT grammar descriptions 114, 128
corpus-informed grammar descriptions 25, 34, 37, 39, 40, 80–82

declarative vs. procedural knowledge 13, 14
descriptive grammar 3, 11, 12, 13, 34, 39–40, 42, 44, 122
discourse and discourse structures 2, 29, 49, 50, 82, 97, 119, 175

EAQUALS Core Inventory for English 28–30, 109
Eckersley C.E. 26n, 95
ELT coursebooks, nature of 2, 4, 6, 12, 19, 20, 21, 22–25, 28, 41, 50, 85, 175–179, 181
ELT examinations and examination boards 2, 4, 18–20, 22, 29, 72–73, 85, 86n, 90, 177
ELT journal 37–38, 48, 174
ELT publishing industry 22–26, 28, 85, 98–104, 175–176, 179
English Grammar Profile 67, 110–113, 117–118, 123–124, 128–131, 132, 133, 176–177
English Language Institute (ELI) 38, 39
English Testing Service (ETS) 19
explicit knowledge and instruction 1, 14, 36

Fries, C.C. 35, 38–39, 40, 43, 51n
functional-notional approach 48–49, 51n, 98, 175
future forms 29, 32, 33, 81–82, 91, 93, 107, 124–131, 132, 133, 134, 157–169, 171, 172n, 175

grammar as choice 13, 171
grammar items: selection of 11–13, 14, 46, 48, 59–63, 66, 67, 68, 70–73, 74, 76, 78, 79–80, 81, 82, 84, 92–94, 178; sequencing of 3, 15–17, 21, 26, 44–45, 48, 59–63, 65, 67, 68, 70–73, 74, 76, 78, 79–80, 81, 84, 91, 92–93, 98, 99, 100, 101, 103–104, 109, 176–177

grammatical terminology 13, 125, 137, 144, 148, 151, 158, 171
grammar-translation method 1, 15
Great Tradition, the 27, 33–35, 42, 44, 174

Halliday, M.A.K. 40, 49, 174
Hornby, A.S. 35–38, 51n, 89, 173
Howatt, A.S. 1, 4, 6, 7, 15, 26n, 31, 32, 35, 38, 41, 48, 51

Institute for Research in English Teaching (IRET) 37, 38, 174
Interagency Language Roundtable (ILR) 19
internal syllabus 17, 133

Jespersen, O. 34, 35, 89, 125, 171, 174
Jonson, B. 31–32, 170

Kruisinga, E. 34, 89

Lado, R. See 'Contrastive analysis hypothesis'
learnability. See 'internal syllabus'
learner corpora 133, 179, 180
Leech, G. 11, 40, 81, 161
level assignments. See 'grammar items: sequencing of'
level system 5, 17–22, 44–45, 52–53, 59, 61–62, 63–65, 68, 72, 75, 76, 77, 82–84, 96, 99; origins of 90, 95–96, 105, 181

market research 22, 62, 64, 70, 74–75, 85, 90, 95, 102, 103, 175
McCarthy, M.J. 2, 20, 32, 34, 49, 81, 82, 116, 130–131, 161, 175
modality 25, 29, 32, 66, 115, 125, 159, 162, 165, 172n
Murray, L. 32–33, 136

natural order. See 'internal syllabus'
norms 59–61, 62–63, 85, 104, 120, 140, 176, 178

O'Keeffe, A. 2, 28, 111
Ollendorff, H. 15
O'Neill, R. 62, 66, 86n, 94, 99

Palmer, H. 15–16, 17, 35–38, 41–43, 45, 46, 50, 51n, 173
passive voice 14, 25, 31, 32, 163
past: simple 71, 96; perfect (simple and continuous) 43, 79, 142
patterns 36–37, 38–39, 42, 46, 48, 116, 138, 140, 141, 145, 157, 173

pedagogical grammar: definitions of 11, characteristics of 11–17
Pienemann, M. 17
prescriptivism and prescriptive grammars 11, 33, 44, 46, 70, 74, 145, 148, 150, 152, 157, 165, 170, 171, 173–174
present: simple 13, 16, 43, 78, 82, 92, 93, 101, 114, 126, 129, 160, 162, 164, 165; continuous 43, 71, 81, 84, 92, 93, 101, 125, 126, 127, 128, 129, 130, 142, 143, 158, 159, 160, 161, 162, 163, 164, 165, 166, 167, 168, 169, 172; perfect (simple and continuous) 14, 25, 43, 51n, 60, 76, 79, 93, 109, 110, 111
procedural knowledge. See 'declarative vs. procedural knowledge'
processability theory. See 'internal syllabus'
publishers and the publishing industry 4, 22–25, 26, 28, 48–49, 53, 59–60, 62–63, 64, 65, 66–70, 74–75, 76–77, 79, 82, 84–85, 90, 93, 95, 98–105, 170–171, 175, 176

Quirk, R. 35, 39–40, 42

Reform Movement 1, 173
relative clauses and relativisers 91, 118–124, 132, 134n, 145–157, 170, 171, 175, 177
reported speech 25, 73
Richards, J. 4, 10, 16–17, 37, 41, 48, 51n, 176

school grammars 32–33, 37, 40, 46, 170
Skill Acquisition Theory 14
Smith, R. 7, 37, 51n, 135, 180
spoken grammar 25, 40, 81, 97
structuralism 38–39, 173, 174
subjunctive 138, 141, 145
substitution tables 36–37, 38, 43, 46
Swan, M. 12–14, 35, 39, 51n, 79, 80, 89, 116, 171, 174
Sweet, H. 34, 42, 51n
Systemic Functional Linguistics 40, 174

Thomson, A. 45–46, 137, 170
Thornbury, S. 28, 176
Threshold level 21, 26n, 51n, 112
TOEFL examination. See 'English Testing Service (ETS)'
traditional grammars. See 'school grammars'
Trim, J. 21

usage-based models 177

Wilkins, D. 51n, 105n

For Product Safety Concerns and Information please contact our EU Authorised Representative:

Easy Access System Europe

Mustamäe tee 50

10621 Tallinn

Estonia

gpsr.requests@easproject.com